Other Books by The Author

Love and Loathing in the Islands, Searching for Gauguin

Love and Redemption in the Tropics, Missing Gauguin

CONFESSIONS OF A HIPPIE

ALWAYS SEARCHING FOR LOVE

~ ADRIANA BARDOLINO ~

iUniverse

CONFESSIONS OF A HIPPIE
ALWAYS SEARCHING FOR LOVE

iUniverse books may be ordered through booksellers or by contacting:

iUniverse
1663 Liberty Drive
Bloomington, IN 47403
www.iuniverse.com
844-349-9409

Because of the dynamic nature of the internet, any web addresses or links contained in this book may have changed since publication and may no longer be valid. The views expressed in this work are solely those of the author and do not necessarily reflect the views of the publisher, and the publisher hereby disclaims any responsibility for them.

Any people depicted in stock imagery provided by Getty Images are models, and such images are being used for illustrative purposes only. Certain stock imagery © Getty Images.

ISBN: 978-1-6632-1359-4 (sc)
ISBN: 978-1-6632-1361-7 (hc)
ISBN: 978-1-6632-1360-0 (e)

Library of Congress Control Number: 2020925766

Print information available on the last page.

iUniverse rev. date: 04/08/2024

We do not all walk along the same path in life, but life itself can be the path.

CONTENTS

PREFACE

The main story of this book focuses on an eight-year period in my life, 1967 to 1975, when I was in my twenties. I kept journals that have great detail of my experiences and my feelings. After my mother passed away, I found the journals and the letters that I had written to her during those years, which she had kept. I am not sure what her motivation was in saving them, but I am thankful she did. Reading through my letters and journals was a roller coaster ride of emotions—a lot of laughter and a lot of tears.

During that time, the Vietnam War was still raging, although it was nearing its end. The war began in 1955 and ended in 1975 amid huge protests. The country was divided, and it was a time of upheaval and unrest. A counterculture developed, where the catch-phrase "Turn on, tune in, and drop out," made famous by Timothy Leary, was adopted by many people, myself included.

A love movement was going on and something called "Flower Power," which was displayed sometimes at antiwar demonstrations by hippies giving a flower to a soldier holding a gun. It was also the beginning of the free-speech movement, which began in Berkeley, California, where I was living in the late sixties. Free love was a general practice, and the word *freedom* was in the lyrics of many songs that were popular at the time. It was a time when psychedelic drugs were the rage, which drove people toward introspection, questioning society's norms, and the meaning of life itself.

My journals include poems I'd written, watercolors, and drawings. I jotted down excerpts from books I was reading and described dreams I had. I copied lyrics of songs with words that expressed what I was feeling, perhaps better than I could express them myself. Some paragraphs in this book are directly from the entries in my journals. I have thousands of photographs and slides—some are black-and-white photos I developed myself when I had my own darkroom. In fact, when I discovered I'd written very few journal entries in 1969, I was able to fill in the blanks with my letters, photos, and slides, which were stamped with dates. I found letters from friends glued in the pages, and there were drawings and passages they had entered themselves. Of course, I also had my memories.

When I began reading through my letters and putting them together with the journals of corresponding years, I found an outline I'd written for this book, which was almost exactly the same as the outline I had just jotted down. At some point, many years ago, I guess I had attempted to write this book, but life got in the way. After I retired I had plenty of time to delve into the project.

I want to confess that I fell in love with the characters in my life all over again. I was tossed into the past in such a way that I felt love, anger, happiness, hurt, and depression, just as if it was happening now. Some of the people in the book are dead now, and some are still friends today. Names have been changed, but I imagine that those who experienced these years with me will know who they are. I ask them to remember that these were my experiences and feelings, and may not have been theirs.

Siri and Alexa became my assistants with dates and places of events from those years. I also had help from friends who read my original drafts of chapters. A few of the main people, who experienced a great deal of this right along with me, contributed their memories and stories. We are all tied together by the experiences we shared.

There was so much more, and so many more people I could have included. I attempted to limit the story to concentrate on the events, the people, and the relationships that were the most important to me during that time in my life. I would ask readers to keep in mind that I recorded these experiences when I was in my twenties; it was how I perceived the world, the people around me, and love itself. For me it was a time of innocence, hope, mysticism, and idealism. Of course my youth played a big role.

I hope that readers can relate to my story written from a woman's perspective. Those who are too young to be familiar with that era will learn something about that time, and about some of the young people who lived in it. All in all, writing this book was a joyful process, and I loved every minute of it. Looking back, it was certainly a wild and beautiful ride.

Adriana Bardolino

It was a beautiful, warm, sunny day. A group of us dropped LSD and walked across the road to the stream.

I lay nude on a large, flat rock running my hand through the rippling water, peacefully listening to it gurgle past me over pebbles and branches. A soft breeze rushed past my body raising the hairs on my arms and legs.

It's hard to explain the euphoric place I went to on the psychedelic drug. We stared at each other's faces as if we knew a profound secret that no one else knew. He stared down at me as if he was seeing into my third eye. Then he began painting my body. I wasn't aware that different rocks created different colors. It was spiritual at first, but soon became erotic.

Hours went by. As the sun was setting it cooled down quite a bit. We got dressed and drifted back to the house and congregated in the living room. Music seemed to be in order. Someone put an LP of the Edwin Hawkins Singers on the stereo, and we began dancing wildly to "Oh Happy Day." We formed a circle and locked arms swaying together as one body, the differences between us disappearing.

It had been a glorious day, followed by a glorious night. There were many days and nights like that that summer.

ONE

THE DISCOVERY

"Secret Love" by Sammy Fain and Paul Francis Webster

*Just like in the song I was hiding a secret, a secret love. I held
the secret for many years until one day it was set free*

It was October 1995. I was visiting my mother in the Bronx. It was her birthday, and we were planning all the things we wanted to do while I was there. She recently had spent three months with me in Hawaii, where I had been living for a long time. We were discussing the possibly of her moving there permanently with me.

She had called me about a month back, telling me that she wasn't feeling well.

I had only been in the Bronx a few days when she had a stroke and was hospitalized. After five depressing and grueling weeks, during which my mother slowly deteriorated, she passed away.

I received the phone call from the hospital informing me that my mother had died. I rushed there, wanting to see her one last time, as if I could catch her spirit before it left her body. I touched her face and neck which were still warm. I hugged her and cried. I kissed her goodbye and stroked her face. I sat on a chair next to her bed for a while. She had such a peaceful look on her face, despite what she had been through over the past weeks.

Eventually I got up and touched her lifeless body again. I turned to her and said, "I'll see you on the other side." I closed the curtain around her bed and walked to the nurses' station. I thanked them for all the attention they'd given my mother, and I left the hospital. I walked to the bus stop in a daze.

The next week was filled with funeral arrangements and calling family members, which I seemed to get through like a robot whose wires had been short circuited. I am an only child, and my father had died less than two years earlier. I went through my mother's dresser drawers and observed how neatly her undergarments were placed, and how orderly her clothes were hung in the closets. It was almost as if she expected someone would be going through them. Just a few days before her stroke she had shown me a dress she had set aside for her funeral, which I thought was weird.

She had said, "Adriana, I don't want anyone to see my feet. I want a half-opened casket."

I turned to her with a frown and said, "Ma, what are you saying? She didn't answer me. Perhaps she'd had a premonition.

It took three months to go through the apartment where my parents had lived for thirty-two years. I found crazy things in the closets—Styrofoam heads with wigs, a gas mask, and boxes of fabric she had saved for me from her dress factory. The fabric was so old it disintegrated as soon as I touched it.

In the closets I found tissues crumpled up in the pockets of jackets with her jewelry. On a shelf at the top of one of the closets was my father's accordion. There were shoeboxes filled with family photos. Looking through the liquor cabinet, I found six bottles of twenty-five-year Ambassador Scotch. I immediately called my mother's youngest sister, Camille, who loved scotch. She came to the apartment, and we marveled at the fact that by then, it was probably fifty-year Ambassador Scotch. She took all six bottles home.

I opened a large drawer at the bottom of the dresser. It was filled with all my parents' important papers. I found a certificate from Hartsdale Pet Cemetery, where all three of their cats had been buried in tiny little coffins. I opened a large manila envelope and found it filled with all the birthday cards I had ever sent my mother, as well the baby cards my parents had given to me as a small child. My mother saved everything!

Then, there it was—I noticed a stack of letters held together with a rubber band. For a moment I thought that maybe they were love letters. I looked at the return address of the letter on the top. It was the address of the first commune I lived in, on Charming Way in Berkeley, from 1967 to 1968. I thought, *what the—?* I took the rubber band off and fished through them. At the back were some letters from Colombia, South America, where a group of us from the commune had spent the entire three months of the summer of 1971. Memories flooded my brain. *Why would she save these letters?* I began to cry uncontrollably as my emotions finally caught up with me—emotions I had been holding in over the past weeks.

As I began going through the letters, I remembered that I had journals somewhere. I rummaged through piles of paperwork in the drawer and found them. There were nine journals, all different-sized notebooks in various colors, all tied together with a ribbon.

I sat down on the floor in my parents' bedroom and untied the ribbon. For a moment I forgot where I was, and delved into what was in my hands. I was thrown back into the past and thought of the years I'd lived with a group of people—my years of communal living. I opened the first journal and flipped through the pages. There were drawings, poems I'd written, watercolors, excerpts from books I was reading, and there were pages of text about my experiences and feelings. I began reading one of the entries from Berkeley 1969:

> This music has so much soul. The guy standing next to me knows it's good. His wispy brown hair swaying to the music, and his feet are stomping. Soon, he takes off his glasses. I turn to look at this man beside me. His soft, sensual, and exciting face is smiling at me. Then he becomes very intent. I look again, and he is just a boy. He takes my hand tightly in his. His hands are cold. He is enjoying watching me groove to the music. He tells me he is tired and wants to leave. I am thinking he wants something else.

I put the journal down and thought, *this was not my boyfriend, Noah Bernstein. Who was it?* I was interested but reluctant to read further, wondering what I would rediscover about myself and my past. I had so much packing to do, so I took the letters and journals and placed them in a box on top of the important family documents.

My parents' old apartment was filled with so many memories that flooded back to me over the three months I was there. I couldn't help but reminisce about my family and growing up in the Bronx. I decided to sleep in my parents' bed. It made me feel close to them, and in a strange way it gave me comfort.

The next day I called my oldest childhood friend, Robby Noble. Robby and his brother, Joshua, lived upstairs on the second floor of the four-family house I grew up in. We played together on the streets, and shared each other's holidays. Joshua had a weight problem, and his mother put a lock on their refrigerator. I never knew anyone else who did anything like that.

Robby and I talked on the phone for a long time. His mother was still alive, and I told him that was a blessing. As we were talking I pictured the lilac bush that was outside the window of my parents' bedroom in that first house. It had the most wonderful aroma that would drift in on the breeze in the spring. In summer, when it was unbearably hot inside those apartments, our neighbors would bring beach chairs out onto the street, and we'd all sleep outside. There was no air conditioning in those early days.

Packing up my elementary school class photos, I noticed that my mother had saved my report cards. I remembered her being called to school because I was caught passing a book around with my girlfriends—*Lady Chatterley's Lover* by D. H. Lawrence. Another time, it was for writing a racy letter about a boy we all liked. Someone gave the letter to the teacher, and she read it out loud to the class.

My mother always had a frown on her face when she read "Defies authority" on my report cards. In first grade she came to school for Parent's Day. My teacher held up my finger painting and told my mother I was going to be an artist.

I took a break from packing, made myself dinner, went into the living room and sat on the couch to eat. The couch was where I slept when I visited my parents. I walked to the box with my journals and took out the same notebook from Berkeley that I'd been reading.

The sun's lost some of its bottom, and it looks like a Chinese lantern. It's lighting up a room for someone. Maybe Dean's room, red and warm. I can see fir trees swaying on a cliff in the distance. It's going to be a foggy night. I really can't live just in the *now*, because I'm all of those things that happened before. It's all me. Everything

I've ever felt, everyone I've ever loved, and all I've ever done. I'm all that and more. I try to be in the *now, now, now*. The sun has disappeared. But it's somewhere else, for someone else.

After reading that, it was obvious who the first journal entry was about. I looked around me, and the apartment seemed so empty—my family gone and our memories being packed away. All my artwork, which my mother had framed, hung everywhere around the apartment. *Funny*, I thought, *because she never really praised my work when I was younger.*

The day I was born the doctor told my mother she'd drawn her own picture. She was thirty-one at the time and as beautiful as a movie star. Her hair was brown, like mine, but she always dyed it red, like that popular actress, Rita Hayworth. Her name was Vita, which means *life* in Italian. My mother was full of life, and everyone loved her. I carefully packed her photo away.

Vita owned a dress factory in the Bronx with her brother, Victor. I spent a lot of time there as a child. I learned how to sew on those fast and powerful industrial machines. Sometimes we stayed late into the night, setting up bundles of dress parts for the operators for the following day. Occasionally two rats would appear at the end of the cutting table, which ran almost the entire length of the factory. These little creatures were not fazed by us at all. My mother named them Tom and Jerry, after the popular cartoon. They were as large as rabbits and were very cute. They had been displaced when the adjacent lot next to the factory was turned over to build a gas station. I remember inviting the neighborhood kids into the factory after hours to watch the rats run over my feet. The kids squealed with joy and horror. I wasn't afraid. I knew they wouldn't bite me; they never did.

My mother was a very independent woman, and I think it rubbed off on me. Most of her siblings were born in Bari, Italy, but she was born in the Harlem section of New York City. I drove by that house a few times with my cousin Giovanna, whose mother had grown up there with mine. They told us spooky tales about a ghost in that house. Giovanna Ferrari, Gia for short, was like a sister to me. Our mothers were sisters and always together. They even dressed us like twins when we were children.

I looked down at a gem I had found in one of my mother's jacket pockets. It was her sapphire ring, a large center stone with diamonds around it. Gia was on her way over to the apartment to give me the certificate for the cemetery. Sapphire was Gia's birthstone, so I gave the ring to her. Our parents, who were to be buried together, purchased a plot in Woodlawn Cemetery when Gia's father, Faustino, died a fairly young man. My aunt Porciella was still alive, thank God. Gia handed me the certificate, and we held each other and cried. When she left I felt depressed. I walked to the box with all my journals, which by now had become a habit. I picked out one from 1972.

> Bodies of splendor. Nude, strong, and shining in the sun. Beads of water trickling over hair and breasts. They painted my body with earth-tone colors of brown, yellow, and green. It felt holy yet sensuous. I felt like an ancient queen being decorated with spit and rock. I swam out into the water to rinse the paint off, and he followed me in. The paint wouldn't come off so we kissed under the surface, and it sealed the bond. We swam to shore together. It's a beginning. It's new. Yet it's ancient.

I needed another drink after reading that. The memory of that day flooded back to me.

My father once told me that his life began the day I was born. He was forty years old at the time. My mother told me I was the apple of his eye. My father, Andrea, had come to America from Sicily when he was ten years old. His family were sharecroppers in the old country. Andrea told me he slept in a barn and would be woken up by rats running under him through the hay. My father called me *Cookie*—well, all Italian girls are called Cookie— being a sweet young thing. I was definitely Daddy's little girl. My mother never took me anywhere, but my father took me everywhere.

Andrea learned barbering and eventually got his own shop. The barbershop was another place I spent a lot of time while growing up. I'd swing around on the barber chairs until I was dizzy. I loved watching my father cutting the guys' hair in the newest styles of the day—the DA (Duck's Ass) and the flattop. When I was a teenager, my father kept my high school photo on the cash register. If a guy would stare at it too long he'd say, "Don't get any ideas. She's my daughter!" There was no hope of my ever meeting a guy in the barbershop! I chuckled at the sweet memory.

I carefully packed my father's shaving kit. I was sure that the straight razor and brush were antiques. I walked to the liquor cabinet to make myself a drink. I was hoping the drink wouldn't prompt emotions and tears. Of course, I rummaged through the box and picked out another journal. I flipped through the pages and came across a poem I'd written:

New Year's Eve
Blissful thoughts of times gone by
Streamers, horns, and lovers kissing with stars in their eyes
A new year dawns with only a hint of the past
Yesterday's gone but for the memories that last

I took another long sip of my drink and lay on the couch feeling the effects of the alcohol. I thought of the gas mask I had put in the pile for the Goodwill, and began to laugh. I wondered how I'd ever grown up normal—or had I?

My father had a phobia—that's what everyone called it. He had a sensitivity to gas fumes and odors in general, perhaps resulting from two operations he had on his nose as a young man. He told us he smelled gas fumes in our home, insisting that it was killing us, but we didn't know it. True, there was a gas boiler in the basement of the building, but it didn't affect anyone but him. He suffered actual physical symptoms—nausea and headaches. He even wore a gas mask in the house at one time. My mother persuaded him to see a psychiatrist, but after his appointment he told us that he was sane, and the psychiatrist was crazy.

This called for an exorcism, Italian-style. My cousin Ariel was married to Bruno whose mother was born with "Veronica's veil" (also called a caul). This is when a baby is born with the amniotic sac covering (or partly covering) it. The Italians believe such people possess special powers. This woman kept part of the placenta from her birth, and wore it in a pouch around her neck. My mother summoned her to our house, hoping the woman could rid the house of my father's scourge.

She came into the living room as we all stood around in a circle, waiting to see what would happen. At some point, her expression changed, and she began pacing around the room like a woman in a trance, touching things and spitting into a bowl. I was just a child, but it seemed nonsensical at best. All of a sudden, she pointed to my Castro chair-bed, screaming, "Whose chair is this? It throws me!"

Well, everyone knew it was my chair. Perhaps she felt me resisting her.

I was sure she could see it in the snarky expressions I was making. In the end, she left the house without any resolution to my father's scourge. This "Allergy," as my father called it, began to affect everything in his life, even his barbershop. He moved from one shop to another, because at each one he would eventually smell gas.

As I was packing the Italian antiques and cut-crystal champagne glasses from the forties, a train went by outside the bathroom window rattling everything in the china cabinet. I stopped and thought, *I never noticed that when I lived here.* I walked to the box that held my journals and took out a blue one from 1970. I sat at the dining room table and began to read:

> I haven't written out of my head for a while. There has been so much living and loving done this summer. We swam in streams, played on mountains, and made love everywhere. The man I am in love with is beautiful, but I wonder where his head is at right now. Something is not there anymore. Maybe it's all in my head. I want to see him standing there in his overalls again. It was all right there, in that moment, and I felt it. I don't feel it from him anymore, and it makes me sad. We were friends, lovers, and partners. We're due for a trip out west, and I wonder what changes will evolve. I'm not even sure I should go with him. Maybe it will be like Siddhartha's river. Constantly flowing and changing but still the same river.

After reading that, those emotions came back to me. I remembered how I'd felt writing that passage so many years ago. I knew who it was about, and I felt loss all over again.

I was also dealing with a lifetime of guilt. A woman named Filomena Genoa had taken care of me since I was six months old, from the very beginning. My mother was a busy woman with a business to run, so she found someone to take care of me during the day. Filomena lived in a five-floor walk-up across the street from my mother's dress factory. She had the most striking blue eyes. She was a wonderful woman, and was like a mother to me. In fact, I imagined she was my real mother, and that Vita, my real mother, had adopted me. There was a popular song at that time called

"Secret Love" sung by Jerry Vale. Whenever I heard that song, I thought of the secret love I hid inside of me for Filomena. I couldn't tell my family or my friends; they wouldn't understand.

When I was in elementary school, Filomena would pick me up after class and take me to her house, where I remained until my mother closed the factory and would come to pick me up. My fantasy about Filomena being my real mother came to a head one day when my mother closed the factory early, and showed up at school to pick me up. I was annoyed and threw a temper tantrum. I yelled at her, "You're not my mother! Filomena's my real mother!" My mother was very upset and began crying. She grabbed my arm and took me to Filomena's apartment. We walked up the five flights of stairs. Filomena was surprised to see us.

They sat me on a chair, and Filomena straightened me out to the facts, gently but firmly. She said, "Adriana, I love you—you know that—but I'm not your mother. You know that honey; don't you?"

I was crying, but nodded my head. I accepted the truth, but I didn't like it. After all, I couldn't help how distant I felt from my own mother. I was a confused kid with a very vivid imagination. I eventually woke up to reality—although I was emotionally numb for a long time.

I still felt guilt, even after all these years had passed. After seeing all the things my mother saved, I realized just how much she loved me. She once looked at me and said, "You're my life!" I hadn't understood back then.

Liquor was getting me through this rough time. I walked to the cabinet and made myself a Tanqueray and tonic. I reached in the box of journals and took out one from 1971.

> We danced all night in that café in Cali. We were high on tequila and high on life. I think I'm in love. The night was so hot and humid. I felt as if I was living in a movie. This Bolivian revolutionary swept me off my feet, and I don't know how I will ever come back to earth. Here in South America, the line between fantasy and reality is getting blurred. The way he looked at me and held me. I couldn't wait until we were back in the hotel room.

I walked back to the liquor cabinet and made myself another drink. I took out a different journal, a yellow one. I sat on the couch, put my feet up, and began reading.

Mescaline ... Runnin' 'round my brain. It was all so beautiful. But it wasn't the drug; it was the people and the vibes. Bodies draped over each other, warm, swaying, some nude. Souls melting into each other, dripping off chairs and flowing onto the floor. It felt warm, felt high. Lots of beauty and love floating between us.

The journal entries were drawing me further into my past, and I was feeling at home in the pages.

The next day I went to the bank to close Vita's accounts and empty the safe deposit box. Among the birth certificates in the box, I found my baby jewelry, and my graduation ring from the High School of Art and Design. At some point, when I was younger, I'd told my mother I didn't want the ring anymore. I was so happy she'd saved it for me. I slipped it on my pinky finger, which is where it fit me now. I had always planned on attending my district high school, Henry Hudson, in the Bronx, but my mother enrolled me in the High School of Art and Design in Manhattan. That art school orbited me into a different world. I wonder if my life would have been different if I'd gone to my district school and stayed close to my childhood friends.

The trip to the safe deposit box, and my high school ring, caused a flashback of my first serious boyfriend, Jamie Fitzpatrick. We dated for a few years, and I wondered whatever had happened to him. Jamie Fitzpatrick was everything parents could want for their daughter—but I was so young, perhaps fifteen. Jamie's father was Irish, and his mother was Polish. He was very tall—six foot four—with blond hair cut in an Elvis-style— with locks of hair cascading down his forehead. He was very handsome, in a classic James Stewart way. My parents took us to the Roseland Dance Hall in New York City, where they had met. A woman passed Jamie, staring at him longingly. My mother squeezed my arm and remarked, "That woman almost melted when she saw Jamie." He was beautiful to look at, and I was definitely smitten.

At that time however, my life was going through changes, and I didn't see that at the beginning. Jamie wanted to get engaged, but my parents were dead set against it. My mother said, "Adriana, you're too young to be thinking about marriage." Of course, the more my parents were against it, the more I wanted it. So, at seventeen years of age, I was engaged to Jamie Fitzpatrick.

That same year President John F. Kennedy was assassinated. I sat on the couch in our living room, watching the state funeral on our new color TV. I couldn't help crying as I watched the president's little son saluting his father's casket as it went by in the motorcade. Jamie didn't share my political sympathies, which was one of the things that drove a wedge between us. There were riots that summer in some of the major cities, and the country was in turmoil. The National Guard was called up to keep the peace.

But politics wasn't the only thing on which Jamie and I differed. I was an artist, and he was what we called *straitlaced* at the time. My mother bought me a guitar for my birthday, and sent me for guitar lessons. Jamie remarked, "What are you—a hippie now?"

Jamie enlisted in the National Guard to avoid the draft. I enrolled in The Fashion Institute of Technology in Manhattan majoring in fashion design and illustration. The two year college was filled with fashion shows, French lessons, ad illustration, and garment construction. The instructor of the pattern making class, Mr. Whittaker, was a funny little man. He was heavy set, wore a bow tie, and was subject to frequent nose bleeds. Everyone snickered behind his back while he dabbed the blood with a perfumed handkerchief. I liked him because he claimed I was ambidextrous.

My entire family loved Jamie, and at the beginning so did I. In fashion school my life was changing rapidly. Within a few weeks of his being gone in the National Guard, I fell out of love with Jamie Fitzpatrick, and in love with Zachary Darcy. I didn't tell anyone, and I especially didn't want my mother to know that she was right all along. Jamie was at Fort Dix when I wrote him a Dear John letter.

Zachary Darcy was a jazz musician, a drummer. I had gone to Latin Night at the Village Gate in Greenwich Village with my best friend Salina to see Tito Puente. Salina Rivera was Puerto Rican, and we often went together to hear Latin music. On that night, we got friendly with the two guys who were sitting at our table. Zack was tall with a solid build and curly blond hair. He had a boyish face with dimples when he smiled. He looked like Donovan, the Scottish folk singer whose songs I liked to play on the guitar. He had a funny hip-hop walk. I guess he thought it was cool. Zack opened my senses to the world of jazz, and we frequented the jazz clubs in the Village. I saw just about all the great jazz musicians and singers who were popular at that time—Sonny Rollins, Miles Davis, Nina Simone, Dave Brubeck; too many to name.

CHARCOAL PORTRAIT OF SALINA RIVERA

Salina was dating Zack's friend Cory, and we would often double date. The four of us spent that New Year's Eve together. I still remember the blue dress I wore that evening. It was a sample dress from my mother's dress factory, and I looked like a model in it. I smiled shyly when Zack told me I was "So damn beautiful."

I wasn't ready for a sexual relationship, so Zack and I drifted apart, although I never forgot him.

I sat on the couch and tried to remember how I felt at that time, but that was hard to do. I was a girl becoming a woman, which is always a confusing time. I was eighteen years old. A string of guys came into and went out of my life. I was disillusioned with the sexual aspect of relationships. After all the love stories and novels I'd read, my experiences seemed bland. Sex was nothing like I'd imagined—there were no fireworks.

I walked to the box with my journals and, as had become my obsession, I took one out. I thumbed through the pages and settled on the following entry from 1972:

> Last night I dreamt that our neighbors, the Tremmels, came to visit us at the farmhouse. In my dream they were poor, backwoods people. We went running towards the barn to get away from them. We had to run through a herd of cows, and the bull began chasing us. We managed to escape by sliding under the barbed wire fence. We found ourselves inside the barn, excited, breathless, and sweating from the heat of the day. I saw you lying there on a wooden plank and began kissing you all over. I wanted to make love to you. I remember touching you very tenderly, but then I woke up.

I knew the dream was about Kelly Cooke, but I didn't remember feeling that way about her—At least not consciously.

After I graduated from the Fashion Institute of Technology, I worked in Manhattan as a fashion designer and illustrator in the fur market. I was happy to be out of school. It seemed as if I had been in school my whole life without a break. I had a few great jobs, but found myself constricted in creativity. I sensed a new direction coming in my life, though I wasn't sure what that was.

FUR COAT DESIGN RENDERING

Zachary Darcy called me out of the blue. After he telephoned me a few times, I agreed to see him. I met him at the Circle Train Station in Parkchester, as we had done many times before. He had his father's van. We drove into Manhattan and went to the Blue Note in Greenwich Village for some jazz. I still had feelings for him, but played coy.

When we left the club, Zack told me he had the key to his friend's apartment on Sixth Street. We walked through the busy streets until he stopped in front of an old building with a glass door. It was a four-floor walk-up, very sparsely decorated, and not that clean. I felt comfortable and secure with Zack; we had some history. There was liquor in a kitchen cabinet and he made us drinks.

I couldn't wait to tell him that I wasn't a virgin anymore, but I never got the chance.

He said, "Damn, I've missed you so much. I never stopped thinking about you."

"Me too," I told him. "I felt the same way."

I took his face in my hands and kissed him softly on the lips. We started to make out heavily, and I let him unhook my bra. He began to undress me slowly, watching my face the whole time as if waiting for me to stop him, but I didn't. I took off the rest of my clothes and lay down on the couch. Zack turned off the light. He got undressed in the dark and got on top of me. He made love to me, and it was a very beautiful thing.

This, I figured, was more like making love with someone you really cared for. After we were finished, we lay there quietly. He stroked my arm up and down as he looked at my face and said, "I'm so damn happy!"

I whispered, "Me too." I fell into a satiny sleep.

Sometime during the night I awoke thinking it had been a dream. Then I felt his breath on my neck and his curly locks on my shoulder. His body was so warm, and I could feel the thud of his heart beating. He grabbed my hair gently and pulled me on top of him, and we made love again. When we were finished, he sat up and lit a spliff (the word he used for a joint) and passed it to me. I took a toke even though I wasn't fond of Marijuana. We got dressed and Zack drove me home. I was in a dreamy cloud the whole way. Zack and I dated for quite a while, but he had issues with his father. He moved to California, but I never forgot him.

It was time to close the box with my journals, letters, and important papers. I was going to the post office in the morning to mail a few boxes home to Hawaii. I just had to read one more entry. I picked a black book with pages that were made for watercolors. I flipped through some drawings and watercolors. I settled on the following entry from 1973:

> Tonight is hard. I don't know exactly why, but I feel lonely up here in the country. I've been thinking of working in the city for a month or so, just to get some money together. I need a diversion. Something's missing. It felt really good sleeping next to Bobby, his warm body next to mine. It's been a while since I've been really close to a man, where there is love and tenderness. I want that feeling again.

I certainly remembered Bobby Becker. I put the journal back and sealed the box.

The apartment was all packed up. The furniture was sold or given to family members. As I watched my cousin Cody and his son carry the couch out the front door, I thought of the time my parents came home unexpectedly early from a dinner date with my Aunt Camille. Zack and I had been making love on the couch. We scrambled to find our clothes hearing the key in the door. Luckily it was the Bronx, and there were three locks and a security chain on the front door, which gave us time to get dressed. We sat at the kitchen table while my mother went to the kitchen to make coffee. Zack hid his right foot under the dining table because his shoe was lost somewhere under the couch. My aunt leaned in and whispered in my ear, "Adriana, your dress is on inside out." Mortified, I ran to the bathroom. I laughed sentimentally at the memory. I gave everything that was left in the apartment to the Goodwill.

On one of my last days in New York, I took the train into Manhattan and walked around the city. I wondered if I would ever see the Bronx again. I tried to think back on how my communal life had begun all those years ago. Some of the people were still friends, but we never talked about it anymore. It happened so long ago.

As I walked around New York City, it all came back to me—how my adventure in the counterculture began. I knew that when I was back in Hawaii, I would read all the letters my mother saved, and my journals from the very beginning.

This is how I remembered it:

In Manhattan there are office buildings with floors converted into loft apartments. My friend Reuben Hoffman had just such an apartment, and I loved going there. It was a huge open space that covered the entire length of the building. Visitors had to use a freight elevator to get to his apartment. Ruby, as we called him, loved antiques and the finer things in life. The loft was decorated beautifully, and had a Bohemian feel. Though spacious, it was cozy.

Ruby was a weird sort of guy—heavyset, with reddish-blond kinky hair and a beard. He was very intelligent, political, passionate about life, and a true loner. He wore clear round glasses, and carefully chose his words before speaking. He had a short, snorting laugh. I liked him a lot. He was going on a business trip to Canada for a couple of weeks, and said he'd call me when he got back.

When he returned, he asked me to come to the loft to hang out. I took the subway down to Manhattan and walked to his building. I rode the freight elevator up to his floor, and when the door opened I was right in the loft. We sat on the couch drinking red wine and talking like we always did. We hashed out the world's problems, acting as if we had all the answers to solve them. Then he rolled a joint, lit it, took a drag and passed it to me. I was really just a social toker. We were quiet for a bit.

Suddenly, he pulled out a small, white, oblong box and handed it to me. He said, "I was in an antique shop in Toronto, saw this, and thought of you."

I opened the box slowly. Inside was a beautiful Victorian-style garnet necklace; it looked very expensive.

"Ruby, I can't take this! It's too much!" I said.

"Don't be stupid," he said. "I want you to have it."

Of course I loved it, and he placed it around my neck. Ruby and I had sex that night. I figured that was what he wanted. For some ridiculous reason I felt obligated. After that night though, we were both uncomfortable. We had an uncomfortable conversation and decided we were better off as friends. He insisted I keep the necklace. I still have it, treasure it, and think of Ruby Hoffman every time I wear it.

Through Ruby, I met his friend Noah Bernstein. Noah was a physicist, a brilliant guy. I had to take the bus along Moshulu Parkway to get to his neighborhood in the West Bronx. I was told that just fifty years earlier, the Moshulu Indians held powwows on that very parkway. Now, it had the Bronx Riding Academy. I'd often see people riding horses along the wide stretch of grass and trees.

Noah was tall, well-built, and athletic. He had long, thick, wavy brown hair; green eyes; a large nose; and freckles. His background was Russian Jewish, and he was an only child like me. He wasn't handsome in the traditional sense, but something about Noah made him very attractive. He had a large scar on the right side of his face from the corner of his mouth to his ear. It gave him the appearance of a dangerous swashbuckler. He was a Scorpio, intense, sensual, extroverted, intelligent, and inquisitive.

We fell in love and became inseparable. Sex with Noah-well, let's just say there were finally the fireworks I was waiting for. He wore a military jacket, combat boots, and green seed beads around his neck. My parents called him a hippie. We were into the love-and-peace-movement, the free speech movement, and were against the war in Vietnam. We had a great group of like-minded friends. Noah was politically radical, and I was swept up in the antiwar movement. Life began to get exciting, and a whole new world was opening up. Being sheltered as a child made me rebellious.

Noah kept telling me there was a whole new way of living going on in California, and we needed to be part of it. It was 1967 and people were calling it "The summer of love!" I was terrified and fought the whole idea. The most exotic thing I did as an adult thus far was taking a vacation to Puerto Rico with my girlfriends. The thought of leaving my parents, family, and friends, save for vacations, gave me angst. But Noah Bernstein took off and went to California; of course, with the plan that I would follow.

After many phone calls from Noah, and some soul-searching, I decided to go. How was I going to tell my parents? I'd heard about the "Love Bus" going from New York City to San Francisco for sixty dollars. I was filled with excitement, fear, and every emotion you could possibly imagine. I was twenty years old, and despite my fears and my parents' objections, I hopped on the Love Bus and headed to California.

This is how my journey began........

THE OFFICIAL SUMMER
OF LOVE, 1967

The coldest winter I ever spent was a summer in San Francisco.

—Mark Twain

I was on the Love Bus on my way to San Francisco, not knowing what awaited me. To my surprise, the bus was just an ordinary van. There were five other curious travelers riding along with me in the back. There wasn't much chitchat as we drove for three consecutive days; the only diversions were the rest stops. Crazy visions ran through my head, and I wondered if I had made a mistake. In the end, excitement and wonder conquered fear and doubt. I was always of the mind that you have to leave your hometown, and all the things you are used to, in order to become the person you are meant to be. Get out of your comfort zone!

We arrived somewhere in San Francisco at night. I gathered my belongings and got out of the van. It was dark and the air was chilly. I immediately felt lost. I walked around searching for a public phone. I finally found one and called Noah Bernstein, who was already living in Berkeley. I was so relieved to hear his voice—a familiar voice in a strange place.

He asked, "Where are you?"

I looked up at a street sign, "Van Ness." I gave him the name of the cross street, and the street address of the store I was standing in front of.

He said, "I'm on my way!"

A friend of mine from New York, Violet, was already living in San Francisco. I told my parents that I would be staying with her until I was settled. The truth was that I intended to live in Berkeley with Noah, but I didn't want to tell my parents straightaway.

I waited for what seemed like forever, for Noah to drive from Berkeley to San Francisco. He finally showed up. I watched him get out of a car. He had on his military jacket and combat boots walking toward me with a big stride. As soon as I saw his face, and the way he looked at me, I knew I hadn't made a mistake. He hugged me, "I'm so happy you're finally here. This place is going to blow your mind."

"I thought about you every day since you left," I said.

Violet was expecting us; she was the second phone call I made after leaving the van. We drove to Violet's apartment building in the Tenderloin district.

I didn't bring much with me. Before I left New York I packed a trunk that was to be sent to me as soon as I was settled. Violet opened the door, and we embraced. I was inside her apartment, safe and sound, and had Noah by my side. Since it was late, we decided to stay at Violet's apartment that first night.

Although it was June and the beginning of summer, it was much cooler than I had anticipated. In fact, it was downright cold. The sun was out strong the following day, so the three of us roamed up and down the hills of San Francisco together. We stood on the highest point in Twin Peaks, with the wind blowing wildly. In late afternoon a dense fog rolled in, and the weather turned nasty, so we took a cable car back to Violet's apartment. I could tell by the expression on Noah's face he was eager to show me the place he'd found for us in Berkeley, so we headed out before dark.

NOAH, ON TWIN PEAKS, 1967.

As we drove over the Bay Bridge into Berkeley, it was like driving into another climate. The weather totally changed, and it was warm and sunny. I can remember the smell of unfamiliar flowers in the air, and seeing quaint and ornately painted Victorian houses on almost every street. We turned onto Charming Way and stopped in front of an old pale yellow Victorian. It had a really steep and wide staircase, with a large front porch. As I got out of the car, I smelled something wonderful that wasn't familiar.

I asked Noah, "What is that luscious smell?"

"It's that big eucalyptus tree in the yard," he answered.

An older woman with very long, messy blonde hair and glasses met us at the front door. She wore a flowing dress in Madras fabric, heavy beaded jewelry around her neck, and was very pale. She made me feel welcome right away. Her name was Sage. Standing next to her was Manuel, a Mexican guy, who seemed a lot younger than her. I didn't know if he was a friend, a boyfriend, or her husband.

Entering the house I was overcome by the eclectic beauty of the place. Noah opened the door to a room off the side of the house, which he said was our bedroom. He placed my things on the floor, and we glanced at each other in anticipation. In the center of the room was a large bay window, and below it a bed that was so low, it was almost on the floor. On the wall behind the bed hung a medieval romantic tapestry. I loved it all immediately.

In the kitchen, Sage was preparing supper, something in a large pot. I could tell it was Mexican by the aroma of cumin, coriander, and other spices. Every once in a while, she'd toss a fruit that resembled an apricot into the pot. We all sat at a round wooden table and had dinner together. After dinner Manuel placed a bottle of tequila and some shot glasses on the table. Noah lit up a joint, which was passed around. We drank, toked, and talked, for a very long time. Manuel had been quite, then said,

"Adriana, is this your first time living on a commune?"

"I've heard of group living before, but yes."

"I know you will love it," Sage said.

Noah nervously watched my facial expressions. He stood up, took my hand, and led me into our bedroom. This is what I had been waiting for and dreaming about on that long, boring, three-day ride in the van. I lay down on the bed next to the bay window, and Noah lay down beside me. We stared at each other for a time.

"It's going to be wonderful here," Noah said, with a crazy, melty look that set me on fire.

I smiled at him. "I know; I can feel it."

It all seemed magical, like a dream.

We lay there, holding each other, and I was filled with joy. Then we began undressing each other, and soon we were making love. I couldn't get enough of him, and all seemed right with the world. Afterward I drifted off into a blissful sleep, with the smell from the eucalyptus tree drifting in through the open window.

When I awoke the next morning I explored the house in early light. I heard music in the living room; it was Jefferson Airplane's song "Today." The words expressed how I was feeling: My love for Noah was real, and my dream was coming true. I noticed all the items that made the house a home. There was a branch of bay leaves hanging over the kitchen window. Sage told me it was from a tree in the neighborhood. I saw exotic spices on a shelf, and glass jars of Indian teas. There was an old toaster—the flap-up kind. You had to open the flaps on either side and turn the bread around to toast the other side. Sage made her own bread from scratch, and that toaster was perfect for those thick slices. On another shelf was an antique coffee grinder, an earthenware teapot, and handmade dishes and bowls with various painted designs.

Later, I learned that Manuel had made the dishes and painted them himself. He had a potter's wheel, along with a lot of other tools and items on the front porch. The floors were redwood throughout the house. In the living room was a fireplace with a large mirror over the mantle. A Chinese lantern hung from the ceiling over the round wooden table. It all looked dreamy with the morning sun streaming in. I peered out the window down at the yard outside and saw fresh blackberries, which Noah told me made a great jam. I fell in love with the house the minute I walked in.

The four of us had the upstairs part of the Victorian, but there were other rooms and separate apartments. There were about eight people, and we often ate our meals together. Out-of-towners often stayed with us. Noah was close with Sven, a Scandinavian guy who lived in one of the downstairs rooms off the yard. Sven often invited us for a dinner he'd make on a hot plate.

It was my twenty-first birthday, and after one of Sage's dinners, I was surprised with the most phenomenal birthday cake. It was a three-tiered strawberry shortcake which was assembled on the round wooden table right in front of me. Walking out of the kitchen were Sage carrying the layers of cake; Manuel, with a bowl of freshly sliced strawberries; and Noah, still whipping the cream. Later on, Sage told me the layers were a spice cake made with blackstrap molasses, wheat germ, with whole wheat and soy flour—a no-guilt cake.

Sage and Manuel were going to Woodstock in Upstate New York for six months to house-sit for a friend, at which time Noah and I would take over the house on Charming Way. Sage asked us if we would take care of their cat, an orange tabby named Zoey, while they were gone. Of course, we said yes. Noah didn't get along with Zoey, or maybe she didn't get along with him, but she was in love with me. She followed me everywhere, even in the street. I often would have to turn around, take her back to the house, and lock her inside before I continued on my way.

I'd never really cooked before I lived in the house on Charming Way— my mother was very fussy about her kitchen, and didn't let me cook while I was growing up. Occasionally she'd let me stir the tomato sauce as it was simmering on the stove—so I was amazed at how good a cook I turned out to be. Noah seemed to love everything. We often had friends over and shared whatever we had.

Money—or rather the lack of it—was a huge issue. Noah was teaching a class called "Science and the World" at the Free University of Berkeley. His students paid at the beginning of each class, but it wasn't very much.

He also maintained the yard along the side of the house, for which we received a reduction in rent. I loved watching him work in the yard, his arms pumping, and his sweat glistening in the sun. We got our favorite records from the public library, rather than buy them. Noah brought home a new album by the Beatles—*Sgt. Pepper's Lonely Hearts Club Band*. It wasn't my cup of tea, even though I loved the Beatles.

There were days when we only had canned beans to eat for dinner. We joined a local food co-op to help with groceries. It was the first time I experienced real hunger.

A friend told us we could make decent cash by selling a local newspaper, the Berkeley Barb. It was a political rag, very popular with the students on campus. We would set the alarm for 3:00 a.m., head over to the editor's house, and wait for the papers to arrive from the printer. There was always a bunch of guys there; usually, I was the only girl. We'd divvy up the papers and head out to Telegraph Avenue, the main drag for the Berkeley campus. It was dark and chilly that early in the morning. We'd each pick a corner, my favorite being the doughnut corner, so called because at 4:00 a.m. a baker would make doughnuts for the day in the shop on that corner. There was something comforting about watching him in the kitchen.

The guys hated when I was out there on the avenue because all the delivery vans and truckers would stop at my corner and buy the paper from me because I was a woman. When the doughnut shop finally opened, customers would feed me doughnuts on their way out the door. I usually sold out my papers before the guys.

One Saturday, there was an art fair on Telegraph Avenue. After I sold out, I put one last Berkeley Barb in my backpack, with the intention of reading it with Noah later that evening. I had been watching all morning as the artists set up their tables. I cruised around and check it out. I noticed a large candle on a display table. It was shades of green, yellow, and white. I picked it up and turned it around in my hands, examining it very carefully. I knew I couldn't buy it; we really needed the cash I'd just made for groceries.

Eventually, the artist asked, "Do you like it?"

"It's beautiful," I answered.

"I'll take a little less for it if you really want to buy it."

I set the candle down on the display table. "Oh, I do love it, but I just can't afford it right now. I was really just admiring your work."

The artist had a funny look on his face as I browsed through his other crafts.

After cruising the other artists' tables, I headed home.

Noah was home when I got back to the house. I told him I'd saved a Barb for us to read together, which put a big smile on his face. I reached inside my backpack to get the paper out, and to my surprise the green candle fell out. The artist had slipped it into my backpack while I wasn't looking. That's the way it was in Berkeley, California in 1967.

After Sage and Manuel left for Woodstock, fire inspectors came by and told us we had to clean off the front porch, which had junk stacked everywhere. There were art supplies, piles of wood for the fireplace, stacks of marble, bamboo shades, paintbrushes, all sorts of tools, and much more. Sage and Manuel were junk collectors. We stacked everything in a shed behind the house. We wrote to them in New York to let them know about the inspectors. We did leave Manuel's potter's wheel out there though. The porch was much neater, and we could sit outside and enjoy it. We rented their bedroom to a guy who was from Miskolc, Hungary. He had intentions of sailing around the world and liked to talk about his plans. He was an avid hiker, and we'd often go for hikes in Strawberry Canyon behind the university. Occasionally, we'd take longer weekend trips to Big Sur or Los Padres National Forest, and camp out for a few days. We seemed to have settled into a daily routine that was quite nice. I was enjoying communal life.

LOS PADRES NATIONAL FOREST

Adriana Bardolino

During this time, I wrote many letters home to my parents—sometimes two letters a week—and called them every other Sunday. I finally told them that I was living with Noah Bernstein in Berkeley, which I doubt was a surprise to them. Most of the letters I received from them were disturbing, in that they were not happy for me at all. They wanted me to come home, which I was not going to do. I was happy in Berkeley, and despite our struggles I liked our way of life. I sensed I was at the beginning of something unique and monumental, and I wasn't about to stop now. My parents needed constant reassurance that I was not going to become one of those starving artists they always warned me about.

Noah came running up the front porch steps, breathless and excited. "We're invited to a Hasidic wedding!" he shouted at me.

I looked at him with a blank expression.

"It's a big celebration, a feast that goes on for days."

"What is Hasidic?" I asked.

"It's a religious, Jewish, ultra-Orthodox sect," he said.

We found a gift to bring the bride and groom and set off for their house. When we arrived, the house was filled with people dancing in circles to klezmer music. The wedding ceremony itself was over, but we heard that the bride and groom had been hoisted on chairs and paraded around by the crowd.

The first thing I noticed was that the men and women were celebrating separately—at the beginning anyway. The whole scene was wild and intense, maybe even a bit chaotic. Noah joined the other men dancing around in circles. Then they began jumping up and down to the music while standing in place. One of the men hoisted the groom on his shoulders, and the other men danced around him with lively and joyous abandon.

We ate and drank and joined in on the joy of the bride and groom. After a few hours I was ready to leave. "Noah, let's go," I said. "I'm ready to go." I grabbed his hand. "Noah, I want to go." I'd had enough, but Noah acted as if I'd stopped him in the middle of his euphoria.

The groom reminded us that the celebration would be going on all week, and invited us back. Noah was brooding like a little boy when we left, but I wasn't going back.

Some friends in the neighborhood invited us to their house for dinner. After dinner we sat around listening to music. One of the songs had an extended intro with howling wind, which went on for a very long time. Listening to the howling wind, I had a flashback to a night my mother and I were walking home late from her dress factory in a snowstorm. I saw it very clearly, even though I was a child at the time. I could almost taste the snow on my tongue. We turned a corner, and the cold wind hit us. I could feel the snow stinging my face. Our legs were freezing as we held each other up against the wind. The memory flashed before my eyes a few times before it disappeared. It was as if I was living it over and over again, like in the movie *Groundhog Day*. I pictured my mother's face, just the way it looked that night. I don't know why that scene was so vivid and profound that it stood out in my memory. It left me feeling nostalgic. The very next day I wrote a letter to my mother, telling her I was coming home for the holidays. I didn't mention that it would be only a visit.

Weekends were a big deal in our neighborhood. Provo Park, also known as "The People's Park," was just a short walk from our house. On Saturdays there was a huge art extravaganza with tie-dyed clothing, paintings, jewelry, sculpture, pottery, and so much more. It's where I found four beautiful and unique espresso cups, hand-thrown and painted. They were perfect for Noah's Israeli coffee. He made it in a carafe with a cone filter. Of course, he used Sage's antique coffee grinder to grind the beans.

On Sundays there was free music all day long. All the hottest new bands would play in Provo Park—Jefferson Airplane, Charlie Musselwhite and his blues band, the Grateful Dead, Mike Bloomfield, Country Joe and the Fish, and many more. I stood right in front of the stage, listening to Grace Slick belt out "Somebody to Love." I was overcome with the thrill of the moment, the togetherness of all the people, and the love movement. People of all ages, colors, and backgrounds came together to enjoy the music, and to let loose with freestyle dancing. Life seemed so full at that moment in time. I bought Jefferson Airplane's album *Surrealistic Pillow* and must have played it thousands of times in the house on Charming Way.

CHARCOAL SKETCHES NUDE MODELS

I was taking art classes—those I could attend for free, or pay for on the day of the class. There were life-drawing classes with nude models—sometimes a male, sometimes a female, sometimes both, and sometimes wrapped in cellophane. There was a class on Psychedelic Anthropology, and another in Romantic Poetry. Noah and I attended an evening lecture on Transcendental Meditation. None of these class topics was offered in either of the art schools I attended in New York City. It was a completely eye-opening experience, and I was hungry for new ideas. I loved the creative innovation of Berkeley and California at that time.

My uncle Rosario, one of my father's brothers, and his wife, Lavinia, lived in San Lorenzo, about seventeen miles from Berkeley. Noah and I paid them a visit. I had forgotten how much Rosario was like my father Andre, and it freaked me out. He talked like my father, had similar facial expressions, and even laughed like him.

After dinner we sat in their living room. Lavinia played tunes on her piano, and we all sang songs. Lavinia told us she used to play piano for the tracks on silent movies. She was a little older than my uncle, but they seemed very well suited and happy together. They sent us home with a bag of fresh peaches from the tree in their yard.

In turn, we had them over to our house for dinner a few times. The first time I made all my uncle's Italian favorites, lentil soup with toasted garlic, and eggplant parmigiana. My uncle Rosario said it tasted just like my mother's. Noah's Israeli coffee was a hit, but the dessert I baked collapsed into candy bar status, which everyone ate without comment. It was wonderful to get together with family. In a way, I think it gave my parents peace of mind, knowing that I was all right on the other side of the country.

We heard about a Be-In (also called a Love-in) in Golden Gate Park in San Francisco. We were meeting Violet and her new beau, Jonas. This time we decided to try the Provo Bus, an old converted yellow school bus painted with psychedelic art and fake flowers all over it. The best thing was that it was a free ride given by the hippies.

The bus dropped us off on Haight and Ashbury in the city, where we met up with Violet and Jonas. The air was heavy with marijuana, and a group of guys were playing bongos at the bus stop. That area became ground zero for the hippie love movement. It was a base camp, of sorts, during the Summer of Love and beyond. Men and women had long hair adorned with headbands, flowers and beads. Hippies were everywhere, and greeted each other with the peace sign. Live music played on street corners, and people smoked joints right out in public. Someone was carrying a radio and I heard Scott McKenzie singing that John Phillips song, "If you're going to San Francisco, be sure to wear some flowers in your hair." We saw buses filled with tourists, stopping to take photos of the hippie freaks. There were news crews from various local and national affiliates taking newsreels of the street scenes. We wondered if we would be on the national evening news.

The Be-In was filled with crowds of people sitting on the grass smoking pot, dropping acid, and doing hashish from large glass hookahs. Others were dancing wildly in groups. I saw women bare breasted, some nursing their babies, and couples having sex as if they were in a private hotel room.

There was a free clinic, started by David Smith, MD, for people who couldn't afford to pay for a visit. Doctors volunteered their services on their days off. I used the clinic a few times myself. Something different and special was definitely going on; we could feel the love vibes in the air.

In later years, every time I heard Buffalo Springfield's song "For What It's Worth," I'd flash on those early days when I first lived in California.

The four of us hitched a ride to the Cliff House on the ocean, where tons of seals hung out. The air was brisk but salty and fresh. We walked along the beach, which was deserted, except for the squawking seagulls and barking seals. It was an amazing day. When the fog rolled in, the weather turned cold, so we hopped a trolley back to Violet's apartment. That evening we went to a new club called the Steppenwolf. It was an odd place with a castle theme. Waiters and waitresses dressed in medieval garb served beer in oversized beer steins. We danced the rest of the night away. It was too late to drive home, so we stayed at Violet's, and headed back to Berkeley in the morning.

A friend was giving away kittens, so we adopted a beautiful black, furry Persian male with green eyes. I fell in love with him immediately and named him Boo. Zoey wasn't so happy about the kitten, and she took off. After a few days, she reappeared in the middle of the living room, apparently reclaiming her territory. Boo followed me everywhere and sat on my lap when I was writing or drawing. He slept in bed with us, which Zoey never did.

I was taking Zoey back to New York with me. Sage planned to pick her up at my parents' apartment in the Bronx. She and Manuel had decided to stay in Woodstock well past the six months they had originally planned on. From the way Noah smiled at that news, I wondered if he still wanted to go back to New York.

The Berkeley campus was abuzz with the free-speech movement. There often were demonstrations against the war in Vietnam. Draft cards got burned, effigies of political figures were torched, and draft-age men picketed the induction centers. Women tossed off their bras, and for some crazy reason, there was a general boycott of underwear.

Noah told us he saw a girl sitting on the steps of Sproul Hall with her legs wide open, and she wasn't wearing any panties. I had the feeling he was trying to make me jealous.

Hanging out in the cafés on Telegraph Avenue students would engage in heated political arguments. There were huge demonstrations against the war, not only in Berkeley, but in San Francisco as well. Noah was passionate about the antiwar movement. I was more about the peace-and-love movement. He was of draft age, and lived in fear of receiving an induction notice to serve. Most of the marches and demonstrations were organized by the Students for a Democratic Society (SDS). Noah and I participated in a rather large one, ten thousand people, on the Berkeley campus. It made national news. There was push-back by the campus police, windows were smashed, crowds scattering with tear gas in the air, but I had no fear in those days. Noah stayed close to make sure I was safe.

There were similar marches and demonstrations in every major city in the country. The lyrics to Bob Dylan's song "Masters of War" gave me chills, and put words to what I was feeling. Now I realize that there's a war going on somewhere in the world on just about any given day, and people are suffering and being oppressed somewhere on a regular basis. But at twenty-one years of age, I was swept up in the whirlwind of protest and the counterculture.

Noah was reading the newspaper while I made dinner. He walked into the kitchen reading to me. "Muhammed Ali declared himself a conscientious objector and was stripped of his championship boxing title. He was given a five-year prison sentence." Before I could respond, Noah added with a strained expression, "I've decided to be a conscientious objector." His announcement took me by surprise, although I knew he was dogged by his military status. I wondered what our future would look like.

It was autumn and Halloween was upon us. We bought a large pumpkin, carved it into a jack-o'-lantern, and displayed it on the front porch. We had our costumes planned well in advance. Noah was a pirate. He darkened his mustache, put a black patch over one eye, and wore boots, a hoop earring, and a wide red sash. His long, wavy brown hair and the scar on his face added to the total effect. I was an Indian squaw. I entwined feathers in my braided hair, and war-painted my face. I wore moccasins, beads, and a fake-suede fringed dress I'd picked up at Sally Ann's.

Someone told us that at midnight there was to be a "happening" at Eucalyptus Grove on the campus. We cruised Telegraph Avenue in costume for a while. Around eleven o'clock a bunch of us headed to the grove with wood to make a fire. The grove had huge logs placed in a circle around a fire pit. Each log had a quarter chunk carved out of its length, and were used as benches. We made a fire and hung around joking and laughing. At midnight the bells in the campus bell tower rang twelve times, and we waited to see what would happen. A procession of men and women wearing flowing garments entered the grove. They were holding candles, and one carried a flaming skull. We watched them perform their ritual. We were told that they were devil worshipers, and their mission was to conjure up the devil. They seemed very serious in their endeavor. I found it fascinating, but I didn't believe in that sort of thing.

After they finished the ceremony, they dripped wax from their candles onto one of the log benches and fastened the candles in the hot wax in a row. We went on with our own celebration. For some unknown reason I felt compelled to lie down on the bench where the candles were placed. I closed my eyes and drifted off into a pleasant trance. I awoke when I heard Sven talking to me. I opened my eyes but soon became aware that he wasn't speaking to me at all. He was speaking to a strange young man who was standing over me looking down at my face. The man was dressed in a three-piece suit. He had dark hair very neatly tied back, and a short beard that came to a point under his chin.

Sven asked him, "Are you part of the group that was performing the ritual?"

The young man had a faraway look in his eyes and replied, "You could say that!" He soon disappeared into the eucalyptus trees surrounding the grove. It was totally spooky.

Sven said, "I walked over to you when I noticed that man staring down at you. I mean the guy just appeared out of nowhere in the dark."

"I guess those worshippers were more successful than they ever imagined, and actually conjured up the devil tonight," I said.

"Creepy," Sven said. "Let's get the hell out of here."

It was all so mystifying. Something I couldn't fathom.

"The most beautiful thing we can experience is the mysterious" ~ Albert Einstein

In November, my mind drifted to my upcoming visit with my family in New York. Sage had a small kennel for Zoey, who was coming with me. I didn't want to leave Noah or Berkeley, but I had promised my parents that I would spend the holidays with them. I was dreading the trip—not the plane ride but my family's interrogations, which I knew were coming. The thought of leaving Noah in charge of the house and our new kitten, Boo, filled me with anxiety. But in the end, I knew it was something I'd committed to, and didn't want to disappoint my family.

Sven and Noah drove me to the airport. They assured me that all would be well while I was gone. Sven said, "The six weeks will fly by, and before you know it, you'll be back on Charming Way." Still, it was an uneasy goodbye.

THREE

FEAST OF THE SEVEN FISHES

"Alfie" by Burt Bacharach

*After seeing the Movie "Alfie" the theme song stuck in my head.
I did wonder what life was really all about. Was I just living
for the moment, or did I have a plan for the future?*

Zap! There I was, on the corner of University and Eighth Street in New York City—Greenwich Village, my old stomping grounds. It was as if I'd never left. The scene in the city is forever exuberant and filled with promise. It was quite impressive, even for someone like me, who'd been navigating the city streets and subways in Manhattan since high school.

On the subway ride downtown, I noticed a few new trends. There were mostly older people, and I wondered were all the younger ones had gone. There were numerous ads inside the subway cars. I saw a poster of Twiggy, the British model, who made miniskirts popular, and there were ads for FDS (Feminine Deodorant Spray). I noticed girls wearing hot pants, another new trend, some even shorter than the miniskirts. Even though I had been in the fashion Industry, I was never into those particular trends.

When I got out at my stop on Eighth Street, on the platform was a trio of guys playing jazz. This was a common occurrence. Live, impromptu music on the streets of New York City, or on a subway platform, was always a possibility. I walked up the stairs and into very dense, murky air. A cacophony of noises surrounded me which didn't bother me at all. Young girls walked past me dressed as if they were on a meat rack waiting to be plucked off the assembly line. Men followed them with drooling eyes. I stopped in a deli for lunch. Standing at the counter waiting for my order, I observed people sitting at tables scarfing down their food as if someone was about to take it away from them. After I ate my ham and Swiss cheese on rye bread, I walked back out into the busy street. I was in the midst of life itself—city life that is.

This trip was more of a compromise than a vacation. I'd promised my mother I would spend the holidays with the family, although now I felt that Noah and Boo were my family. My parents didn't understand any of this.

My mother said, "Adriana, after all your education, what are you doing with your life?"

My father added, "She doesn't see danger."

I listened but didn't respond.

My mother had her stockbroker sit down with me for a serious talk. He said, "Think of your money as a money tree. If you don't water it, it won't grow." I just zoned out.

My parents constantly compared me to my cousins, some of whom were already married and had children. It was going to be a long six weeks for sure.

My mother and I had a strained relationship for many years. I harbored resentment about the time I'd spent in fashion schools. I had been accepted to a number of fine arts colleges—The Rhode Island School of Design, Pratt Institute in Brooklyn, and Parsons in Manhattan—but my mother's fear of my becoming a starving artist prompted her to nudge me in the direction of becoming a fashion designer and illustrator. She was paying for it, so I respected and followed her wishes. I felt bitter about it, but for a while I made it work. I was also subconsciously punishing her for an affair she had with another man when I was a child. My father threatened to leave us a few times, and my mother would send me into the bedroom while he was packing to beg him not to leave. He did get his own apartment for a while, and I felt abandoned. My father forgave her, but I never did. Their relationship clouded my trust in people, and made me insecure in relationships with men.

While I was in California my mother adopted a kitten, a beautiful chocolate point Siamese. She claimed the kitten was for me; I suppose that was to lure me into staying. After watching the way she held, kissed, and fawned over the cat, I could tell they had already bonded, and he was definitely her cat. Besides, I had Boo. She named the kitten Alfie, after the character in the movie of the same name which was a hit in theaters.

Noah Bernstein called from Berkeley. He seemed to be struggling back there. Perhaps there was also a little resentment on his part that I wasn't there with him for the holidays. He told me that his parents received a letter from the draft board with a date for his physical. The physical was to take place on Whitehall Street in New York City. Apparently the draft board was not aware he was living in Berkeley. He was upset and confused as to what to do.

"I'm going to the draft board in Oakland to try and get my physical transferred to California," he said.

"That's a good idea, Noah."

"I also filled out the conscientious objector form and will bring that along with me."

I listened intently to what he was saying, but I felt an uneasiness in Noah's voice, as if he was trying to convince me of something.

"Even Martin Luther King went public with his opposition to the war," Noah continued.

"I know, I saw that on TV."

I called Noah a few days later to check on him. He'd received a letter from a friend who had moved to Canada to avoid the draft. He began reading his friend's letter to me. "Things in Canada are really great, although I miss my family and friends. I'm making new friends here."

As Noah was reading the letter to me, I knew that leaving the country was not an option for me, but I didn't want to voice that to Noah just yet. I was hoping, by a miracle, that things would iron out.

Thanksgiving was a big event. Two of my mother's sisters, their husbands, and my cousins, came to our house for dinner. As my mother was getting special glasses out of the china cabinet and setting the table, I sketched Vita in her new dress with a ruffled collar, which she made herself on her Singer sewing machine. She had her hair up in a French twist and wore gold earrings.

CHARCOAL SKETCH OF MY MOM THANKSGIVING DAY

Before the traditional turkey dinner with all the trimmings, there was a full Italian spread with lasagna. The holiday was a lot of work for my mother. She wanted it to be special because I was back home. She made sure everyone got to see me, and of course interrogate me. She even invited two of her neighbors in the building to join us. It was all wonderful, but I was happy, and somewhat relieved, after everyone went home. Vita and her three sisters had a very tight bond. For them, it wasn't a holiday unless they were all together. In a way I was jealous of that bond. My mind however, was still reeling from Noah's friend's letter.

Sage telephoned from Woodstock, saying she was coming to the Bronx to pick up her cat, Zoey. Their plans had changed yet again, and they were not intending to return to Berkeley any time soon. That meant that the house on Charming Way would be ours. That should have made me happy, but my mind was filled with doubt and questions about the future.

When Sage arrived at my parents' apartment, we embraced and were happy to see each other again. Zoey immediately perked up when she heard Sage's voice. My mother didn't quite know what to make of Sage, with her wild hair and hippie clothing. My clothing hadn't changed much since I moved to Berkeley. My father welcomed her warmly. His motto was, "Any friend of Adriana's is a friend of mine." Sage told me that she and Manuel were living in an A-frame in the woods, and that it was incredibly beautiful up there in the country. Woodstock is about four hours north of New York City, and the winter weather can be more severe. Sage mentioned that there was a lot of snow, and it had been very cold.

"Come visit us while you are here on the East Coast," she said.

"I'd love to, if I can find someone to ride up with."

Between Thanksgiving and Christmas, I mainly roamed around New York city going to museums and my favorite music haunts. I loved rummaging around the secondhand stores in Greenwich Village. On one of these mornings I was planning to meet my cousin Gia and her husband, Stu, at the Metropolitan Museum of Art in Manhattan. It was raining really hard so I took a cab to the train station. When I got in the cab, I thought the driver's profile looked familiar, but I didn't say anything.

The driver stared at me in the rearview mirror and asked, "Do you remember me?"

"With that profile," I said, "how could I forget you?"

We both laughed.

Ronny Donnelly was one of my first boyfriends from the old neighborhood. He was a "hood" (short for hoodlum). I was about fifteen years old at the time. He was a tall, good-looking Irish guy. He had dark hair, dark eyes, and a hook on the bridge of his nose. He spoke with a lisp, but that just made him more attractive to me. He was the neighborhood heartthrob, so I didn't think I had much of a chance with him. Most of the neighborhood guys were on a last-name basis, so everyone just called him Donnelly. He finally asked me to go out, and there it was—I was hanging out with Donnelly and all his hoodlum friends, much to my mother's chagrin.

My father liked Donnelly; my mother, not so much. Whenever he came to pick me up at the house, the doorbell would ring and my father would yell out, "It's Dick Tracy!" That was my father's nick-name for Donnelly because of his nose—Donnelly's profile looked a lot like Dick Tracy's.

Donnelly always bragged that his nose had been broken a couple of times in fights, I suppose to impress me. He was wild and crazy, a most sought-after guy. He gave me an ankle bracelet for Christmas that year, which my father referred to as a "Slave chain." It meant we were "Going steady." One of my girlfriends, and my cousin Gia, also received ankle bracelets from their boyfriends. I have a cute photograph of us girls in front of the Christmas tree with our left legs up, displaying our ankle bracelets with big smiles on our faces.

Back then, the girls seemed to have their future lives planned out—they would graduate high school, get engaged, and get married. I knew I was different at that point, because as they talked, all I felt was a cold chill run up my spine. I wasn't so sure that the life to which they aspired would be my life. I didn't feel it was my destiny, that something else was out there, and I was going to find it. The path I had chosen was definitely not conventional, and I was determined not to go with the flow of society's norms. My mother was relieved when I met Jamie Fitzpatrick, a very nice run-of-the-mill guy, at a church dance.

As the cab drove on I wanted to ask Donnelly a million questions about his life, like did he ever get married and have kids, but we'd arrived at the train station. I got out of the cab and waved goodbye. He called after me, "It was good to see you again, Adriana."

I smiled, waved, and rushed up the stairs to the train platform dodging the rain.

Because I was an only child my cousins were important to me. Our family was very close on my mother's side; on my father's side, not so much. My cousin Jeremy was the son of my father's youngest brother, Red. He was the only cousin on that side of the family with whom I remained close throughout the years. Jeremy and I double-dated when we were teenagers. I dated a close friend of his, a British guy, Jude Walker. We liked going to the clubs in Brooklyn, and it never failed—something crazy always happened.

One night, Jude borrowed his father's car and picked me up in the Bronx, with Jeremy and his girlfriend. We drove to their neighborhood in Brooklyn, and went to a popular nightclub. We were sitting at a table having drinks. Jeremy was telling us how his father escaped death when he was in the army during a deployment to Korea. Jeremy said, "Yeah, my dad was the sole survivor of his whole regiment. There was a big battle, and my dad woke up to find everyone around him dead. He put his hand in his shirt reaching for the crucifix he wore around his neck, and was shocked to find the figure of Jesus gone from the cross. My dad said "'Jesus sacrificed his life for my life.'"

We were intently listening to Jeremy's story about my uncle Red, when we noticed a group of guys sitting at another table giving us the evil eye.

Later on, when we got up to leave, we didn't notice they had followed us out. We got into Jude's father's car and headed home.

While driving along the parkway, a car sped up and came alongside us. They passed us, cut us off, and blocked us in. A bunch of guys got out of the car and walked over to our car. That's when we noticed they were the same guys from the nightclub. They opened the two front doors and dragged Jude and Jeremy out onto the ground. Jeremy's girlfriend and I sat in the back seat frozen with fear. They began pounding the car with chains—the car that Jude Walker begged his father to take for the evening, assuring him we'd be careful. There seemed to be no rhyme or reason for the attack. Finally, they walked off, got back in their car, and drove off. The four of us were stunned. Thank God none of us was hurt, but we had to face Jude's father later that night, with his car all banged up.

I called Noah back in Berkeley to find out how things were going back on Charming Way.

He told me he came down with a bad case of poison oak. "My face has swelled up so much it's disfigured."

"Noah, go to the clinic for a cortisone shot—please!"

"The fire inspectors were around again. This time they had an issue with the shed in the backyard. They're claiming it's a fire hazard," he said, ignoring my comment.

"What do they want us to do?" I asked.

"It needs to be emptied out or at least cleaned up."

I felt that the fire inspectors were harassing us because we were hippies, most likely thinking that if they harassed us enough, we'd move out of the neighborhood.

Noah wasn't finished telling me his woes. "We received an official notice in the mail from the landlord. I'll read it to you: "As of January 1, 1968, there will be a fifteen percent rent increase.""

"The first of the year is only weeks away," I said.

"Yeah. There's men outside working on the roof."

"Noah, remind the landlord that the fireplace chimney needs to be fixed, and the yard needs attention, if he plans to raise our rent."

"Yeah, I'll tell him."

I wondered if Noah was up to the task. His voice was a little shaky, and I could tell he was somewhat depressed. Even though he'd known a draft notice would eventually come, he still wasn't prepared. My not being there for him was difficult. We had just heard that my cousin Pauley had been sent home from Vietnam in a body bag, which made both of us nervous. Pauley hadn't been in any live combat; he had cancer. But I couldn't help wondering if there were chemicals used that might have caused his condition. So many families were going through the same tension and heartbreak during the war in Vietnam.

Noah and I had mutual friends who were also in New York for the holidays. They were often at our house on Charming Way in Berkeley. Maxwell Robinov, whom we called Max, was a chemist who had gone to the same college as Noah. He had dark curly hair and a beard. He reminded me of Trotsky, the Russian revolutionary, with his political rants and raves. Adam Hirschfeld was an architect, another friend I met through Noah. Adam was gay, and we seemed to like a lot of the same things. The three of us roamed around New York City together on that holiday trip. We decided to drive upstate and spend a weekend in Woodstock at Sage and Manuel's A-frame. We heard Bob Dylan had a house there and hoped to run into him at a café in town.

Sage wasn't kidding when she said there was a lot of snow in Woodstock, and it was very cold. The wood-burning stove didn't keep the A-frame that warm. I was happy to have a heavy Air Force parka with a fur trimmed hood, which kept me toasty. We had a great time with Sage and Manuel. I always thought they were such a hip and unique couple. On the night of the full moon we hiked into the mountains behind the A-frame. It was very bright outside with the moonlight reflecting off the snow. There was no wind, and the deep snow created an insulation, so we stayed warm. We never ran into Bob Dylan, but I always thought Adam Hirschfeld looked a lot like him. When the weekend was over, we drove back to New York City.

Christmas was upon us, and there was so much preparation. It was slightly toned down, now that most of us cousins were adults with boyfriends and spouses. When we were kids, Christmas lasted three or four days. My mother and her sisters would rotate the holiday hosting. All the women, and us kids, stayed at the host house, while all the men stayed at another house. We never quite figured out what the men did all day long; probably drank and played cards. But my mother and her sisters spent days baking special Italian holiday cakes and cookies. In winter, a lot of the food was kept outside on the fire escape, as there was only so much room in the refrigerator.

My mother and I combed the neighborhood for a Christmas tree. In those days fresh evergreens were lined up outside many of the local markets. We found the perfect tree. We took it home, and I carried it up the stairs. We got the decorations out and had fun hanging all the lights and momentous ornaments, my favorites being the glass lights filled with liquid that bubbled when plugged in. Alfie had never seen a Christmas tree and tried to climb it a few times. In the week or so that followed, I made a gift list for Christmas shopping. My father gave me money to buy my mother something. My mother gave me money to buy my father something. And they both gave me money to buy myself something. This was not a new practice; it had been the routine since I was a teenager.

Christmas Eve was at our house, just my mother, father, Alfie the cat, and me. The Italians eat only fish on Christmas Eve. The Sicilians call it "the Feast of the Seven Fishes," though we rarely had all seven fishes. My mother made lobster tails fra diavolo, in a spicy hot tomato sauce served over linguine. On a platter was battered and fried shrimp, scallops, and baccala, a cod fish sautéed in olive oil with lots of garlic. At midnight we exchanged gifts like we always did. For me there were no surprises, as I already knew what was in all the packages. After midnight it was considered a new day with the Christ child having been born. We had Italian sausages to celebrate the birth. Going to midnight mass on Christmas Eve was not a tradition at our house. A sadness was developing within me about leaving my family. Despite our dysfunction at times, I loved my parents deeply, and missed the familiarity of home.

Christmas Day was at my Aunt Porciella's. My mother brought her famous Sicilian cake, an Italian sponge drizzled for days with bourbon and rum, cannolo cream between the layers, topped with a semi-sweet chocolate glaze. It was always a hit. She placed it out on the fire escape to keep it cold. There was Italian music playing. On the table was red wine, trays of olives, fresh fennel, and hot cherry peppers. There were loaves of crusty Italian bread—the kind it seems I can only find in a bread store in Italian neighborhoods back East. Noah wasn't with me, but once I got into the wine and sampled the food in the kitchen, it was all joyous.

During the raucous dinner, with the clanking of silverware, and everyone talking, my cousin Gia's baby swallowed a walnut and couldn't breathe. I looked on in shock, but Gia grabbed the little girl, held her upside down by her feet, and smacked her hard on the back a few times. The walnut popped out onto the floor, and everyone went on with dinner.

I'd set up my return flight to California before New Year's Eve, so Noah and I could spend it together. Max and Adam had already gone back to Berkeley. I was a little apprehensive about what I would find at the house on Charming Way. So many things had happened while I was gone. I knew that I would miss my family, but I was looking forward to getting back to Noah, Boo, and the commune.

Packing my suitcase a few days before my scheduled departure, I'd often find Alfie sleeping in it, almost as if the cat didn't want me to leave either. It was a tearful goodbye with my parents at the airport. I mentioned that Noah had been offered a teaching position at a university in Brooklyn in the fall, and that we planned on moving back to New York in June. I prayed that would give my family hope that we'd be moving back to the East Coast in the summer. Inwardly, I feared there would be resistance from Noah.

FOUR

SURVIVAL BREAD

Whoever has loved knows all that life contains of sorrow and joy

George Sand, French novelist

I landed at the airport in San Francisco and found the weather cold and rainy. Luckily, while staying at my parents' apartment in the Bronx, I'd come across my reversible brushed-suede jacket in the back of a closet. I had purchased it at cost when I was working as an assistant designer in the fur market.

Walking back into the house on Charming Way was a bit of a shock. Unfamiliar people were living in the house, along with those who were already there when I left. There were sleeping bags and mats in every available space on the living room floor. Clothing was strewn everywhere, and the house was filthy. Dishes were piled in the sink; pots and pans were all over the kitchen counters. A dinner had been prepared for my homecoming, but I had no appetite for it. Noah could tell by the expression on my face that I was freaked out. He must have spoken to a few of the guys, because some of them quickly disappeared. No doubt they felt my vibes. Noah and Max cleaned up the kitchen, and I closed myself in our bedroom.

Boo had grown so much in the six weeks I was gone that I hardly recognized him. He was bigger and had very long black fur, and his tail stuck straight up like a bushy tree branch. He seemed to not remember me at first, but soon was following me everywhere around the house.

So as not to provoke a revolution, I didn't put up a fight. Within the next week or so, most of the temporary boarders disappeared. We had an empty bedroom again, which we rented to two of the guys who were already staying in the house. They were from Rumania, spoke English well, and were very neat and respectable. They didn't mind doing chores around the house, and often purchased groceries. Communal living was a challenge, but eventually I calmed down, and it all seemed to fall into place.

It was February 1968, and the Berkeley scene hadn't changed much. Noah and Max were attending an astronomy class at the university, and planned on going to the movies after class to see the new release of *Planet of the Apes*. The other guys were probably cruising the cafés on Telegraph Avenue. Besides students, the cafés were now inhabited by hippies and Hell's Angels.

I had the house all to myself, which was rare. I decided to listen to Spanish Renaissance music. I sat in the living room on my favorite large straw chair next to the fireplace. I slung my legs over the side arm, and gazed toward the bay window. I could see the rain coming down pretty hard. I was finally at peace.

I managed to come down with the flu. The guys had it and passed it on to me. I was hoping it wasn't the Hong Kong flu, which was a worldwide pandemic in 1968.

Noah went to the editor's house to pick up the Berkeley Barbs. He'd be selling his share and mine, as we needed the money. I had absolutely no strength, and my brain was in that foggy state you get when you're ill. I lay in bed, reading *The Lord of the Rings* by JRR Tolkien, with Boo snuggled at my feet.

Something had changed about Noah while I was gone. He seemed very different. He became visibly upset after a phone call from his parents, something about their receiving another letter addressed to him from the draft board. I was under the impression that he had gone to the Oakland draft board to request that his physical be transferred to California. Apparently, he hadn't, not if he was still receiving letters at his parents' address in the Bronx. I saw him getting more and more frustrated, confused, and agitated, and there seemed to be nothing I could do for him.

We were watching a newsreel on TV of the My Lai massacre. Vietnamese women and children had been napalmed and were screaming. It was horrific and physically upsetting to watch. I could tell by the expression on Noah's face that he wanted no part of that.

"Noah, talk to me," I said. "Tell me what you're feeling. For God's sake, Noah, share it with me."

He stood up ignoring me and said, "I'm going to the avenue. I'll be back later." He disappeared out the front door. At times, he descended into a strange place where I just couldn't follow. It was creating a distance between us.

Three months after I returned from New York Maxwell Robinov moved in with us. Max had an insane laugh and was a very funny guy. He was a welcome addition to the commune. Max loved baking bread, and we were all more than happy to try all the recipes he came up with. The last bread he baked was made with rye and soy flour, walnuts, and dates. It was so good toasted in that flap-up toaster, with butter and cream cheese. But his mainstay was the garlic rye, which he referred to as "Survival bread."

I was taking a class called An Introduction to Chinese-Character Writing. I'd loved calligraphy in high school, and this was somewhat along the same lines. Chinese character writing is a language of pictures. A particular character resembling a house means *house*, with a few strokes of the brush. I also sat in on a criminology class. The instructor said, "We are all criminals at one time or another in our lives." He explained how the law was sometimes applied diversely to different classes of people, how penalties were administered to subjects in courtrooms according to how they appeared, and who came to court with them. The instructor had a wonderful sense of humor, and I found the class interesting and thought-provoking.

Noah, Max, and I had just gotten back from a hike in Strawberry Canyon behind the university. We stopped on Telegraph Avenue to have a coffee in one of the cafés, and that's where we heard the news. Martin Luther King Jr. had been assassinated. The whole campus was talking about the horror of it. We had just been on a joyous hike, but were brought back to the reality of the madness going on in our country. The shock and sadness hung around for weeks.

Although Sven usually ate with us upstairs, he invited us down for dinner at his place, as a friendly gesture. He had quite the wine and liquor collection, as well as an incredible stereo system. Noah and I loved to hang out down there and play our favorite records. He had a black girlfriend, Tanika, and she and I became friends. It was nice to finally have another woman in the house again. Women never stayed that long. Tanika made jewelry. I fell in love with a pair of beautiful, long, beaded earrings, Native American in design. Noah was crazy about them too, and bought them for me. He'd watch them swing on my ears, and couldn't resist the temptation to play with them. He'd gaze at me with a soft, but very hot, loving expression. In the coming weeks, a cloud finally seemed to lift from above Noah's head.

One day in particular stands out from that time. Noah and Sven were downstairs in the yard playing ball. I was upstairs in our bedroom trying to take a nap, but I couldn't fall asleep. I knew we had to pick up the Berkeley Barbs from the printers at three o'clock in the morning. Through the open window I heard them sparring and laughing. I could feel the thud of the ball against the side of the house. An uncontrollable wave of sexual desire came over me, so strong that I felt as if I had no power over my own body, like an animal in heat. I was lying in bed, writhing around, wanting Noah badly. I hung my head out the window and shouted down to him a few times to come upstairs.

I finally got his attention. I heard his heavy footsteps running up the staircase to the front porch. He stopped in the doorway of our bedroom. He looked so very sexy standing there. Noah narrowed his green eyes and smiled at me. His eyes began to dance and melt. He approached the bed, got undressed, and got on top of me. We made love like two wild animals, which orbited me into another time and space. When we were finished, we both lay there next to each other breathing heavily and laughing out loud.

Dharma and Mickey moved into the house adjacent to ours on Charming Way. They had a rock band and practiced at all hours of the day and night—two electric guitars, a piano, drums, and a guy who played harmonica. I was still playing my guitar but mostly to accompany my singing. I wasn't a particularly good guitar player, but I did have a good voice. I loved to sing, especially the blues and folk music. I was into Joan Baez, Nina Simone, and Bob Dylan. Dharma often asked me to sing with the band, but I was insecure and always declined. Then, during one of their jam sessions, Mickey passed around shots of tequila. After a few shots I just got up and started singing. The tequila gave me the courage I needed. That was the beginning of a good thing. I regularly sang with the band and had a blast. Some of my favorite times were when Dharma and I were alone. She'd sit at the piano barefoot, her long red hair below her waist, banging honky-tonk music on that old upright piano.

Things in our commune were forever changing. I learned that if there's one constant in life, its change. One of the guys was leaving for South America, and another was going to Hawaii. Years later, I heard about Taylor Camp on the island of Kauai, which was supported by Elizabeth Taylor's brother, Howard Taylor. It was one of the first communes in Hawaii. I knew that Hawaii was one of the remotest places on the planet. It was said that Taylor Camp was a commune on the "Last point of the world." But at that time, a tropical island was the last thing on my radar.

Max had plans to check out a commune we'd heard of that was about fifty miles north in Sonoma called Morning Star Ranch.

"Noah, why don't you go with Max? Get out of your head for a bit," I said.

He gazed at me. "I think that might be good for me."

"We can see how a real commune works," Max said.

"Yeah, I need a change to reset my head," Noah said.

So they set off on a trip to a place we had heard so much about. It was one of the first big self-sustaining communes, where people lived in harmony off the land. I looked forward to their returning with details. Around that same time, Adam Hirschfeld moved into the house on Charming Way. He and I were already tight friends. Adam was an artistic and spiritual addition to the commune.

ADAM CHANNELING, OSCAR WILDE.

I received a letter from my father. He didn't write that often, but when he did, the envelope was stuffed with newspaper clippings. His letters were always filled with predictions, platitudes, and a lot of preaching. He also enclosed two dollars in cash—God only knows why; probably for stamps so that I'd write back. That would cover a lot of letters with postage stamps being six cents. I also received a box from my mother that was filled with all sorts of goodies—homemade cookies, chocolates, peanut butter, and assorted jams. I guess she thought we were starving. There was a note enclosed with Zachary Darcy's phone number and address in Sausalito, California. Zack, my old boyfriend, the jazz drummer. The note said he was trying to get in touch with me. I thought that was strange. Why would he be looking for me after all this time? I threw the note with his phone number in our junk drawer.

I sat down and wrote a thank-you letter to my mom for the box of goodies. I also asked if she could please tell me the exact time of my birth, because Noah wanted to draw my astrological chart and calculate my rising sign.

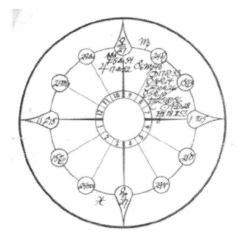

ASTROLOGICAL CHART

Adam Hirschfeld was into meditation, and while Noah and Max were gone, he took me along with him to a meditation center not far from the house. At that time, I found that it paved a path for me to a peaceful state of mind. I hoped it would help me to accept those things in life that I could not change. We repeated a mantra, over and over, to clear our minds of all external things, until that word or phrase was the only thing that remained in the mind's eye.

The yogi remarked that ego was the source of our unhappiness, tension, and feelings of a life unfulfilled. I found it difficult to clear my mind of outside thoughts, but I continued to try. There was no particular religion or prophet involved, just with whomever your spiritual connection was. The mantra could be Jesus Christ or Krishna, or you could just recite a Hail Mary, if that is what moved you. The instructor also claimed that joy and happiness came from giving to others and forgetting the self. We should look for God within ourselves, he told us, not without.

I woke up to find a tiny kitten sleeping on the straw chair in the living room. She was a tortoise shell, and her coat was beautiful shades of black, tan, orange, and white. I imagined Boo had dragged her home with him during the night. Boo looked up at me as if to say, "Can we keep her?" We named her Pepper, and she was a joy and a wonder. Boo and Pepper played together and slept together. Our bed was getting very crowded.

Along with a new pet came some good news. Noah received an official letter from the draft board saying that his physical had been transferred to San Francisco, and that he would soon be notified of the date. This made me happy, but Noah remained apprehensive.

Noah's cousin Harold came to visit from Boston and he rented a car. Not having a car of our own, we took advantage, and were able to visit some of California's landmarks. We spent a day in the quaint town of Sausalito on the Bay. On another, we drove south to Carmel and Big Sur. The ocean and the scenery were spectacular, the likes of which I'd never seen. The beaches along the coast were pristine and deserted, truly a feast for the eyes. We went on a weekend camping trip to Yosemite—oh my God, the rustic beauty of the place. We hiked around and set up camp in a valley at the foot of a very steep waterfall. It was magnificent. The rush of the water was so loud that we could barely hear each other speak. It was still winter and very chilly. In the distance we could see snow atop the surrounding mountains.

Our campsite was next to the river, so the weather was milder, but there were patches of snow on the ground. We passed through a redwood forest which really impressed me—trees that were hundreds of years old; some so large that a car could drive through them. There was a movement in the works to create a redwood national park, its aim being to protect the California redwoods.

It had been a whirlwind of a week with Noah's cousin Harold, and I saw a definite change for the better in Noah. Harold was able to communicate things to him that I could not. I had a hunch that Noah's parents had something to do with Harold's visit. They were as worried about him as I was. After Harold went back to Boston, Noah and I had a talk.

"I've decided to take that teaching position in Brooklyn in the fall," Noah said.

"I'm so happy, Noah. You know, I heard that teachers are so needed that you could probably get an exemption from the draft."

He looked at me and half smiled but didn't say anything.

We'd heard rumors of a party at the Carousel Ballroom in San Francisco, hosted by the Hell's Angels. Everyone we knew was going, so we had to check it out. As we approached the ballroom, we saw hundreds of motorcycles parked on the street. Waiting on line outside the ballroom, the loud rumble of the motorcycles sparked a memory.

Guy was the first man I had sex with. He had a Harley-Davidson chopper—with the high handlebars and low seat. This excited me to no end but gave my parents agita. Guy was short, though taller than me. His blond hair was slicked back with a lot of grease, and was on the longish side but neat. Something about Guy was mesmerizing. He was attractive in a rough yet quiet way, like the Jax Teller character on the television series *Sons of Anarchy*. I was terrified to ride on the back of his chopper, but excitement won out, along with the thrill of holding on to Guy at high speed. There was a group of bikers and their girlfriends we rode around with. I was totally smitten with Guy. I wrote a short poem:

> You could hear them coming,
> A sound as bold as thunder,
> Speed as fast as the wind,
> A shine as silver as the moon they ride under.

I'd be sitting at the kitchen table in the Bronx, and could hear the loud rumble of the motorcycles pulling up to the apartment building. My father would frown at me; then he'd get up and walk to the window. He'd look down to the street, eyeing the pack of noisy bikes. "Adriana," he would say, "Don't think you're going!"

I'd answer, "Dad, I am going!"

"You're not going with Guy again."

"Oh yes I am!" I'd say snidely.

At eighteen I felt empowered, and despite my father's objections, I went. I loved the feeling of being on the back of the chopper—the power of the machine underneath me, the wind in my hair, and the attention it attracted as we rolled through the streets.

There was a horrific accident that involved a number of motorcycles on a parkway, not far from our house. It was all over the local news. A portion of the parkway was closed to clean up the debris. We didn't see what had happened, but we heard there were body parts strewn all over the roadway. My parents were terrified for me, but I was not fazed or deterred by that horrid event. I'd always been rebellious, sometimes even reckless.

Guy picked me up one evening without any of the other bikers. We cruised around until we reached a popular hangout. There was no one there that particular evening. He rolled the chopper up on the grass under the Throgs Neck Bridge—it's where all the teenagers went to make out and such. We got off the bike, and although it was a warm summer night, I felt chilled from the breeze coming off the Long Island Sound.

Guy put his arm around me, and we walked a bit further under the bridge. He threw his leather jacket onto the grass, and we lay down and started to make out, as we had done many times before. Then he pulled my pants down and his as well. That's when it happened—I went from a girl to a woman in a quick, numb, dumbfounded act. I wouldn't call it *making love*; I'm still not sure what I can say about it. I lay there very still and let Guy do everything, since he seemed to know what he was doing. It was weird, but I had no feeling down there. Afterward, I pulled my panties and pants back on. He did the same. We sat on the grass and made out for a while.

Eventually, we got up and walked back to the bike. Before he started it up, I asked, "Did we do it?"

He stared at me with a blank look on his face; then he laughed a little and stroked my cheek. "I hope I didn't hurt you too much."

Hell, I felt something, but nothing like the fireworks I was expecting. I was a little disillusioned about sex. I wasn't sure if I liked it; it wasn't what I had anticipated in any way.

I continued dating Guy until my mother began questioning me.

"Adriana, why can he only see you on certain nights?"

"I don't know ma. Maybe he has things to do on the other nights."

"Adriana, I'll bet he's married."

I couldn't accept that as a possibility, but soon it began to make sense. I did some investigating, and it turned out that Guy was indeed married. *My mother was right*, I thought. *Damn it! She's always right.* That was the end of my affair with Guy. Years later I heard he died of a heroin overdose, as so many in the Bronx did back then.

After my little daydream about Guy, prompted by all the motorcycles, the line began to move.

Inside the Carousel Ballroom people were drinking liquor and beer, smoking joints, and dropping acid. On the screen at the back of the stage was a psychedelic color-and-light show. I had never taken LSD, but this seemed like the perfect time. A friend of Noah's handed me a small blotter laced with LSD. I held it in my hand and asked him, "What will it be like?"

He said, "It's like God in a bottle!"

Janis Joplin was the headliner with her band, Big Brother and the Holding Company. By the time the music started, I was in a plastic fantastic world of colors and wonderment. I was not afraid; rather, I was filled with joy. Watching Janis that night was something spiritual. She came on stage wearing purple velvet pants, a white flimsy unbuttoned blouse, and beads hung loosely around her neck. Her hair was long, frizzy, and wild, with feathers randomly tucked in here and there. The psychedelic light show behind the band was synchronized to the music, and added to the effect. Janice stomped all over the stage, and her raspy voice hit the right pitch. She made me feel every emotion she felt.

After her performance a fight broke out between some of the Hell's Angels. Noah found me in front of the stage staring off into space. He took my hand, and we made a quick exit as fists were flying. Once outside, we saw police cars everywhere. We found our way back to Sven's car amid sirens, which was trippy on LSD. We headed over the Bay Bridge to Berkeley. All in all, it was a night of which legends are made.

In the days and weeks that followed, all hell seemed to break loose between Noah and me.

For some reason, Noah agreed to let someone live in the shed in the backyard—the same shed that contained all of Manuel's tools and junk that we had cleaned off the front porch. We had a huge fight over it.

"Noah, you just can't say no to anyone, can you? We can't be responsible for a tenant living there. We could get into trouble with the county." I brought up the fact that the fire inspectors were looking for an excuse to chase us out of the neighborhood.

"You just don't like anyone or want people around."

"That's not true," I insisted.

We went back and forth over it for a week or so. In the end, the fire inspectors came around on their harassment campaign and made the decision for us. They told us that the shed was a fire hazard and had to be torn down. I was relieved, but this was only a momentary reprieve from troubling events to come.

The basic rub between Noah and me was that I sensed he didn't want to move back to New York. It didn't help that he'd received an official letter from the Selective Service classifying him 1-A, and the conscientious objector form he'd filled out and sent in was rejected. He had thirty days to appeal. Noah's draft status scrambled his brain. Our future life plans seemed to be going down different paths. He was visibly troubled and, at times very depressed. Every exchange between us ended in a conflict.

"Two persons cannot share a dream, except in darkness, as in make believe."
~ Daphne du Maurier, English novelist

Noah became needy, insecure, and possessive of me, while at the same time bragging how the girls on the campus loved him. He began not trusting me, yet I had the feeling he was cheating on me. One day, Noah locked me in our bedroom before leaving the house. I went crazy and yelled out the window. Luckily, Sven was home, came upstairs, and let me out.

About a week later, Noah locked me in the bedroom again. No one was around that day, and I was angry and frustrated. I found a hammer on the dresser, which I had used to hang a picture, and I broke the doorknob off. We had a big fight when he returned, which resulted in his blurting out, "I'm not going back to New York."

"Noah, we've discussed this, and you said you were taking the teaching job in Brooklyn in the fall."

"Well, I changed my mind."

He stormed out of the house, and I ran after him. Then, the strangest thing happened. I yelled out after him, "Daddy, don't leave!" Just like I had done so many times as a child when my father threatened to leave us. A Freudian slip for sure.

Noah spun around with a confused look on his face. He stood there staring at me for a moment tossing my words around in his head. Then he turned away and walked toward the avenue. I was in a state of shock. A flood of emotions washed over me. I stood there crying in the street outside that lovely house on Charming Way. I felt we had somehow lost each other.

Later that day I walked to the avenue and sat in one of the cafes. I ran into a guy I'd seen a few times. We'd had friendly conversations over coffee before. I knew he had a thing for me, but I also knew he had a girlfriend. I went home with him. We had sex in his bedroom. I guess I thought I was getting even with Noah in some fucked-up way. I didn't realize at the time that once you cross that line of infidelity, there's no going back.

Adam Hirschfeld and I enjoyed going into San Francisco to roam around Haight-Ashbury, as it was now called. We often visited a famous bookstore, City Lights. We were told that Allen Ginsberg frequented the bookstore. But we never ran into him. Before hippies there were beatniks. Allen Ginsberg hung around with other poets and writers like Jack Kerouac and William Burroughs, all popular during the Beat generation. We also got a big kick out of old black-and-white movies that played in an avant-garde theater. We howled with laughter when Mae West said, "It's not the men in your life; it's the life in your men!" Adam told me that he often traveled back and forth between New York and California, and it was no big deal. But convincing Noah of that was another thing altogether.

Adam was the first gay person I was ever close with. I had many casual gay friends in high school and college—the schools I attended were art- and fashion-driven and had a large gay student body. Adam and I were riding a similar wave. Even though Noah knew Adam was gay, he seemed jealous of our friendship, though he never expressed it verbally. Perhaps Noah felt he was losing me—or at least control of me—in some way. So many things had chipped away at my love for Noah that a deep wedge developed between us. I no longer felt the same love for Noah that I had at the beginning of our magical journey together in Berkeley.

I searched through the junk drawer for the note my mother had sent me with Zachary Darcy's phone number and address. It took me such a long time to get over him that I wondered why I was calling him. I almost hung up the receiver, but then he answered—and I heard Zack's voice. He seemed happy to hear from me. He told me to come by his place in Sausalito, and I told him I'd try. Somehow, I convinced Adam to go with me. I was anxious as we drove over the Golden Gate Bridge into Sausalito.

We found Zack's house and I knocked on his door. Zack opened the door, hugged me, and kissed me on the cheek. I sat on the couch with Adam and looked around Zack's apartment; I didn't see a set of drums anywhere. He was in the process of ironing a shirt when we arrived, which he claimed he needed for a gig he was playing. There was an awkward silence for a while. Then Zack said, "I've been living with a girl named Squeak for a while."

"That's nice," I said, wondering why he'd contacted me.

We engaged in a nonsensical back-and-forth conversation; I wasn't sure to what end. The whole episode was weird, and I felt estranged from him

"Well, we have to go. We're meeting someone for lunch in town," I said, lying.

Zack walked us to the door and kissed me goodbye on the cheek. He said, "Sorry I'm in such a rush, but I have a gig to play."

"It was good to see you Zack," I said, "and I'm glad you are loving life in California." I walked out the door feeling puzzled, as if I'd been slapped in the face. It was a strange sense of closure. Adam and I had lunch at a quaint restaurant on the Bay in a converted houseboat, then we headed home.

On the drive back to Berkeley, I thought of Zack and how in love with him I'd been a few years ago. He was my first real lover. That visit was strange, and Zack was cold and detached. I was sorry I'd gone to see him. I would have rather left our love affair as a beautiful memory. I closed my eyes as we drove over the Golden Gate Bridge. In my head, I was hearing Zack's favorite song, "Cristo Redentor" through Donald Byrd's trumpet. I pictured us walking out of the Blue Note jazz club on a rainy night in Greenwich Village; then I dozed off.

The next thing I knew, we were riding on the Bay Bridge into Berkeley. I took Adam's hand and thanked him for coming with me.

He smiled affectionately and said, "Any time."

Months went by, and it was June. Adam and Max had already moved back to New York. Noah and I were at an impasse. We sat together on the bed but were silent. We still had the sex thing for each other, but the oneness and love was not there for me anymore. I wanted to go back to New York, and he wanted to stay in Berkeley. We had just heard of the assassination of Robert F. Kennedy. The country was exploding in race riots and antiwar demonstrations, and I wanted to be near my family.

Before Adam Hirschfeld left for the east coast, he mentioned that he had an apartment with a friend on the Upper West Side of Manhattan. He told me I could stay there if I didn't want to live with my parents when I got back to New York.

I was seriously considering that option when Noah said, "I'm staying here, and I want you to stay here with me."

"I want to go back to New York. We can always come back here in the future," I answered.

Another week went by, but there was no break in our impasse. I began packing a suitcase. Boo was coming with me to New York, and Pepper would stay with Noah in Berkeley. Noah had to find someone to sublet the house in case we wanted to use it in the future. He watched me take all my things out of our dresser and empty my side of the closet. It killed me. I took the handmade green candle off the dresser—the candle that was given to me at the art fair on Telegraph Avenue in happier times. I wrapped it carefully in a sweater and placed it in my suitcase. I looked over at the bed where Noah was sitting, and thought of all the times we'd made love there. My eyes welled with tears, and one rolled down my cheek. It was a heart-wrenching thing. The plan we agreed on was that Noah would come to New York when he was ready. I was relieved but apprehensive. We held each other for a long time. Then our lips touched. It was a beautiful kiss. I knew Noah loved me very much, and it pained me that the magic was gone for me.

I didn't want Noah to come to the airport. I thought it would be too difficult for both of us. I asked Sven to drive me. When I got in his car, I couldn't look back at the house on Charming Way that had given us so much joy. I was filled with sadness over love lost. I knew Noah was standing at the bottom of the porch steps, but I couldn't turn around. If I looked back, I might not leave.

I put my hand on Boo's kennel in the back seat and listened to him meow all the way to San Francisco International Airport.

FIVE

THE TREE WAS ALIVE, LIKE ME

The Lord giveth and the Lord taketh away.

—Job 1:21 (King James Version)

Summer on the East is always a beautiful thing. I was back at my parents' apartment in the Bronx, only now I had Boo with me. I wondered if Noah would make it back to the East Coast. It was a moot point anyway, because the damage had already been done between us.

We wasted no time in making the most of the warm summer weather. My parents and I headed straight to Connecticut to my aunt Mari's for two weeks in the country. My mother drove because my father, Andre, was a very nervous driver. If he had to drive, even a short distance, he followed a specific routine before he started the engine. My mother and I would sit in the car waiting for him. He'd circle the car a few times, kicking each tire as he went along. He'd adjust all the outside mirrors to make sure they were in the right position, and clean the front and back windshields. My mother would begin to boil over, muttering and cursing under her breath. Then he'd open the driver-side door and get in. He'd squirm around a few times until he was in just the right position. He'd make the sign of the cross, kiss his fingers and touch the statue of the Virgin Mary on the dashboard. His hand would swipe across the Saint Christopher medal, the patron saint of travelers, clipped to the sun visor. Whatever other aid my father might have needed for security was loudly interrupted by my mother yelling, "Goddamn it! Start the car, and let's go already!"

Luckily that day my mother was driving the three hours to Connecticut. I had the two cats, Alfie and Boo, in a kennel with me in the back seat. The further north we drove, the greener the scenery became. About halfway there, we stopped at the Three Judges Restaurant for pancakes, and then continued on our way. After another hour of driving, we saw the Three Judges again.

"We must have taken a wrong turn," Vita said.

My father and I didn't dare say anything. Once we were in Connecticut, we drove past farms, horses, and rolling hills, and I could breathe again.

We finally arrived at their house and parked on the grass. My mother and I rushed into the house to greet my aunt and uncle. Everyone wondered where my father was—he was supposed to be bringing the suitcases in. Then my aunt Mari yelled, "Oh my God! The geese!" She ran outside, and we all followed.

Two very large geese were holding my father hostage in the car. The geese belonged to my cousin Arlo. He was able to coax them away with food, and my father was finally set free. I never realized geese could be used as watchdogs. We all laughed, although my father didn't see the humor in it. I thought the geese were a big improvement over Rex, a German shepherd that my cousin had on a runner chain the last time we visited.

My cousins were home from university, so it was endless fun for me. They took me along with them everywhere they went. At night, we went their favorite hot spot hangouts for dancing. I'd had a crush on one of Cousin Cody's friends, Jethro Huddleston, when we were younger. We called him Jet. He had written me a couple of letters when I first moved to Berkeley, California.

On one excursion, we went to a place called Gillette's Castle. I was happy that Jet was coming with us. I hadn't seen him in two years. The castle was on a small island at the mouth of the Connecticut River. It was built by a Shakespearian actor named William Gillette. It was a quirky castle with secret passageways. The piano in the main room was on tracks so that it could be moved from one room to another. Jet and I marveled at all the ingenious inventions in the castle. A small railroad went around the whole island, and we spent the better part of the day investigating.

My cousin Arlo played piano, and his brother Cody played guitar. When I was a teenager, my cousins took me to the folk festival in Newport,

Rhode Island. The festival exposed me to traditional folk music, and also to the blues. It's where I saw many great artists of the time play, like Bob Dylan, Joan Baez, Pete Seeger, and Dave Van Ronk. I attended workshops with some of the old blues legends, like Mississippi John Hurt, Lightnin' Hopkins, and John Lee Hooker, just to name a few. There was always music at their house, and I was having a summer blast!

Some crazy things happened on that trip. My mother's cat Alfie had a fight with a feral cat. I attempted to break up the scrap and got scratched pretty badly in the process. I still have faint scars on my left forearm. My father ended up in the emergency room with sun stroke, after spending a whole day on a beach chair in their yard, slathered with baby oil and iodine (old tanning method). He spent a week of his vacation in a Connecticut hospital.

After my cousins went back to university, there was not much for me to do. I asked my mom if I could take the car and drive back to the city. My parents were a little skeptical. Aunt Mari said that she and my Uncle Giuseppe would drive my parents back to the city. They were planning on spending a week or so in the Bronx with us anyway. It was agreed that I could go home after the weekend.

On Monday morning, I started out on the road. As I drove onto the New York State Thruway, the weather changed. The sky turned very dark, and I could hear thunder and see lightning in the distance. Then it began to pour rain; it came down in sheets. I fumbled around for the windshield wipers, but it was raining so heavily that the wipers didn't help much. I considered pulling off the road, but there was so much traffic that it seemed too dangerous to attempt. I slowed down and moved steadily with the flow of traffic. I could feel myself tense up at the wheel, but I forged ahead. The rain subsided, conditions improved, and I calmed down.

Suddenly, the slick of the rain on the hot, greasy, road sent the car careening. It went out of my control and spun like a top. I gripped the steering wheel and held on. I stared straight ahead, wondering where I'd end up. My parents' car was a big, heavy Oldsmobile, and after it spun a few times, the car miraculously straightened out on its own. God must have been watching over me that day, or maybe it was Saint Christopher on the sun visor.

After that incident, I had the road all to myself, because the other cars stayed well clear of me. The rest of the drive home went smoothly. When I saw the George Washington Bridge, I knew I was almost back in the Bronx.

I never told my parents about that experience; they would have never let me take the car again.

I received a call from Noah Bernstein, who was still in Berkeley. He told me he was coming back to New York very soon, and that he had decided to take the teaching position in Brooklyn. I told him I was happy, but I was very cautious so as not to sound excited. I wasn't sure how I would feel when I saw him. I didn't want him to read too much into our conversation.

About three weeks later, he called me from his parents' apartment in the West Bronx, wanting a reunion. I was very nervous about seeing him. We hadn't been apart too long, but we'd left things at an impasse. I still loved Noah, but I didn't feel the same way about our relationship.

I took the bus along Moshulu Parkway, observing the horses and riders alongside the bus route. A million memories ran through my head, and I had a difficult time focusing on the present. I kept seeing our past, and how much in love we were. Our time on Charming Way in Berkeley was so intense. I thought of our showers together, and how we'd dry each other off. I'd sit in front of Noah on the bed, and he would dry my hair. Perhaps it evoked a pleasant memory of my father drying my hair when I was a child. It was a very simple act, but a close and loving one. It always gave me a feeling of security.

I rang the bell in the vestibule of Noah's building, and he buzzed me in. I walked up the stairs to his apartment, and he was waiting at the door for me. I was indeed happy to see him. We hugged and kissed and went inside. His mother was in the kitchen and embraced me. She had that "you're the one" look on her face. It was something she told me a few times in confidence. I didn't say much, and neither did Noah. She mentioned having grocery shopping to do, but I knew she wanted to give us time alone. She left the apartment, and when we heard the door close behind her, we walked along the hallway to Noah's bedroom. I was familiar with everything; I had been there many times before. We both were a little awkward. He showed me some formulas and projects he was working on. I was glad he didn't drag out that article in Scientific American Magazine about a model rocket he built, although I saw the periodical laying on his dresser. After we talked for a while, we both relaxed.

Suddenly, one thing was on both of our minds. We stopped talking and gazed at each other. He sat down next to me on the bed, leaned over and kissed me. Then he began touching my breasts, and I responded. I reached my hand down to his crotch and could feel how hard his member was under his jeans. It turned me on. Despite all the things that had gone wrong with our relationship, we still had that sexual fire for each other. Soon we were making love; we couldn't help it. God, it was so good.

For some reason, after I climaxed, I felt immediate regret and was disgusted with myself. I pushed him off. I felt like a black widow spider that wants to kill her mate after sex. I don't know what got into me. I was overcome with self-loathing and was angry at my own weakness and desires. I stood up and quickly got dressed. I said, "This was a mistake, a big mistake!"

Noah sat up, a little shocked and probably disappointed at how our reunion was going. He watched me get dressed with a blank stare.

I ran out of his apartment and down the stairs.

Noah ran after me, crying and grabbing onto me saying, "Adriana, I love you. Adriana, I love you!"

I ran out of the building and left him standing on the street. I just kept running until he was out of sight. I hated myself. I hated what I thought I had done to him and to us. I was filled with guilt and overwhelming sadness over love lost, the love I once felt for him. But god, how could I help the way I felt?

By the time I reached the bus stop I was shaking. The bus finally arrived, and I got on. I looked around at the faces of the people as I searched for a seat. I don't remember anything about the ride home. I was in a complete daze. I didn't remember the walk back to my parents' apartment either. I felt numb and stayed that way for days. I began keeping a journal. This poem was the first thing I wrote in it:

Love is like the warm glow of a flame
It fills a heart with passion that knows no shame
Comes a cold wind, a bitter word, or a warm tear
And darkness shall fill the heart
Where once a flame did appear

It was a difficult time and I was somewhat depressed. I needed to work. I found a job in Manhattan at a small fur-coat design house called Kooky Furs. There was no pattern making or garment construction involved, just sketches and renderings of the designs. I also ran errands and got coffee for the owners, if that's what was needed. *The Devil Wears Prada* was a movie that brought back memories of what my job was like. I was in no way a fashion icon, but I was lucky to find such a great job in my field. Chasing the owners for checks was an issue at times. The daily commute into Manhattan from the Bronx was something to which I was immune. But I had tasted a different sort of life in California, and I didn't enjoy the routine anymore. Living with my parents again, after living on my own, was also very trying.

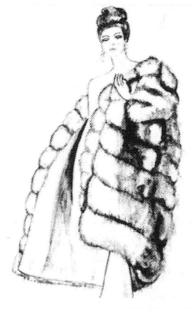

FUR COAT RENDERING.

My years studying fashion design and illustration prepared me well for the fashion world, which turned out to be more like Hollywood. I thought back to my senior year, when I was sent on a job interview by the university office. I brought my portfolio of sketches, and went to the address I was given. The man who interviewed me was waiting for me when I arrived. I took note of how well dressed and formal he was. I followed him into his office, and watched him sit down at his desk. He flipped through my portfolio of renderings and designs. He seemed very pleased. Then he asked me, "Would you be willing to do some modeling if that was required of you?"

I was flattered and answered, "Of course."

He said, "Well, you'll have to take your blouse off so I can measure you."

I went along with it, thinking it was part of the interview. Then he unhooked my bra and told me to take it off as well. Even though my gut told me it was wrong, I numbly went along with it.

He explained it away by saying, "Some of the dresses you will be modeling require no bra."

"I do understand," I said, but felt violated in some way.

When the interview was over he left the office. I dressed myself, folded up my portfolio, and walked out to the desk in the showroom. I was totally embarrassed and felt foolish.

He shook my hand, "I'll let you know about the job."

As soon as I got on the elevator, I knew it was all wrong. I reported it to the university office, but they did nothing.

Boo, being an outside cat was hard to keep indoors. He'd yowl, tug at the blinds, and climb the drapes until we let him out. There were a number of private houses on the same street as my parent's apartment building, and Boo played in their yards. This went on for quite a while and became his routine. Often, when I'd get off at the train station, I'd walk the few blocks to the apartment house, and Boo would be waiting for me in the street, just like a dog. He seemed to know what time I got out of work. He was a remnant of my happy times in Berkeley, and I loved him so much. I felt guilty about taking him to New York with me, and it crossed my mind that subconsciously, it was a way to punish Noah.

Boo was looking peaked and wouldn't eat, so I took him to the veterinarian. The vet told me he'd been poisoned. I stared at the vet in disbelief, trying to wrap my mind around the gravity of what he was saying. He told me that Boo was suffering, and that the humane thing to do would be to put him to sleep. I stood there in total shock and denial. I began petting Boo and crying. I felt as if God was punishing me for abandoning Noah. I told the vet that if he couldn't save Boo, I wanted him put down. I didn't want him to suffer any longer. I wondered which of our neighbors would do such a thing. My mind was tumbling into a very dark place. I had to shake it off somehow but not that day. My love for Noah had died, and now my beloved Boo was gone too. I left the vet's office in a thick dark cloud.

I wrote this poem for Boo:

I'll remember you running through fields of green
Fur so black and shining
Occupied with moths and climbing trees

Stalking butterflies behind flowers
I'll remember your eyes, green as they were
Brightness and life within them
Your tail, tall as a redwood tree
Bushy and straight as an arrow
I touched and held the life I loved so much
As it left with but a whimper
And watched the sparkle in those eyes
Fade from me forever

I went around for weeks in a gloomy state, going through the motions of what my life had become. I kept working for Kooky Furs, and I morphed into a dull pattern of daily drudgery. One of the few things I looked forward to each morning was the toasted bagel with butter and American cheese that I picked up at the deli by the train station where I got off in the city. The hour-long ride into Manhattan for work every day, and the same ride back to the Bronx, was filled with shades of gray—gray subway cars, men in gray suits, a city filled with gray people racing to and fro with lifeless expressions. Even the air was gray. It seemed as if the sun never came out anymore. Or maybe it was just me. An escape from the dullness was reading a book on the subway ride. I would drift off into a faraway place or get lost in someone else's life or adventure. It would give me a short reprieve from the place in which my mind was dwelling. California, and my life there, had permanently changed me.

I ventured downtown to Greenwich Village searching for anything that would make me feel emotion again, anything! I stood there numb on the platform waiting for the next train. The subway car had a familiar stale odor. I was used to it, having ridden these trains since high school. I got out on Eighth Street and walked past Cooper Union, the art school my mother's brother Victor attended as a young man. I had an emptiness that no one seemed to be able to fill. I stopped at a deli for a tuna sandwich and a coke to go, and walked to a club that had blues all day long. I sat there and ate my sandwich listening to blues artists hoping to be discovered

It was the fall of 1968, and my friend Adam Hirschfeld called to remind me that I was welcome to stay at his place. Although I'd met him through Noah, we remained good friends. I decided to take him up on his offer, and began hanging out in Manhattan after work. Soon, I stopped going back to my parents' apartment in the Bronx. He and his roommate, Lonny, had a great apartment on the Upper West Side. It was in an up-and-coming neighborhood with outside markets, and was close to both Riverside Park and Central Park, where we'd often go for walks.

Although my friends were gay, there were a lot of straight guys hanging around their apartment. Lonny Marcum, Adam's roommate, was a university professor. There were often students, some from other countries, who hung out there. I was sitting on the floor of their apartment, when I overheard some students talking about the Tet Offensive that was in the news. Interesting and provocative conversations were the norm, and Adam was forever fixing me up with guys. Sometimes I had the impression he was vicariously living through me with the straight guys he couldn't have.

Maxwell Robinov was also still in the picture, and we often all did things together. We did not discuss Noah—at least, they didn't speak about him in my presence. We went to plays, avant-garde live theater in SoHo, museums, concerts, and all sorts of interesting happenings that were going on in the city. Adam and I took a pottery class in Greenwich Village. I loved working with clay on the potter's wheel, and was introduced to the slab method. I did spend a night with my parents in the Bronx once in a while, but not often. After Boo's demise it depressed me to be there. Within a few months, I was basically living at Adam and Lonny's apartment.

SLAB PIECE VASE GLAZED AND FIRED

We heard that a new band was playing at Carnegie Hall, the Rolling Stones. They were part of the British Invasion. We all took LSD, got on the subway, and headed to the concert. I felt the drug coming on (taking effect) while we were still in the subway car. A little girl was sitting across from me holding a big orange balloon. I asked her, "Can I have a bite of your orange?" Her mother stood up and quickly ushered her to a seat far away from me.

Adam put his hand gently over my mouth and smiled at me. Lonny and Max started laughing, and Max's laugh was just crazy, like a high-pitched machine gun. We got out at the stop nearest Carnegie Hall, and everything around me became trippy, vibrant, intense, and dramatic. The Rolling Stones were fantastic, and we had the most epic night. Acid always had a way of making everything we were doing more intense. People said that LSD was a mind-altering drug, but I often found it to be mind-enhancing.

Timothy was a musician from England on vacation. He was very tall, with dark hair in a shaggy Beatle cut. He hung around the apartment, and I loved his British accent.

Adam said, "Be prepared because he's probably not circumcised; most foreign men are not."

Being gay, Adam considered himself an expert on the subject. The comment caught me off guard, and I didn't know what to say. Then he added, "Don't worry; once it's hard, there's no difference at all!"

Tim and his bandmates were always at the apartment, so we were basically thrown together. Maybe I was using Tim to get over Noah. You know what women say: "The best way to get over a man is to get under another one." Was it working for me? Not really, but in those days of youth and beauty, romance was so easy to come by. When one guy exited, there seemed to be another one waiting in the wings, sometimes even before the curtain closed.

Soon it was the Christmas season, and Timothy went back to England. Even though Adam was Jewish, he appeased me with a Christmas tree. We picked out a nice one from a line of fresh cut trees in front of a bodega, and Adam carried it home. The doorman watched disapprovingly as he dragged it through the lobby and onto the elevator leaving a trail of pine needles behind. There were no decorations, but we adorned the tree with lights we picked up on the way back to the apartment. When Christmas was over, Adam put the twinkling lights inside his headboard, and the evergreen remained on the living room floor until spring.

In February there was a huge snowstorm—which came to be known as the Blizzard of 1969—it virtually closed down New York City. Three feet of snow fell. Trains and buses were not running, stores were closed, people didn't go to work, and kids stayed home from school.

Adam made breakfast and Lonny fed the cats. There was a knock at the door, and Max drifted in cold and wet from the snow, followed by two of his friends. We figured that this was a day that New York City probably would not see again for many years, so we all took LSD and headed to Riverside Park to go sledding.

As we left the apartment building and headed out into the street, the snow was still coming down heavily. All we could see for blocks in front of us was a world of white. When we reached the park, it seemed as if everyone in the neighborhood had the same idea. We didn't have a sled, but we'd picked up a large piece of sturdy cardboard that we found next to a restaurant dumpster on the way. The cardboard worked well. We all piled on and went sliding down the hill laughing hysterically. We did this over and over again. I looked up at the sky, and the sun was shining through the clouds. The LSD made everything sparkle and pulse with a dreamy quality. It was intense.

Something else happened that day. As we were playing on the snowy hills in the park, I had an epiphany, probably sparked by the acid. It was as plain as day, right in front of my face. Why hadn't I seen it before? It wasn't Timothy, or some new guy Adam was fixing me up with that I wanted; it was Adam. We stared at each other, our eyes connecting like magnets. How could this be? My best friend. My gay best friend. I wasn't sure if anyone else picked up on it at the park, but Adam and I surely did. Adam wrote in the snow with his finger: *Triad > Adam, Adriana, and Max.* It was very suggestive, although it wasn't exactly what I had in mind.

We were frozen from the cold. We said our goodbyes to our friends and left the park. Max, Adam, and I walked along the same path that we had arrived on. Suddenly Adam stopped, grabbed my jacket, and pulled me so close that our faces were just inches apart. He looked straight into my eyes, and for a moment I thought he was going to kiss me. The expression on Adam's face let me know he was feeling the same thing I was. A shudder ran through my body. Then he let me go, and we continued on our way.

WITH ADAM IN RIVERSIDE PARK.

The three of us finally reached the apartment house and entered the vestibule. The doorman followed us with his eyes as we walked through the lobby. He was frowning because we were beginning to melt. We got on the elevator, puddles of water forming around our feet.

Lonny wasn't home, and the apartment was empty, save for the cats. With the warmth of the apartment, I felt the blood rush back into my cheeks. We took off our wet clothes and left them in a pile on the floor. We were still buzzing from the LSD. The three of us lay on Adam's bed, nude, with me in the middle. My body was tingling all over. We hugged each other and started giggling, arms and legs everywhere. I had a vision that they were the brothers I never had. We lay there talking and laughing. I gazed up at the rainbow headboard, which Adam had designed and constructed himself, and got lost in the twinkling lights. After a while Max got up and quietly slipped away.

Adam raised himself up on one elbow and gazed at me. He began fondling my breasts, then ran his hand over the rest of my body with curiosity. I wondered if I was the first woman he'd touched. Then he kissed me very tenderly on my lips. We made love as I stared up at the twinkling lights. It was all surreal. I slept in Adam's bed that night.

The next morning when I awoke I wondered if we would feel the same, or if the love bug had worn off with the drug. Adam opened his eyes and smiled at me. He stroked my hair and said, "I think this will be a very different year. I'll go make us breakfast."

The day was off to a beautiful start.

Jimi Hendrix was playing at the Fillmore East, and a bunch of us went to the concert. Watching Jimi was a religious experience. The guy was an amazing guitar player with lots of charisma. I heard that he and Janis Joplin had a thing. They seemed well suited for each other. They had music in common, as well as talent and stardom.

Adam and I became a couple. I got flak from the gay community— not from Lonny or Max, but from our friends at the commune we visited upstate on the weekends. They treated me as if I were corrupting Adam in some way. That seemed to be the twisted politics of the time. We couldn't help that we fell in love. You don't choose who you love. It's just a feeling, and it doesn't have rules. Love hits you like a bolt of lightning when you least expect it. It's not something you plan. It's the domain of the heart, not the brain. I was very well aware of Adam's sexuality, and never lost sight of it. Even though our friends loved us, some had a difficult time accepting us as a couple.

Adam found a Romanian robe in a second hand store, which he liked to wear around the apartment with nothing under it. I teased him, saying, "Maybe we should have a Bed-In Peace Week, like John Lennon and Yoko Ono."

He also got into the habit of wearing an essential oil called patchouli, which has a medicinal pungent scent. It reminded me of incense being shaken in an urn, inside the temple of a distant land. Soon I was wearing it too.

We loved the music of the Incredible String Band, a British group. I often walked around the apartment singing the lyrics of their songs… "You get brighter every day, and every time I see you." Sometimes I'd watch Adam as he sat in a chair by the window, quietly reading, with one of the cats on his lap, totally in another world. The sunlight streamed in the window, lighting his curly blond locks and the stubble on his face. That was love.

We were spending our weekends at our friends' commune in Aliceville in Upstate New York. I loved it up there in the country. Spring was approaching, although it was still rather cold. It was time to visit our brothers and sisters from other mothers. We loved to hike in the surrounding woods, and sit by the stream behind their house.

A group of us took mescaline and walked to the stream. It was chilly, but the sun was strong. I sat on a rock on the edge of the stream, which seemed more like a raging river that day. The winter snow atop the mountains was melting and rushing into the surrounding waterways. As the drug came on, I began seeing beautiful images. Adam was sitting on the rock next to mine. I noticed a chunk of ice in the shape of wings floating his way. I imagined they were wings of freedom. He smiled at me as if he knew what I was thinking. The sunlight on his curly blond hair and mustache resembled a Van Gogh painting, with swirls of different-colored brush strokes. We wandered into the woods, with colors of yellow and purple following us.

We rolled down a grassy hill, lost our shoes, and began laughing uncontrollably. We kissed like children.

Adam said, "I'd like to fly like a bird! Would you want to fly?"

"But you wouldn't take me along."

"Well, you can come for a little while!" Adam said.

"Then I'd rather not fly at all!"

In reality, I was already on that flight, despite my better judgment. I looked at my hands, and the flesh appeared sacred. In the woods I had a profound vision. I stared at a tree that was on the hill in front of us. I saw how it was the same above as it was below. The top of the tree covered with leaves, was taking in sunlight and air. Below the earth, it had roots that were taking in water and food. The image was burned into my mind's eye, and I never forgot it.

THE TREE OF LIFE WATER COLOR

That night, we all sat around in their living room, and I played guitar like I'd never played before. It was as if I was playing with my whole being, not just with my hands. Everyone around me felt it too. I played Bob Dylan's song "Mr. Tambourine Man." One of the guys sang the words as I played the music. There was a union of souls in that room. We all felt it. I walked outside and looked up at the stars sprinkled in the sky. The night air was brisk but refreshing, and I felt content. After that weekend, when Adam and I were back in the city, we had a serious discussion with Lonny about getting our own commune upstate.

When spring finally arrived, Adam and I took a walk to Central Park. At the northernmost end of the park, there's a large trellis covered with wisteria. As we approached it, we were overcome by the fragrance. It was so luscious and beautiful to look at, and the scent was heavenly as we strolled underneath. We also saw the bronze fountain—Untermeyer Fountain— with a statue called *Three Maidens Dancing*—such a beautiful reminder of the celebration of spring after a long, cold winter.

"The original sculpture is in Germany, and the artist is Walter Scott," Adam said; he always knew details about things like that.

On our way back to the apartment, we stopped at an outside market to pick up some fresh vegetables. Adam wanted to cook us a nice dinner; he was quite the chef now.

The next thing I knew, he was shaking me awake. I had completely blacked out. I found myself on the ground amid the vegetables, with a crowd of people standing over me. I didn't know what the hell had happened. It crossed my mind that maybe I was hungry, and hadn't eaten enough that day. As soon as we got back to the apartment, Adam started dinner. Lonny seemed puzzled by my fainting spell.

Lonny had friends, a gay couple, who had a cabin near Cape Cod. There was much anticipation as we drove to Massachusetts for the weekend. Their cabin was in the middle of the woods shaded by trees. Spring was in full swing with flowers blooming everywhere. It was the most relaxing few days I had spent in a long time. Adam and I came back from a walk in the woods to find the others lounging in chairs on the front porch. With drinks in their hands they resembled a group of Southern aristocrats. Lonny Marcum was from the South, and on the porch that day, it was obvious.

The sun was shining and the weather was warm, almost like summer. Vivaldi was playing loudly on the stereo. Lonny's friends had an incredible sound system, with speakers that reached every corner of the property. Adam and I took acid, took off our clothes, and went romping through the woods, naked, as Vivaldi blared through the speakers. Everything in the woods seemed to come alive—so many vibrant colors, with different shades of green. The trees were rustling and swaying in the warm breeze. I lay down on a grassy patch and looked up. The sunlight streamed through the forest above us, and the air was filled with the luscious scent of pine.

I thought I saw a tree move; maybe it was alive, like me. I ran over to the tree and put my arms around it. I could feel it breathing and thought I felt a heartbeat. I was overcome with a feeling of oneness with the tree, almost as if the tree and I were one entity. I said to Adam, "The tree is alive."

Adam grinned from ear to ear.

I felt as if the tree was my mother, and I was a mother too. Adam gently pried my arms from around the tree. Soon, we were off discovering other fantastic things in the woods.

Over the next week or so, back in the city, I began feeling queasy. While visiting my parents in the Bronx, I told my mother about passing out and feeling queasy.

"Is there any possibility you could be pregnant?"

I looked at her blankly. After rolling it over in my head, I answered, "There is."

I could tell my mother was upset with me when she said, "Don't say anything to your father."

Fear came over me, and I promised I'd go to the doctor the very next day. I prayed that this time my mother would be wrong, but as usual she was right. Damn it; she was always right. I thought of all the drugs I had taken and the fact that Adam, despite loving me, was gay. I definitely knew I wasn't ready to be a mother. I flashed on that quote from D.H. Lawrence, "We fucked a flame into being." After much tormented thought, I decided to have an abortion.

When I told Adam I was pregnant, he smiled, almost as if he was happy about it. I don't know what exactly was going through his mind. I was twenty-two years old, and my life was unstable. I didn't know from one year to the next, who I would be with. I didn't think it was a good idea to drag a child into the free-spirited way of life I had chosen. In the end, Adam told me that it was my body, and whatever I decided to do, he was with me.

Abortions were illegal in New York State at that time, so I had to fly to Pittsburgh, Pennsylvania. The clinic I attended had given me the name of a doctor. I was afraid, but I knew I didn't want to be pregnant. Adam flew with me to Pittsburgh. After we landed, we hailed a cab. The taxi stopped at the address we'd given—it was a hotel. We walked into the lobby and saw the doctor's office straightaway. I knocked on the door.

The doctor answered it and hurried us inside. He looked at Adam and said, "Wait outside; she'll be fine."

Adam handed him the money, briefly gazed at me, and reluctantly left the office.

The doctor closed the door behind him. "Relax," he said. "I'm going to help you."

I didn't know what to expect, but I wanted it to be over as soon as possible. I was afraid because I'd heard that women who went to backdoor abortionists died due to infection from the procedure.

The doctor said, "Get undressed, and put on this hospital gown, open in the front. Did you follow the directions you were given not to eat anything this morning?" I nodded.

"Try to relax because I can't administer an anesthetic. Right after the procedure, you are to get up and leave immediately."

The pHisoHex he covered my genital area with felt cold, but I was relieved he was using a disinfectant.

I closed my eyes tight, grabbed the sides of the narrow table, and readied myself. I didn't lose consciousness during the procedure, but I zoned out from the pain and loss of blood. I kept telling myself it would be over soon. Well soon couldn't come soon enough.

Finally, the doctor took my hand and said, "It's all over."

I lay there with tears streaming down my face and running into my hair. The doctor let me lie there for a short time, until I regained my composure. He handed me a prescription and said,

"You'll feel cramping for a while; it's totally normal. You have to quickly leave the office, as soon as you feel able."

The doctor helped me off the table, and though shaky, I was able to stand up. I thanked the doctor; he opened the door and showed me out.

Adam had been sitting on a couch in the lobby and stood up as soon as he saw me. He put his arm around me and told me to sit down. "I could hear you all the way out here," Adam said. I didn't answer. We sat on the couch together. He held me and just let me cry. Eventually we left the hotel lobby, and Adam called a cab. We went directly to the airport and were soon on our flight back to New York. I think I was in a form of shock.

When we arrived back at the apartment in Manhattan, Lonny was waiting. He put his arms around me and hugged me with love and sympathy. They put me in Lonny's room because his bed was larger than Adam's. They lay on either side of me, and the cats lay at my feet. Lonny brushed my hair, and Adam stroked my face. I was relieved the ordeal was over. I soon fell asleep, feeling loss, but very loved and cared for.

SIX

AMERICA THE BEAUTIFUL

~~~~~~~~~~~~~~~~~~~~~~~

Every man has two lives, and the second starts when
he realizes he has just one ~ Confucius

With summer approaching, our plan was to get out of New York City. We took a short trip back to Berkeley, which we now referred to as Berserk-ley. We anticipated a reunion with our friends for some California dreaming. The plan was to fly to California and then drive back to New York, hitting all the West Coast and northern Border States. Adam arranged for us to stay with a friend who lived in student housing at the northern end of the Berkeley campus. Lonny Marcum had a boyfriend now, Mitchell Dosky, and the four of us were flying to California together.

Before leaving, I visited my parents in the Bronx. My mother told me she had something for me—it was a letter from Noah Bernstein. She wanted me to read it there, but I told her I wanted to read it by myself. The next day, when I was alone at the apartment in Manhattan, I put on my favorite LP from that time, Jefferson Airplane's *Surrealistic Pillow*. Memories of the house on Charming Way in Berkeley with Noah and Boo flooded back to me. I pictured that beautiful, warm, eclectic, house, and all the joy we experienced in it. I'd watched Noah slowly deteriorate into a weird headspace to which I couldn't relate.

When I heard the song "Comin' Back to Me," my eyes filled with tears. I opened the letter and began reading. Noah sounded lonely, confused, and destroyed. It was painful to read. He'd signed it **"Napoleon in Rags."**

I tried to be upbeat, and think about our upcoming trip back to Berkeley, but the words to that song played over and over in my brain for days.

I'd forgotten how cold San Francisco could be, even in the summer. As soon as we drove over the bay bridge into Berkeley though, the weather warmed up. I avoided the house on Charming Way, not wanting to dredge up beautiful memories that had gone to hell in a handbasket.

Telegraph Avenue was the same as I remembered it. I was happy that the doughnut shop was still there on the corner where I used to sell Berkeley Barbs. I stopped in for coffee and a Bismarck for breakfast every morning.

Our days in California were filled with picnics in Tilden Park, and excursions into San Francisco. But Adam and I were drifting apart in the love department. There was an essential piece missing, and we both knew it. There could never be total fulfillment for either one of us. He was into men sexually, and it gave me feelings of inadequacy. I did know the difference between having sex with someone and making love to someone, but ours was a unique and difficult situation. I knew we had to end the couple thing.

Sonny Terry and Brownie McGhee were giving a live folk concert on the campus. I headed there alone to check it out. I had seen them at the Newport Folk Festival in Rhode Island, and I loved their soulful music. I met a guy at the concert, Dean, who was from Upstate New York. He had short wispy brown hair and a pleasantly sensual face. I began a little romance with him—on the sly; it might have been about evening things up with Adam. Dean and I seemed to have a connection. We walked to his place off campus and had sex in his room. It wasn't anything special, but he was into me, which was self-affirming in a screwed-up way.

Adam and I hitchhiked down the coast to Big Sur for a music happening, with lots of bands scheduled to play. The coastal beaches, which used to be empty and pristine, were filled with sleeping bags, tents, and smoke from campfires. There were people on LSD, magic mushrooms, and who knows what else. People wandered around lost, looking for the friends they came with, only to sit down in frustration with a group of strangers. We found a spot for our sleeping bags. A guy on a blanket next to us was pounding on his bongos, which added to the tribal effect of it all. This was definitely not a good environment in which to take hallucinogens, but we enjoyed the music of people like Crosby, Stills, and Nash, Joni Mitchell, and Joan Baez, to name a few.

The following day, we wandered through the crowd and decided we'd had enough, so we hitched back to Berkeley. When we got back, the talk in the cafés on Telegraph Avenue was all about Woodstock, the Aquarian Festival Exposition. It was a huge happening in Bethel, New York, on Max Yasgur's six-hundred-acre dairy farm.

(Later, we learned that so many people had showed up that it became as populated as a city for the few days of the event. It was said that 350,000 people were there. We saw newsreels on TV, with cars abandoned along the roadways. Then came the rain and the mud, with people sloshing around in the muck. How the hell did we miss that?)

Back at the house we were staying in, we found new people hanging around. It was almost the end of August and figured we would just roll with it for a few more days. Adam told me he was going to visit a friend in San Francisco, and would most likely stay overnight. I figured he was going to cruise guys. I walked to Telegraph Avenue to hang out in one of the cafés. I ran into Dean, the guy I'd met at the Sonny Terry and Brownie McGhee concert, and invited him back to the house. Adam would be gone for the night; this was the perfect time.

When Dean and I arrived at the house it was empty. He had psychedelics, so we went to my room and took LSD together. The room began to get really trippy with the walls breathing and pulsating. We sat on the floor facing each other for a long time. We stared into each other's faces noticing every detail, and laughing. We got undressed, got into my sleeping bag, and had sex. It was pleasant on the drug, but I felt nothing emotionally.

At some point I wandered off nude to the bathroom in the hallway. I put the light on and gazed into the mirror. I stared at my face and then at my breasts. The image faded in and out. Then I saw my mother looking back at me. It was the strangest thing. Dean came into the bathroom, stood behind me, and put his arms around me. I said, "I'm my mother." He smiled at me and chuckled. When I glanced back at the mirror my mother had disappeared, and ours were the only two images in the mirror.

We spent the day together daydreaming and talking. Then we got dressed and went for a walk toward the campus and sat in a café on the avenue. The coffee was strong. We were like two clandestine Bohemian lovers, sneaking steamy episodes in secret. He was leaving soon for New York. His classes at the University of Syracuse would begin in September. I promised him I would visit, and we exchanged our personal contact information.

It was late when I got back to the room. I found Adam sleeping in his sleeping bag, which was next to mine. I was surprised to see him; I'd been under the impression that he was staying in San Francisco overnight. I slipped into my sleeping bag trying not to wake him. I felt guilty about Dean, even though Adam was cheating on me with men. He reached over, took my hand, and held it close to his heart. We fell asleep without uttering a word.

We posted a notice on the bulletin board in the student union, hoping for someone who was driving cross-country and looking for riders. Adam said he was feeling "Anticipatory." That was the word he always used when he felt anxious. But I told him not to worry; something would develop, and we'd find a ride back east. As it turned out, unbeknownst to us, Lonny Marcum had purchased an old Jeep Commando. He said we could take turns driving, take our time, and see as many states as we wanted on the way back to New York.

The next day coaxed Mitchel Dosky into giving my friend Dean a ride to the airport for his flight back east. Adam didn't come along, and I figured he sensed there was something more than friendship between me and Dean.

Although I knew a change between Adam and me was coming, on that particular night, we made love in my sleeping bag, and I fell asleep content.

Too soon, it was our last day in Berkeley. I went to all my favorite haunts by myself. Dean was gone, and Adam was busy making arrangements with Lonny for our road trip. I had lunch at Giant Hamburgers, a popular place at 3:00 a.m. but just as good during the day.

I wandered back to our room and found a spaced-out chick sitting on my sleeping bag. She was playing with the black kitten that hung out in our room. She was really skinny, had sores around her mouth, and I could tell she was on something. She asked, "How long can we go on like this?"

I didn't answer her, just stared.

Then she asked, "Can you float?"

I played along so as to not upset her.

"Yeah, I can float."

"Cats can float too," she said, petting the kitten. "My old man took off to Canada, just like that, without a word. I'm just waiting for the end."

She had a beautiful face, but looked sad, haggard, and lost. She collected cigarette butts from the ash tray, painstakingly lit each one with a match, and took a drag.

I went into the kitchen and made her a chai tea with milk and honey. I came back to the room and handed it to her. "You need to get a grip on yourself," I said.

She stared up at me blankly and thanked me for the tea.

I had a hard time sleeping on our last night in Berkeley; I tossed and turned all night. The moon was still up when we awoke in the morning. I looked up at it with the realization that someone had just landed there; I'd seen it on TV.

I knew we were leaving rather early, so I rushed to the doughnut shop and got us coffee, doughnuts, and two Bismarcks for me.

The four of us headed out after breakfast. Driving through Berkeley, I looked at all the quaint houses and breathed in the exotic scents of flowers and eucalyptus trees. I became nostalgic, missing it already, and we hadn't even left yet. Mitchell Dosky was driving the jeep, his wild, curly red hair flying all over the place as we went over the Bay Bridge. Nearing the coast I could smell the ocean and the native wildflowers that grew on the mountains.

We could see Mount Tamalpais in the distance, and I flashed on the day Noah and I hiked to the top. We passed Goat Rock Beach, then Jenner-by-the-Sea, and memories bombarded me. When we reached the place where the Russian River meets the ocean, a flood of emotions came over me. My eyes welled with tears, and I turned my face toward the window so the others wouldn't see.

As we drove farther north along the coast, the landscape became more and more dramatic, with huge rocks jutting out of the ocean. I looked at it, wondering if Ulysses' boat could be seen offshore.

THE RUSTIC COASTLINE

Adriana Bardolino

As the sun was setting, the sky turned a beautiful shade of orange. It dropped lower and lower until it was just a sliver. Deep pinks and purples replaced the orange in the sky. The sheep grazing on the hillside didn't even stop eating to look at the glorious sunset.

We searched for a place to camp. Berkeley was well behind us, and tomorrow was another day of driving.

From my journal:

> Slept in a redwood forest last night
> Felt super good.
> Swam in a river this morning
> The water was clear and cold.
> The sun is feeding me energy
> But I could still use a battery charge!

By the next day we were much farther north. The scenery was filled with dense green forests and tall redwoods as far as the eye could see. There were yellow wildflowers on either side of the highway. I was looking out the window when a flatbed truck rushed past us. I caught a long glimpse of a woman standing in the back of the truck. She was bare-breasted, stripped to the waist, and barefoot, holding on with both hands and laughing. Her long hair was flapping in the wind. To me, she exemplified total freedom.

Not long after the truck passed our jeep, we saw a guy and a girl on the side of the road with their thumbs out. We slowed down and asked them if they wanted a ride. Donny and Suki were their names. They were traveling farther north, so we told them to hop in. Suki had long brown hair and soft brown eyes. They both seemed really cool.

As the evening approached a fog rolled in, and we stopped at a stream to regroup. We drove to the nearest town for groceries and then headed back out on the road. Suki had picked up a local newspaper at the grocery store, and was reading us an article about the recent Charles Manson murders in California. What a scary cult that was.

Through the fog the image of the redwoods on the mountains along the ocean resembled a Japanese watercolor. We camped right on a cliff by the ocean and walked along the beach as seagulls dipped and dived overhead. Our plan was to get an early start in the morning and hit Oregon by the end of the next day.

It was still foggy when we woke up in the morning, cold and wet. We could hear the ocean but couldn't see it anymore. We rolled up our damp sleeping bags and headed out on the road. We could make out a giant red barn with some cows grazing nearby, but not much else. It was difficult driving because we couldn't see very far in front of us. We were heading into timber country. As the fog lifted, we began to pass mountains with only tree stumps. They had been logged and left that way. It was a horrible and disturbing sight, as if the mountains had been raped. I tried to wipe the image from my mind.

Before leaving the state of California we hiked to the top of Mount Lassen. We were plagued by bears, and had to hang our backpacks from trees. But the vista at the top was phenomenal, like being on top of the world. We could see thunder and lightning crashing off the faces of distant mountain ranges. We slept up there, and were back on the road the following day.

ON TOP OF MOUNT LASSEN.

Soon, we were driving through scenery that looked like the dawn of creation. The Oregon coast resembled a surreal landscape painting, truly mystical. There were farms right on the ocean, with cows atop cliffs. We stopped to rest and had lunch beside a mountain lake; the cool breezes were a treat. We were very much enjoying the company of the couple we'd picked up. At that time, I didn't realize what a big part of my life Suki Rosmond would become. We drove inland toward Portland, and camped in the woods along the road that night.

While making camp a Red pickup truck stopped and a handsome guy got out. I could tell he was Native American by his features. He was clean-cut, with a short haircut in a modern style. He was wearing jeans, work boots, and a hoodie. I figured, based on his physique, that he was probably a lumberjack or a logger.

In that slow, careful way that some Native Americans talk, he said, "My name is Henry Wadsworth, named after the famous American poet, Henry Wadsworth Longfellow."

Yeah, right, I thought, *and I'm Pocahontas.*

"If you guys are camping here for the night, could I hang out with you?" he asked.

I immediately said yes; the guys rolled their eyes, but Suki smiled.

We set up camp, made a fire, and sat around in the dark, talking and telling stories.

Henry said, "In the winter, when there's a lot of snow, the Indians say that if too many people are on the mountain, the snow forms a white buffalo." Henry was a true storyteller, and we were all captivated as we listened to him.

He walked to his truck and brought a drum back to the camp. He began pounding on it in various rhythms, and he sang Native American chants. I sensed that Henry had more than a friendly interest in me, and I was intrigued—he was unique and very attractive. Lonny took some weed out and we all got stoned. It crossed my mind that marijuana was the possible motivation for Henry's wanting to hang out with us. With the tribal atmosphere of the drum, the marijuana, and the campfire, everyone began cheering on Henry and me, as if wanting to initiate an orgy. I had the feeling that the guys were interested in Suki's boyfriend, Donny. It was a totally wild and crazy night. Henry put the drum down, took my hand, and led me away from the camp. We had sex in the woods. Afterward, I slept in my own sleeping bag wondering what the hell that was all about.

When we woke up the next morning Henry and his red truck were gone. We packed up our camp and went looking for a place to have breakfast. Everyone was talking about the Indian poet. I just let them talk as I sat there with a big grin, like the Cheshire cat. I confided in Adam that I felt trashy about the previous night, fucking the Indian. Adam smiled and commented, "Oscar Wilde said, '"We are all in the gutter, but some of us are looking up at the stars."'"

It was Labor Day weekend, but we were on the move, and there was no time to celebrate. We proceeded inland, passing fields of wheat, as well as oats bundled in stacks, already harvested. We drove along the Columbia

River, with its sand barges, and headed for Washington State. We stopped to watch the sunset in a large field. I lay down in the grass waiting for the sun to disappear behind the mountains. I watched the flowers in the field swaying with the wind. The sunset turned them from yellow to red and then to a deep purple. We walked into the forest as it was getting dark, looking for a place to camp for the night. It was spooky. We came across a waterfall, crashing down white in the dark. We heard it before we saw it, and it sprayed a mist on our faces as we passed. We walked a little further and camped there for the night. All we could hear were crickets as we settled into our sleeping bags.

In Washington State we came across the Maryhill Museum of Fine Arts. It was a mind-blowing place on a grassy hill in the middle of a barren landscape. The museum was built like a castle, and had the golden throne of the queen of Romania. We saw various religious vessels laden with jewels, fabrics such as golden brocade, Flemish Medieval paintings, and Greek pottery from 900 BC. There were religious icons from the seventeenth to nineteenth centuries, and some very early photographs of the Romanian queen with her family. To round it all out, there was a collection of early French fashions. This freaky oasis in the middle of nowhere was a good break from driving.

At this point, Donny, Suki's boyfriend, decided to hitchhike back to California. Suki, never having been to New York State, decided to stay on the trip with us. She planned on meeting up with him after the summer. We had become friends, and I was happy she was continuing on the journey.

As we left Washington State and entered Montana, we drove through flat plains and saw snowcapped mountains in the distance. We were near the Blackfoot Indian reservation with herds of buffalo up on the mountains. I thought I'd gone back in time and pictured early pioneers, covered wagons, and Indians on horseback.

We stopped at the trading post along the Flathead River to get some information. Our plan was to enter Canada through Glacier National Park which ran along the border. We got back on the road, and soon the weather turned stormy and cold. There were dark clouds, with thunder and lightning, and we were hit with a hailstorm. We pulled off the road and sat in the jeep for a long time waiting for the storm to pass.

I lay back and closed my eyes listening to the storm outside. The sound of the hail beating against the windows prompted a flashback to a winter snowstorm many years ago when I was a young teen about fourteen years old;

There was a shopping mecca in the North Bronx, about a half mile from our neighborhood, where all the teenagers hung out. It was a large residential and shopping complex called Parkchester, with restaurants and stores like Macy's, Lerner's, Woolworth's, and a Lowe's movie theater. Right across the street from Macy's was a large cafeteria. I often noticed a guy there sitting with his friends, sometimes alone. He was a good-looking guy, with strawberry-blond hair that hung over one eye. He always wore a baby-blue leather jacket. He never acknowledged me or anyone in our group. I tried to make eye contact with him a few times, but nothing more than a return glance happened.

One day, he suddenly got up, came to our table, sat down, and engaged in small talk with the guys in our clique. My heart stopped beating for a few seconds. I heard him say his name was Ryan O'Connor, but everyone just called him Ry. He seemed like a guy of few words, but had tons of sex appeal. He put his arm on the back of an empty chair exposing the bright-red corduroy shirt he wore under his jacket. Someone told me that red is a powerful color, and Ry sure had some sort of power over me.

He had a funny way of looking at you, with his head cocked to the side. A crooked smile on his face revealed a chip in one of his front teeth. When he tossed his head back and flipped his hair, I saw his beautiful blue eyes. I thought I would melt right into my chair. After a while, he got up and walked off. I watched him walk away in that baby-blue leather jacket. I could hear the leather creak with every step he took.

It was the middle of winter, and we were in the midst of a snowstorm. We all met at the cafeteria after school and were hanging out at our table avoiding the weather outside. I looked around and there he was, sitting at another table in that damn baby-blue leather jacket. I was talking to my cousin Gia when, suddenly, he got up from his table, came over and sat down in the empty chair next to mine. He looked straight at me and began talking, but I didn't hear a word he was saying. I kept staring at his face and watching the movement of his mouth as he was talking. Even though I'd never been kissed, I could only think that I wanted to feel those lips on my lips.

Then I heard him say, "It's snowing really hard out there. Can I walk you home?"

I had to catch my breath for a moment before I answered, "That would be nice"—as if I was just being appreciative of his offer.

I lost all concept of reality and everyone around us. I stood up like a robot and followed him to the exit. He reached over me to open the door of the cafeteria, and I heard his leather jacket creak. Within seconds, we were out in the cold, snowy air of the street. He put his arm around me, as if protecting me from the cold, and we began to walk through the storm. I felt as though I was gliding, as if my feet were not even touching the ground, although I could hear the snow crunch under our boots.

When we reached my house, he turned to me, tossed back that beautiful hair and said, "Wanna go to the movies on Saturday?"

"Yeah, that would be fun," I said, trying to act nonchalant. I curbed the desire to jump up and down, which I did as soon I was safely inside the vestibule of my building.

I couldn't think of much else besides our date for the rest of that week. Saturday finally came; we were to meet in front of the Lowe's Movie Theater in Parkchester.

There he was, standing in front of the theater leaning against one of the movie showcase displays, wearing that damn baby-blue leather jacket. Ry got the tickets, a large popcorn, and two Cokes. We walked inside the dark theater looking for seats. My mind was in a daze and my body was buzzing. I could hardly concentrate on the movie.

At some point he moved closer and put his arm around my shoulders, sort of cradling me. In the darkness of the movie theater I could feel him looking at me. I turned my face in his direction, and our eyes met. He tilted his head and leaned in. I could see that little chip in his front tooth. He kissed me softly on the lips, and then again much harder. I was in a state of bliss. Was this what it felt like to be in love? I wasn't sure, but I knew that I liked it.

Ry and I dated for that entire winter. We went to the movies and hung out at the cafeteria together. It was something very nice.

Ry was a little older than me, maybe seventeen. I can't remember if he was drafted or he enlisted, but Ry went into the service. The last time I saw him we walked to his house. We hugged and kissed goodbye, and I left to go home. I turned to see him still watching me walk away with that funny, crooked smile, his head cocked to the side. I was filled with sadness and loss. I never forgot the smell of that baby-blue leather jacket, or the creaky sound it made every time he moved.

We had been sitting in the jeep for more than half an hour. The storm finally passed, and we began to drive on through Montana. After that memory of Ryan O'Connor, and how I'd felt about him, I had another epiphany. I realized that as much as I loved Adam, I didn't feel that way about him. Perhaps our friendship had blossomed into a romance, but in the back of my mind, I knew it could never be a complete love.

We stopped at an apple orchard for hot cider to warm us up. We looked for a place to camp that wasn't so windy. We found an official campsite that had a picnic table, public restrooms, and a small café on the premises. We made a fire, pitched a tent, and settled down for the night, trying to keep warm. The plan was to stay there for a few days and do some hiking.

We got an early start the next morning and hiked up into the mountains behind the camp. It was a grueling ascent, but the scenery at the top was well worth it. Adam told the others we'd meet up with them at the bottom of the trail. He had a devious laugh as he laid me down in a patch of greenery. We had sex on top of the mountain. It was fun and exhilarating, until I stood up and realized I'd been lying in a patch of Poison Ivy. Hiking down, I wondered what the hell that was about, but I chose not to analyze.

That afternoon we had lunch at the little café on the campground. The waiter recognized me from the previous day. He served us tons of food for practically nothing—our total bill was only a few dollars. Mitchell had gone to the bathroom at the bottom of a long staircase in the café. We sat there for quite a while, waiting for him, but he didn't return. Lonny and Adam went looking for him. They found him sitting on the bathroom floor slightly beaten up. He told us that a group of local Native American guys had followed him into the bathroom and worked him over. That freaked us out. We packed up our gear and headed to North Dakota that very night. During the night, the jeep hit a rabbit, Adam saw two big bucks standing on the side of the road, and a large bird flew into the windshield.

I was sound asleep in the back of the jeep when I suddenly woke up, realizing we weren't moving anymore. Everyone was standing outside, looking up. I got out of the jeep and looked at the sky. What a sight it was— the Aurora Borealis, also known as the Northern Lights. Waves of green were moving in the sky. We stood there silently and totally mesmerized, until the chill prompted us to run back to the jeep.

Driving through Minnesota in daylight, we passed a small sign that read HIBBING—TWO MILES.

"Isn't that the birthplace of Bob Dylan?" I shouted, but no one answered me. We were all getting weary.

Then came Wisconsin, and we just kept driving. We passed a lake that was muddy, and I thought of a gospel song Elvis sang: "I washed my hands in muddy water, and they didn't come clean, no they didn't come clean."

Rows of white birch trees lined both sides of the highway. We were on the original Route 2, also known as the Lewis and Clark Trail. We approached Lake Superior, which was a lovely shade of lavender as the sun was setting, and we looked for a place to camp for the night. We pulled over into what seemed like a good spot. I got out and noticed there was a crescent moon on the horizon. It was a dark shade of orange, but as it rose higher in the sky, it got lighter and lighter. Then I saw a shooting star with a green tail. What a magical spot it turned out to be.

The next day we crossed the border into Canada. For the most part, Canada had a lot of farms and ranches, and was sparsely populated. Everyone we came in contact with spoke French. Suki Rosmond had friends who had a commune in Montreal, and mentioned that we could probably stay with them overnight.

As predicted, we were welcomed warmly by Suki's friends, who invited us to spend the night. It was a refreshing change to sleep indoors.

I was rejuvenated in the morning. We walked around the city, and I found Montreal to be what I imagined a European city was like—narrow, winding streets; ornate cathedrals; shops; restaurants; and quaint little cafés. There were bakeries with crusty French bread. We stopped at a French bakery that had lovely baguettes in the window. We sat at an outside table, drank strong coffee, and ate French bread with lots of butter. On our way out, we bought a box of French pastries to munch on during the last leg of our trip. Suki's friends in the commune shared their home and whatever they had with us, and we were grateful.

We headed toward Niagara Falls, New York, which is where we intended to cross back over the border into the States. We kept driving until we reached the falls. It was truly a sight to behold. I was speechless as I gazed into the vast landscape of rushing water, the spray misting our faces from the sheer force of it. The sun made little rainbows as the water rushed down into the river below. Adam and I hugged each other as we marveled at the sight. We were relieved to have made it back to New York State, safe and sound.

I've been across this beautiful country many times, but that first trip stands out fondly in my memory.

SEVEN
THE ZOFIA LODGE

After reading *Siddhartha* by Hermann Hesse, I had some profound revelations. My life was like a river—ever flowing and changing but still the same river. The river taught Siddhartha that everything exists in the present, and eternity is in every moment.

O ur first thought after entering back over the border into the United States was to drive straight to our friends' commune in Aliceville. We weren't quite ready for the hustle and bustle of New York City. Driving through Upstate New York we passed numerous towns with Native American names. I imagined the names of various tribes that once had inhabited the entire region. It was the beginning of fall. The trees were turning shades of yellow, orange, and brown, truly a feast for the eyes. The air was brisk, and the sun was shining.

We were greeted warmly by our friends in the Aliceville commune, and were invited to stay for the weekend. They wanted to hear all about our cross-country adventure. The first thing Adam and I did was to take a walk in the woods behind the house. We admired all the psychedelic fall colors of the trees and shrubs, which looked very different from when we last visited in late spring. I sat on a large rock at the stream's edge, peacefully watching the water gurgling past. I felt as if I was sitting on the bank of Siddhartha's river, and like him, I struggled to keep my mind in the present.

Driving into the city after the weekend, I was filled with apprehension and uneasiness. How would it all play out—the love affair between Adam and me? I was sure he was feeling something similar. I made up my mind that I would just flow with the changes like Siddhartha's river.

At Lonny and Adam's apartment in Manhattan we had a serious

conversation about getting a place of our own upstate—a place where we could spend weekends, chill out, and experiment with a larger number of us living together. Lonny Marcum, being a university professor, would approach like-minded colleagues to see if any were interested in the idea. It would be a retreat where they could bounce all their philosophies off each other in a friendly, laid-back atmosphere.

I hadn't worked for a few months, and was basically being carried by my friends. It was time to hit up Kooky Furs to see about some part-time work. I also designed a line of shoes for a leather company.

Adam and I were hanging out at the apartment when Lonny walked in. He told us he had colleagues, teachers, professors, and even students at the university, who were very interested in the idea of a retreat in the country. A few days later Lonny told us he'd found a great house near Hunter Mountain. He said that it would be a communal experiment in which we all would share.

I loved the idea, and had a pleasant flashback of the early days of the commune on Charming Way in Berkeley. If nothing else, it would be a place to go in the country when we needed a break from the city.

A few of us drove upstate with Lonny to see the house. He gave us some stats on the drive up. "It's the perfect place, in a great location—a large property right off the main road surrounded by woods."

It was about a three-hour drive north of New York City. Lonny said it was called the Zofia Lodge, and he told us a little history about the place. It originally was built in the early 1900s as a hotel retreat for Polish immigrants, who spent their summers there to get away from the city. More recently, it had been used as a hunting and ski lodge, being it was so close to Hunter Mountain.

Nothing prepared me for the initial sight of the house. Set atop a hill was a rather large, three-story Victorian, with outside porches on two levels that went around it on both sides. We walked around the grounds, which included a large open field that bordered the woods at the back of the property. I thought of all the walks we could take in those woods. As I looked back at the house, I noticed endless bay windows, tower rooms, and turrets.

THE ZOFIA LODGE

Entering through the front door I was hit with a feeling of joy. I imagined all the things that could go on within those walls. There were plenty of rooms for all of us to have our own spaces. We were full of excitement, and began choosing our rooms. I chose a room for myself on the second level. It seemed cozy and was very bright, with the light from a large bay window in the center of the room. Adam chose a room at the end of the hallway. I guessed we were back in the friend zone.

The Victorian had a fully equipped hotel kitchen, very spacious, with high ceilings. From the ceiling hung an oval rack with pots, pans and all sorts of cooking utensils. It was suspended over a long butcher-block table. There was a double-surface gas stove, where I was sure it would be possible to juggle numerous sauté pans and large pots. There was a small walk-in room off the kitchen—a pantry for storing flour, beans, and jars of preserved goods. On the way out I passed a stack of large oval hotel serving trays on the floor in the corner of the kitchen.

The house was fully furnished, and there were two huge stone fireplaces back to back. The dining room had a long wooden table, where I pictured all of us having meals together. Sitting in the corner of the dining room was an old piano, which I hoped Jesse Bob Baker would play. Jesse Bob was a friend of Lonny's from the South. He was gay, spoke with a Southern drawl, and wore red fingernail polish. He loved to sing gospel songs, and played honky-tonk piano. Behind the dining table was a tall bookcase filled with books, a storm lamp, and candles in candleholders. We wandered through the house looking at everything. It all felt warm and inviting.

We checked out the basement to see if there was any wood stacked for the fireplaces. When we turned on the light, an old calico cat stared up at us. I wondered why a cat was living there all on its own.

Lonny said, "The owner died, and the cat hunts for her food in the surrounding woods."

Well, I'll soon put a stop to that, I thought.

"The cat's name is Zofia," Lonny said.

That seemed fitting since it was the name of the lodge. I began talking to the cat and trying to get her to come to me. Zofia just sat there staring at me.

"I was told that she only understands Polish," Lonny said.

I walked up to the third floor while the others inspected other areas of the house in which they were interested. I noticed a room that looked closed up. I pried the door open. The room was filled with personal items, in such a way that looked as if someone still lived there. I saw a hairbrush on the dresser, and men's clothing strewn on chairs and hanging in the closet. It was like someone had left to go to the store and hadn't returned. I got a very cold, eerie feeling, and didn't linger there too long. I closed the door and went downstairs to join the others.

We all loved the Victorian. The plan was to rent it for six months, which would put us into spring. That would give us time to see how we all got along as a group.

After we returned to the city things were changing. Adam met Aiden Wazansky. He reminded me of a gypsy, with his dark curly hair and dark eyes. He had a slight stutter, which I thought added to his appeal.

I wanted to give Adam the space to follow his heart and desires. I decided to move my things out of the apartment in Manhattan, and stay with my parents in the Bronx. This didn't stop me from visiting Adam and Lonny's apartment, which I did often. It was time to come to grips with the love fest between Adam and me, and Aiden presented a natural end to the romantic part of our relationship. We loved each other, but not so much in the carnal sense anymore. The fact that we were good friends before we got involved emotionally and sexually, made it easier to return to being good friends. I still loved Adam; I treasured our friendship and didn't want to lose it.

One evening after work I passed a bookstore that I had passed many times before on the way to the train station. For some unknown reason I decided to wander in. I took a few books out of the art section and sat down at a table in the basement of the store. I got lost in the pages for an hour or so, looking at Chinese art from one of the early dynasties. I looked up and noticed that a rather cute guy was watching me. He averted his eyes as soon as I noticed him. After observing him for a while, I realized that he worked there. The next time he glanced my way, I quietly motioned to him, hinting that I needed his help. When he came to my table, I made up some nonsensical question to break the ice.

He responded and said, "My name is Erik, can I help?"

"I'm interested in Chinese art. Could you suggest any other books for me to look at?"

"I know of a book you might like." He walked to the art section and I watched him with intense interested.

He handed me the book and I began flipping through the pages while he helped another customer.

I got lost in time again, then noticed it was getting late. I went to the art section to put the books away.

Erik rushed over and said, "I'll take care of the books."

"It's late. I have to catch the train back to the Bronx."

"I live in the Bronx too," he said. This was looking promising. "I hope I'll see you again."

"I work near the bookstore, so I'll stop in again."

As I was leaving the bookstore, Erik followed me to the exit. "I'd really like to get to know you. Can I have your phone number, or can I give you mine?"

I liked the way he looked and the way he spoke. I gave him my phone number, hoping that I'd hear from him. I left the bookstore and headed to the train station.

We'd been going upstate to the Zofia Lodge every weekend for a while. It was everything we anticipated and more. People sat around having political arguments and deep philosophical conversations. We cooked meals together in the kitchen, and ate together in the dining room. We went for walks in the surrounding woods. Even Zofia the cat was warming up to us. A steady supply of cat food helped with that situation. She also made friends with the city cats from Adam and Lonny's apartment, who were now living at the Zofia. She seemed happy with their company, and was giving the city cats lessons on hunting and how to survive in the country.

WITH SUKI AND LONNY

Maxwell Robinov and Suki Rosmond were living at the lodge full time. Max made sure the pantry was filled with homemade breads, including his Survival bread.

Lonny found out more information about the Polish man who had owned the Zofia. He had died in that room on the third level—the room I'd wandered into on our first visit that had given me a cold, eerie feeling. Max, for some crazy reason, decided to occupy that room as his own. He began wearing the dead man's clothes that were left in the closet, and even adopted his persona. We tried to convince Max that it was *not* a good idea. Hell, even the cats refused to go up to the third floor. But Max thought it was the perfect room for him—that is, until one night he was awakened by a man standing over the bed staring down at him.

Max later told us, "The man was talking to me, but I couldn't make out a word he was saying, and I was frozen with fear. I tell you it was the ghost of the owner." Max vacated the room and moved his personal belongings to another room in the house. His story confirmed what I had suspected— that we were living with a ghost. We were not afraid and just accepted the fact. We figured the spirit wanted us to know he was still around, watching over his beloved Zofia Lodge.

Adriana Bardolino

Back in the Bronx, I was settled into that boring commute again. My parents were overjoyed to have me with them. They were always welcoming and never turned me away, regardless of the circumstances. I received a call from Erik, the guy from the bookstore. He asked me to meet him in the city the next day after I got off work. We were to meet at a restaurant around the corner from the bookstore.

All day at work, I tried to picture him. I knew I felt an attraction, but I couldn't remember any details, other than that he had straight blond hair, not too long, and that he wore glasses. After work, I walked to the restaurant. No one there looked familiar, and my first impulse was to leave. I had a thing about being the first one to arrive and have to wait for someone. I fought the flight impulse and sat down at a table. The waiter came over, and I told him I was waiting for someone. He returned with two glasses of water; I kept my eyes glued to the entrance.

Less than ten minutes later Erik walked through the door. His eyes cruised the tables looking for me. As soon as we made eye contact he walked to the table. He was taller than I remembered. He was wearing a brown suede jacket, bleached-out jeans, and a jeans shirt; they almost matched. He smiled at me, took off his jacket, placed it over the back of his chair and sat down. He wore clear round glasses and had very fine features. I liked what I saw.

The waiter asked us what we wanted.

We both answered, "Coffee would be fine."

"I don't even know your full name," I said.

"Erik Eschweiler, and yours?"

"Adriana Bardolino."

We began to tell each other about ourselves—nothing deep, just the usual chitchat between people who don't know much about each other. It didn't take long for him to start talking politics, which he seemed very passionate about. We agreed politically, although I wondered if I was as passionate as he was.

He had soft brown eyes, and I liked the contrast with his blond hair. All the while he was talking, I was sizing him up in other ways.

He said, "My parents moved to America from Germany when I was little. I can speak German fluently."

"My father came to this country from Italy, but they didn't teach me the language. I do know a lot of Italian words and expressions, especially the curse words."

He laughed heartily at my comment.

Since we both lived in the Bronx we hopped the train back together. We chatted and checked each other out during the ride. Our continuing conversation on the train proved difficult over the screeching of the train wheels as it made its twists and turns over the tracks. We had to overcompensate by speaking louder.

He got off at a stop that was a few stops before mine. "I want to see you again," he said.

I responded, "I would like that."

"I'll call you soon." He said, smiling and exiting the train.

There was something about Erik that reminded me of one of my first crushes as a young girl; maybe it was the straight blond hair.

In the Bronx, many of the buildings had pigeon coops on the roofs. This was a popular thing in the fifties and sixties, and lots of the neighborhood guys trained and flew homing pigeons. Across the street from my mother's dress factory, on the roof of Filomena Genoa's building, a guy had pigeon coops on the roof. I'd see him sitting on the stoop every day as I entered her building. He never paid any attention to me—I was a kid of ten or eleven at the time. He was tall, very blond, and sort of Nordic-looking. He was definitely much older than me. He always wore black jeans, a thick garrison belt, and a white T-shirt with a pack of cigarettes rolled up in one of the sleeves. I think he knew I had a crush on him.

I was surprised when one day, out of the blue, he said, "Hey, you wanna come up to the roof and see the pigeons?"

I could barely speak or contain my excitement. I nodded and followed him up the stairs to the very top of the building. We stepped out onto the roof, and into the fresh air. There were a few cages with pigeons nibbling and cooing. He opened the cage doors and handed me one of them to hold. He took another pigeon, a beautiful brown-and-white one, and petted it.

Then he gave a signal, and the pigeons raced out of the cages and flew into the sky above us in unison. They circled around for quite a while. He said, "It takes a long time to train them to do that, you know!"

I was impressed but didn't say anything; I was too shy. Eventually, the pigeons came back to their cages.

He was so handsome, and so very sweet to me. I wondered if he knew the thrill he gave me that day, one that I would not forget. After that day, we'd always greet each other when I passed him going into Filomena's building. There was definitely something about Erik Eschweiler that reminded me of that guy.

I took the bus farther downtown after work and rummaged around the secondhand stores, where I found a suede fringe jacket. I put it on and never wanted to take it off. Then I took the bus back uptown to Adam and Lonny's apartment. During our conversation, I told them that I had met someone I liked. They began questioning me about him, but at that point, I didn't know much myself. They were always a little skeptical about straight guys they didn't know. They suggested that I bring him to the Zofia on the weekend. I told them I thought it was too soon.

Adam and Aiden acted like a couple. I couldn't help feeling slighted, although I was happy for them. I had no future in a relationship with Adam, but I missed the closeness we had. I took it I all in stride, knowing we were better off as friends.

Erik Eschweiler and I began dating. We'd meet after work and walk around the city with our cameras taking photos. Our passion for photography was one of the things we connected with. The buildings, monuments, statues, and parks in Manhattan offered us so many great photo ops. After we'd have our fill of photographing everything in our interest obit, we'd go for a coffee, and then hop the train back to the Bronx together.

"To me, photography is an art of observation. It's about finding something interesting in an ordinary place. ... I've found that it has little to do with the things you see and everything to do with the way you see them."
Elliott Erwitt ~ French-American photographer

Erik's parents lived in a different neighborhood of the Bronx, in a single-standing house in the middle of tall apartment buildings. As soon as I walked through the front door, I smelled something wonderful. Erik greeted his parents in German and introduced me to them in English.

His parents were very nice. His mother spoke English with a heavy German accent. She made the most wonderful dinner, filled with home-cooked German specialties that I'd never had. There was a German Town on the Upper East Side of Manhattan with German delis, markets, and restaurants, but they were nothing compared to the meal she cooked. She made rouladen (a meat dish), homemade sauerkraut with red cabbage, and the mashed potatoes were dripping with butter. After dinner we talked in the living room. When it was time to go, Erik walked me to the train station. He gave me a long kiss, openmouthed, and ran his tongue along my lips. It gave me chills that went straight down to you-know-where. I decided, then and there, that I was ready to invite him to the Zofia Lodge for a weekend. We had not been intimate yet, but I figured it was time.

The next time I saw Erik, I invited him to come upstate with me for the weekend. I said nothing about its being a commune. As I expected, he said yes. I could tell that he was thinking the same thing I was. That Friday after work we took the bus from Port Authority, and on the three-hour ride upstate I explained the situation. I told him not to worry, that I had my own room. I couldn't help but wonder how the group would react to him.

We got off the bus at the depot in town, and the cold night air hit us. That far north the weather is much colder than among the tall skyscrapers in the city. Max answered the phone when I called the lodge. He said he'd come to get us at the bus station.

Erik seemed confident—maybe overconfident—about meeting everyone. He sat in the front seat next to Max, and they chatted all the way to the lodge.

When we arrived at the Zofia, Erik was totally awed by the place. It was after Thanksgiving, and someone had put up Christmas lights all along the porches. I held his hand and led him through the front door, following Max. Everyone was sitting in the living room, including a few people I didn't know. They all looked up at us. The women smiled, and the men skeptically checked Erik out. Adam seemed the most skeptical and wary, but I'd expected that.

We took off our jackets and sat down on the couch. I didn't know how to introduce him, but he quickly said, "Hi, I'm Erik."

Everyone said in unison, "Hello Erik," like the introduction of a new person at an Alcoholics Anonymous meeting.

I took Erik upstairs to show him my room, and to leave our things inside. I wanted to put to rest any reservations he had about later. We briefly glanced at each other in anticipation. We did not linger; we went right back downstairs to join the others.

Numerous conversations were going on, and everyone was engaged in laughter and storytelling. Sebastian Warren, a fellow professor of Lonny's, was telling everyone about the students in his homeroom class. Suddenly the front door swung open letting in a blast of cold air. I looked up, and in walked an attractive guy with a full-length fur coat; long, wavy, black hair; and a gorgeous woman on his arm.

I thought, *Wow, this guy really knows how to make an entrance.*

"Hey Ross," Lonny shouted, "I'm so glad you finally made it up here!"

I imagined he was someone Lonny knew from the university. He seemed cocky but in an innocent way, and he was very funny. I didn't know it at the time, but Ross Grant would become a close friend of mine, like a brother to me. Nor did I know that my friend Suki Rosmond would take a romantic interest in him.

Soon, everyone went back to their conversations.

The evening went well, although we'd missed dinner. Erik followed me into the kitchen, which left him speechless. He kept saying, "Wow!" We found some leftovers and a loaf of Max's survival bread. We munched standing at the butcher-block counter.

Erik asked, "How did you ever find this place?"

"Lonny found it."

"Well, it's awesome!"

I made us hot tea, and the tea kettle looked tiny on the giant restaurant-grade gas stove. After we ate we went back into the living room. There was only one empty space on the couch, so Erik sat down. I sat on the floor between his legs. He put his hand on my shoulder and began playing with the back of my hair, which put me at ease. Everyone spoke in soft tones, and all I could hear was the crackling of the fire in the fireplace.

Someone said, "Heavy snow is expected overnight." It all felt cozy and warm, and I was lit up from head to toe.

People began going up to bed. I felt a little nervous, but Erik took my hand and said, "Let's go upstairs."

Max said, "I'll make sure the fire is out."

I led Erik up the stairs leaving Max tending the fire.

The first time you are intimate with someone, it's like a Rorschach test—you follow the signs in an attempt to interpret what each look and movement means.

Instead of a bed, I had a mattress on the floor. Once we left the warmth of the living room the rest of the house was cold. We got in bed fully dressed, save for our shoes. I shivered with cold, and Erik put his arms around me. The room was dark, but I could sense him smiling at me. Then he reached over, unbuttoned my blouse, and put one of his hands inside. His hand was as cold as ice, and I shivered.

He found my chest warm and said, "That feels good."

I laughed. "Yeah, for you—your hands are freezing."

Then he began kissing me. His head moved down to my breasts, and he started sucking on one of my nipples. He pulled away from me and held my face between his hands. He stuck his tongue in my mouth and darted it around examining every part of it. I wondered if he was hinting at what he wanted to do to me on the lower part of my body. We quickly got undressed and tossed our clothes outside the covers onto the floor. He got on top of me, and we rocked back and forth. I knew he was going to be a good lover.

We were huddled together under the covers when I woke up in the morning. Erik was still asleep. I lay there with my head propped up on one elbow, watching him. It was light, but I couldn't see the trees or anything else outside the windows. I reached under the covers and ran my hand down the center of his chest.

As I got lower on his body his eyes shot open. He turned his face toward me and said something in German. He took my hand and pushed it down to his member, which was already hard. He pulled me on top of him, and we started going at it again. Afterward, we lay there smiling. Eventually, we got up, got dressed, and went downstairs.

Just about everyone was already up. Suki was making pancakes in the kitchen, and Max was telling her how she should be making them. I laughed and walked out of the kitchen. It had snowed heavily during the night. We looked outside at a winter wonderland. Erik and I walked out onto the porch and saw two deer on the front lawn. They glanced at us, just for a moment, but soon continued foraging under the packed snow for something green.

"Don't they know this was a hunting lodge?" I said.

Derik laughed and said, "Obviously not."

We were without jackets, so we rushed back inside to sit at the dining room table with the others. The pancakes were great. There was maple syrup from a local market that would have been harvested from the sap of maple trees in the area. I had a flashback of the house on Charming Way in Berkeley. Sage showed me a trick of using molasses, brown sugar, and a touch of vanilla with boiling water, to make syrup, if you didn't have the real thing on hand.

The weekend was going better than I'd anticipated—until Erik got involved in a heated political argument with the university professors. I eventually coaxed him away from the table, saying that I wanted to take a walk outside in the woods. That luckily ended the argument, although I was somewhat embarrassed at Erik's demeanor. Max decided to come along, and the three of us went through the kitchen and out the back door. We trudged through the snow for a while; the sun was strong. Max whipped out a joint which he lit up and passed around, and I began to feel giddy.

Max said, "Let's go sledding."

"I don't remember seeing any sleighs around," I said.

"We can use those waiters' trays in the kitchen"

The three of us figured they would work nicely, and ran back into the kitchen. We fetched some trays and headed out to the hill behind the house. Others in the house saw what was going on and followed us outside. We watched each person careen down the hill and laughed with joy. As the sun waned, the cold began to take over, so we went back to the house. Erik and I thawed out in front of the fireplace, while Max went down to the basement to get more wood. We witnessed some phenomenal winter sunsets from the porches of the Zofia Lodge. The sky turned deep pinks and reds, and we reveled in the beauty of the area. On Sunday we joined everyone at the dining room table for breakfast. When the talk turned to politics, I tugged on Erik's sleeve, and he took the hint. A few of us planned to go into town to look around. We took our bags with us, and had Max drop us off at the bus station in the afternoon. We both had to work the next day.

Erik and I had been a couple for about six months when he suggested that we live together. I was reluctant. He had friends who lived in Manhattan, a little south of Harlem. They were moving and looking for someone to take over the apartment. There is something in New York City called rent control, and you never want to totally give up an apartment. We'd been getting along great, I didn't want to lose him, so moving in together seemed like a natural progression.

Erik took me to see the apartment, which was on West Lenox Street in a run-down area, but I loved the fact that we could walk to Riverside Park. We rode the elevator up to the fourth floor. The building was old and dilapidated, and the apartment wasn't any better; it was basically a tenement apartment. The rooms were large, somewhat furnished, and had all the necessities. The kitchen window looked out to the brick wall of the building adjacent to ours. In the living room I noticed an antique piece of furniture of very dark wood. It had a mirror set in the back, with two ornate posts on either side, with a number of drawers at the bottom. I guessed it might be a sideboard, something you'd see in the dining room of an old Victorian. It was the only piece of furniture in the apartment I liked. The apartment came with two cats, Emily and Jolene. They belonged to Erik's friends, and we adopted them as our own.

Erik had to work late at the bookstore, so I took the bus uptown to Adam and Lonny's apartment after work. Max was there and wanted to see the new apartment. It was such a beautiful day that we decided to walk to West Lenox. Max was wearing overalls over a sweatshirt looking like Farmer John visiting the big city. When we entered the vestibule of the tenement a guy was getting on the elevator. He'd already pushed the elevator button, so we hopped on with him. Between floors the guy pulled a knife and demanded money. Max took out a hundred-dollar bill that he had stashed in a flap of his overalls and gave it to him. The guy got off on the next floor and ran down the stairs. Max wanted to run after him, but I pulled him back yelling, "Don't be stupid, we have our lives." This wasn't the impression I wanted to make on his first visit to my apartment. Luckily, nothing like that ever happened again.

My parents were sad to see me move out, but were happy it was to the borough of Manhattan, rather than to another state like California on the other side of the country. Despite the apartment's being in a run-down area, we fixed it up the way we liked, and were happy there.

On the very next weekend at the Zofia, everyone was discussing another huge antiwar demonstration in Washington, DC. There were buses going from Manhattan to the capitol in DC. We had just heard that the Chicago Seven had been found guilty, and were given five-year prison sentences. The government was cracking down on dissidents, and I was reluctant to go to the demonstration. Erik and everyone else were keen on it, and I certainly wasn't going to be the odd one out. Erik was all hopped up about it, and was all he talked about for the next week.

On the day of the demonstration we boarded one of the busses to the nation's capital. I found Washington DC to be very beautiful. The capital was impressive, but even the surrounding neighborhoods were splendid, and filled with stately homes. Everything was organized for the demonstration, and we were all given tips on what to do if we were arrested by the police. We were directed to carry no identification, and were given the phone number of a lawyer, which we wrote in pen on the insides of our wrists. I was very nervous and thought, *If Noah Bernstein could only see me now.*

We headed into the streets. It was a crazy and chaotic scene with hundreds of thousands of people. There were so many demonstrators that we quickly lost our friends. We marched for hours. Demonstrators carried placards and yelled phrases against the war—"Hell no, we won't go," and "One, two, three, four, we don't want your fucking war." The crowds moved in waves and bodies were close together. I was getting frightened, but Erik never let go of my hand; we saw tear gas coming; the air became thick with it.

Erik yelled at me, "Hurry! Start running!" He steered me away from the crowd onto a side street.

The next thing happened so quickly that I had no time to think about a reaction; I just followed my instinct. Erik and I were walking away from the demonstration, and a cop grabbed him and began leading him away. Without thinking, I ran after them and jumped on the cop's back yelling, "Stop! He's wasn't doing anything!"

The cop was pissed off and tried to shake me off his back, but I wasn't letting go; I held on for dear life. The cop shouted at Erik, "You're going to jail, jerk-off!"

I started punching his back. Some guys saw us and began taunting the cop with a piece of wood. We were soon off the cop's radar, as he turned his attention to the guys who were threatening him he let go of Erik, who then pulled me off the cop's back. We started running as fast as we could and turned onto another street. I was breathing heavily and shaking.

When we were well away from the fray, Erik shook me and said, "Whoa, you were really something!"

It was like being in a Hollywood action movie. We hugged each other relieved, and looked around for anyone we knew. We couldn't find anyone in our group, so we headed toward the place where we had all agreed to meet up. Thankfully none of us were arrested. Erik kept telling everyone what I had done. I had shocked myself, and realized that I had done something reckless without thinking of the consequences. We all hopped on one of the busses back to New York City. I was glad it was over.

When Erik and I got back to the apartment on West Lenox, the cats were right by the door waiting for us. They had no idea what we had been through. I held Jolene on my lap and was overcome with emotion and relief. I was happy to be home safe, and in the peace of the moment.

Erik on the other hand was exhilarated by the events of the day. He took my hand and led me into the bedroom. I knew what he wanted, and I guess I wanted it too. I lay on the bed, with the cats settled near my feet. Erik stood next to the bed watching me as he undressed. When he was naked, I stared at him, up and down. He reminded me of a figure in an old Flemish painting I'd seen in a museum, with his fair skin and straight blond hair. He looked so perfectly beautiful. I was already undressed and anticipating what was to happen next.

The Christmas holiday was wonderful. We celebrated at our apartment, and the Zofia. As spring approached, it was still very cold upstate. There were icicles hanging from the eaves of the porches of the Zofia Lodge, like a scene from *Dr. Zhivago*.

We had a big decision to make. Were we going to keep the Zofia Lodge or rent another house? Lonny Marcum and Sebastian Warren, who were the oldest of our group, were already working behind the scenes to perhaps move the communal experiment to a more country-like atmosphere—a place with a lot more land, where we could have a garden and grow some of our own vegetables. In the summer most of us would be living there full time.

In the end, it was decided that we would not keep the Zofia. Our friends from the Aliceville commune told us of an old farmhouse on ten acres of land for rent. It was outside of a very small rural town, and near a dairy farm. I was always reluctant when it came to change, but this time I looked forward to it. I reminded myself that I would be with the same group of people who had become my family, and that was a constant. So in the spring of 1970, we moved to the old farmhouse.

{A sad note: about a year later, we heard that the Zofia Lodge had burned to the ground. Ross Grant and two other guys drove back to Hunter Mountain to have a look at the damage. They came back and reported to us. They said all that was left visible from the road, as they looked up on the hill where the Zofia had once stood, were the two stone fireplaces.}

EIGHT

THE YELLOW HOUSE

You get drunk when you want to forget something.
You get stoned when you want to be real.

~~~~~~~~~~~~~~~~

—*Jerry Rubin, "We Are Everywhere"*

It had been difficult saying goodbye to the Zofia, but moving to the farmhouse was the direction in which we wanted to go. We were still reeling from the news of the four students shot by the National Guard at Kent State University, and talked about it on the three-hour drive upstate.

The farmhouse was on a rural country road off Route 28 in Upstate New York—an old yellow farmhouse up on a hill right off the road. The surrounding ten acres went far back. There was a large front porch that extended around the side of the house, and right across the road was a fast-running stream. The sound of the rushing water could be heard from inside the house, which was a delight. As we walked around the property, I kept hearing Norman Greenbaum's song in my head: "Spirit in the Sky." I was sensing something spiritual was about to happen.

We walked through the living room into the kitchen, which was a good size. There was a large clock on the wall, and the hands were on twenty-five minutes to six. The time was significant since in the coming months, whenever someone checked the time, the hands were mysteriously always on twenty-five minutes to six. We went outside through another door at the back of the kitchen and found the perfect place to plant a garden.

The house had bedrooms on the first and second floors. I chose a bedroom on the first floor at the end of a long hallway. Any weekend visitors would either have to bunk in with one of us or sleep in the living room, since the bedrooms were all spoken for. We all contributed toward the rent, but those who had more means put in more money. There was a giddy sense of freedom, yet a feeling of oneness that we all shared from the very beginning. Someone donated a very simple stereo system for the living room, with two gigantic speakers. It didn't take much to get us all up and dancing.

That summer we had open house parties on the weekends at what we were calling the Yellow House. There could be forty or more people, including any young people we ran into while in town.

The landlord was an old black guy named Darius Blackwell. He always came by in person to collect the rent. He'd sit on one of the chairs in the kitchen, chomping on a cigar until we paid him. Sometimes, he would be drunk and would linger, even after we paid him, to ogle the girls. True, some of us were scantily clothed, but his ogling made us uncomfortable. I once complained to him about the septic tank. There was sewage flowing down the driveway, and I told him it needed to be fixed. The next day he drove up in his pickup, drunk, and began shoveling gravel over the septic tank runoff. He was shoveling, sweating, and had that damn cigar dangling from the corner of his mouth. He claimed it was a temporary fix until the tank was fixed.

The worst time was a day he came by when we were all tripping on LSD. It was a very intense hour or so until he left. He sat in the kitchen talking away, chomping on that damn cigar. He was interrupting our plans for a fun day at the stream. Darius Blackwell had a habit of showing up at the most inopportune times.

A little way up the road was a dairy. Adam and I usually made the daily walk to get three gallons of milk for the commune. It never failed that Max would sneak the cream off the top. He and Aiden were the bakers in our group. Since they kept us stocked with fresh bread and other baked goods, we were inclined to let the indulgence slide. Max, also being a chemist, set up a lab in the basement and made most of the LSD we took. We knew it was pure, and his personal stamp on the blotter was a dab of patchouli.

I was living at the Yellow House most of the time that summer. Erik only came up on weekends, since he still had his job at the bookstore in

Manhattan. Occasionally I'd spend a few days at our apartment in the city. He and I went to see Leslie West and his band, Mountain. Everyone at the concert sang along to "Mississippi Queen." Erik hooked up a stereo system on the surface of that antique Victorian sideboard. We loved listening to Buffalo Springfield, Led Zeppelin, and the Moody Blues.

One night we took LSD together in the apartment. We sat facing each other on the black and white tiled bathroom floor staring at each other. As the drug was taking effect, I fell down a rabbit hole, and the tiles turned into a winding road leading to a Mad Hatter Tea Party. Then suddenly, Erik turned into Jesus Christ sitting at a table with a bunch of strange characters.

He noticed me acting weird and asked, "What is it?"

I answered, "You're Jesus Christ."

Erik laughed. "Adriana, it's me, Erik."

He took my hand and stroked it.

I turned my face to look at him again, and Jesus had disappeared. So strange the way the mind works on LSD.

Erik and I definitely had shared some beautiful times together, but lately, I found him becoming more and more radical politically. I agreed with him on most issues, but he was like a dog with a bone. It wasn't so much that he felt a particular way about an issue; it was that he would dictate what I and others should think and feel about it. I was not one to let someone tell me what to think or how to feel. His attitude grated on everyone's nerves.

At the Yellow House, my friends began teasing me. They would refer to Erik as "The Nazi," a nickname my mother had given him. (I should have never told them what my mother said.) I wasn't sure if they were referring to his demeanor, or the fact that he was German. Either way, I hated it.

Some new people came on the scene that summer and became part of our family; all were wonderful additions. There were three guys who were tight friends: Matthew Romeola, whom everyone called Romeo; Brent Beachwood, who we just called Beach; and Casey Cutler, who had a black dog named Rocco. They were funny guys, always together and sparring off each other to kept us all laughing. At first impression, they reminded me of the Three Stooges—Moe, Larry, and Curly. Casey's dog Rocco had to learn to live with all the cats. It wasn't easy, but he made a valiant effort.

Ross Grant and I had a natural affinity for each other and had become good friends. He turned me on to the I Ching, the Chinese Book of Changes.

He gave me a copy of the book, for which he embroidered the cover. He got me into consulting it whenever I had a perplexing problem or a heavy decision to make. I carried the I Ching and the three Chinese coins with me wherever I went. I definitely found guidance and words of wisdom in those pages.

CLOTH COVER OF THE I CHING BOOK
(THE CHINESE BOOK OF CHANGES)

There was a tall, mellow, smooth-talking, black guy named Sequoia. He didn't live with us, but was at the yellow house every weekend. He was very handsome and reminded me of Chuck Berry. He dressed like a Native American, wore a headband, and decked himself out in feathers and beads. He was a very spiritual type. Then there was a balding Judd Thatcher. We all knew him from the university. He could be a hothead at times, but he was always good for an intelligent conversation.

Erik and I had been together almost a year, but we were becoming somewhat distant. The fall of our relationship was a slow but steady progression. One evening while I was in the city, we visited my parents in the Bronx. We were discussing politics, which was a bad idea to begin with.

It was around the same time as the signing of the Nuclear Proliferation Treaty by the major world powers. How could an effort to stop the spread of nuclear weapons ever be a bad thing? My mother was a staunch Republican and began challenging Erik's ideas. I knew she was poking a beast, but I couldn't stop her. I waited for a big blowup. We saw things differently than she did, but Erik showed her no respect.

The conversation went from bad to worse and culminated when Erik stood up and switched off the TV which my mother had just turned on to hear the evening news. He began pacing back and forth like a tiger in a cage. My mother muttered an Italian curse. I was embarrassed, and tried to calm him down. I was between two hotheads with opposing political views. Defusing the situation was impossible, so it was time to leave.

I could see by my mother's expression that she was shocked and angry. Erik never apologized or tried to make amends. My father was as stunned as I was. I kissed my parents, and we said our goodbyes. This was the incident that prompted my mother to nick-name Erik "The Nazi."

Neither one of us uttered a word on our way back to Manhattan; the only sound heard was the screech of the train's wheels on the tracks. We got out at our stop, and Erik put his arm around me as we walked to the apartment on West Lenox. Once inside, I threw my suede fringe jacket on a chair and closed myself in the bedroom. I was pissed off; this wasn't the first time he'd made a big scene and embarrassed me in front of my family or friends. It was killing the peace and harmony we had between us, as well as—unfortunately—my love along with it.

Erik and I didn't talk much over the next few days. Before he went to work at the bookstore, I said, "I want to spend some time upstate at the Yellow House by myself."

Erik seemed a little surprised. "What do you mean?"

"I need some time to think."

I felt that the people at the commune were my friends. I'd brought Erik into the group, and he was causing friction and driving a wedge between me and my family and friends. There didn't seem to be any emotional bliss anymore.

Erik said, "I don't like that you want to spend time apart. You'll do it anyway, and I won't stop you."

I hugged Erik and said, "I do love you. I just need some time by myself."

On Friday I drove upstate with Lonny Marcum.

SUMMER OF 1970.

At the Yellow House, I felt at peace as soon as I walked through the screen door. Everyone asked where Erik was. I told them that he had things to do in the city that weekend. Lonny and Adam glanced at each other, and I denoted a sense of relief in their expressions.

Everyone was going to a movie in town, but I stayed behind at the house. I sat in one of the rocking chairs on the front porch, gently rocking back and forth. I could hear the water rushing along the stream across the road. I watched the bees buzzing around a row of tall flowers at the edge of the porch. I wrote a poem in my journal:

Flower so tender caress my cheek
So beautiful are you
So freshly washed with morning dew
Soon to be kissed by the sun
Invaded by bees, and thus be danced on
What a shame you must wither and die
Plucked from your source by someone as selfish as I

I set my journal down when I noticed Romeo, Beach, and Casey walking on the road toward the house. Romeo was in front, and I took note of what a fine form he had. He was tall—over six feet—well built, with dark hair combed in an Afro, and very tan. I tried not to dwell on that, but somehow couldn't help it. He saw me, smiled, and waved as he approached. Romeo walked up the front porch steps with the other two following behind. I noticed that he had a pleasing face, with a birthmark on his left cheek and soft green eyes. I thought of something my father once said to me—"That's your trouble; they're always too damn good-looking"—and I giggled to myself. Beach and Casey passed Romeo on the stairs and went into the house. Romeo stood in front of me, leaning against the wooden porch railing, staring down at me in the rocking chair. I stared up at him continuing to rock back and forth.

I felt an immediate attraction. I didn't know why it hadn't hit me when he first came to the commune, but I was definitely feeling something that day. He told me that he had just gotten out of the service; he had been a paratrooper in the Army, and bragged about jumping out of planes. I listened intently to his story; it seemed to me that guys liked to talk about themselves.

He said, "My friend Beach was in the Marines. We both just came back from Vietnam."

I immediately felt pangs of regret over the way I had thought of our guys in the armed forces. The nasty phrases we yelled at antiwar demonstrations when they came back from Vietnam. I felt shame because I'd just looked at them as killers of innocents after My Lai. But here, this very human soldier was standing in front of me, and he was a warm and caring human being who was just serving his country. Of course, I didn't tell him any of that. I doubted he knew anything about Erik and me, nor was I offering up that information. I listened to him and kept rocking.

He asked, "So what's your story?"

"I'm mainly living up here for the summer."

Romeo nodded. "Well then, I guess we'll be seeing a lot of each other. I'm going to the kitchen to grab a beer. You want something?" he asked.

"No, I'm good."

I heard the screen door slam, and I took the opportunity to disappear. I was troubled by what I was feeling and didn't want to feed into it. I walked across the lawn and onto the road, trying to clear my head. I walked beyond the house until I came upon a grassy field and sat down. I could see a hill in the distance, and thought that it would be nice to climb that hill and see what was up there. I stayed long enough to cleanse my thoughts, hoping for a brain reboot. Eventually, I got up and went back to the house. As I walked into the living room my eyes searched for Romeo. He was sitting on the floor talking with a few other people. He looked up at me, and I looked back at him.

Oh God, I still feel it!

The next day was a beautiful, warm, sunny day. The plan was to take some of Max's patchouli LSD and spend the day across the road at the stream. The stream was hidden from the road by trees and shrubs, so we felt it was safe from passersby. A group of us meandered across the road and walked through the bushes to the stream. I lay on a large, flat rock and ran my hand through the ripples in the water. It was so peaceful, listening to the water gurgling past me over pebbles and fallen branches. One by one, we peeled off our clothes, and a feeling of total freedom came over me. The soft breeze rushed past my body, and I could feel the tiny hairs raise on my arms and legs.

PHOTO OF THE STREAM

Pretty soon I felt the drug coming on. It's hard to describe the euphoric place I went to on LSD. Even though we all seemed to be in our own worlds, we came together at various points. We stared at each other's faces as if we shared a profound secret that no one else knew. I noticed Max standing naked in the stream. He was bending over, doing something with the small rocks he was gathering. This held my attention for a while. He would take a rock, dip it in the water, and then rub it on a larger, flat rock until it created a thick watercolor. I wasn't aware that different rocks created different colors. I thought that it must be an old Native American method, but just how Max came by that knowledge escaped me. When he had a few different colors, he began to paint on one of the nude bodies.

Romeo did the same thing, following Max's example, only Romeo chose my body to paint. It was spiritual at first but soon became erotic. The acid intensified everything I thought and felt. Romeo stared down at me, and I imagined he was seeing into my mind's eye. I felt as if he was branding me. I just lay there on that rock and let him paint symbols on my body. It felt good, and I wasn't about to stop him. Of course nothing held our attention for too long on acid. Soon, we were both into something else at someplace else along the stream.

As the sun was setting it cooled down quite a bit, and my hands were beginning to prune in the water. We each took our time getting dressed and slowly drifted back to the house. We congregated in the living room, and music seemed to be in order. Someone put a record on the stereo, an album by the Edwin Hawkins Singers. We were all smiling and began dancing in a state of joy. When the song "Oh, Happy Day" blared through the speakers, we formed a circle and locked arms. We swayed together as one body, the differences between us dissolving. We began to sing the words in a chorus that sounded like a chant. I felt euphoric. It had been a glorious day, followed by a glorious night.

There were many days and nights like that at the Yellow House that summer. It is true that the official Summer of Love was in 1967, but for me it was the summer of 1970.

This is it

"The very heavens seemed to open and pour down rays of light and glory. Not for a moment only, but all day and night, floods of light and glory seemed to pour through my soul. And oh, how I was changed, and everything became new."

William James ~ American Philosopher

I was getting close with some of the women, especially Suki Rosmond, who we had picked up hitchhiking on our way back to New York from California. She was a level headed woman who was into yoga and smoothies. Star Green was from the Jersey Shore. She had brown kinky hair, expressive blue eyes, a heart shaped face, and was in a romance with Beach, Romeo's friend. We were three very independent women of like mind, and loved hanging out together. Casey referred to us as "The three musketeers." I felt as if I finally had sisters. I had a bond with them that I did not have with the other women in the commune. We seemed to be on the same wavelength and on similar life paths. We remained close friends long after that summer was over.

A powerful thunderstorm hit Upstate New York, and we were without power at the Yellow House. Word reached us that the dairy up the road had lost electricity, and the machinery that milked the cows was disabled. Since we were there every day for milk, we thought it only right to help the farmer. A group of us walked to the dairy to help milk the cows by hand. When we arrived back at the house there was still no electricity. There wasn't much else to do but hang out indoors and wait for the storm to pass.

Different conversations went on in various corners of the living room. I was sitting with Suki and Star in a corner by the window. We were crocheting sexy little multicolored tops, a popular hippie clothing item at that time. Romeo, who had been playing cards with some of the guys, came over and sat down on the floor with us. He kept us entertained with stories about his friends in the Army, and about his family in the borough of Queens. He told us that his mother was Irish and his father was Italian, and that he was the best part of both of them. The three of us girls laughed. Every time he turned his face in my direction, I fanaticized that he was talking only to me. He had funny facial expressions and hand gestures that kept us laughing.

Somewhere during the conversation I got lost in his green eyes. From that point on, it didn't matter what the hell he was saying; I wasn't listening. After a momentary distraction, I caught the tail end of one of his stories and heard Romeo say the punch line: "And the guy looked like he had been hit in the face with a bag of nickels."

Suki and Star began laughing hysterically. I laughed too, even though I didn't have a clue as to what the beginning of the story was. Romeo was funny, charming, and seemed very warmhearted. I could tell he liked me, and I was definitely feeling something.

I tried to push Erik out of my mind, but he kept popping back in. I got up and walked outside and stood on the porch hoping to escape my thoughts, but Romeo followed me out.

He said, "Hey, the weather's cleared. Let's walk down the road to that meadow. There's a hill we can climb to watch the sunset."

I thought, *Isn't that the hill I saw yesterday, where I sat down in a field of flowers?* I knew I shouldn't go, but I convinced myself that I was just going to watch the sunset.

As we walked along the road, he told me a few things that were going on in his head. I kept silent.

"I feel a little lost after coming back from Nam. I'm taking life one day at a time. Been thinking about checking out California too."

Hearing that, my heart sank a little, and I hoped that remark would keep him at a distance from my feelings.

"I liked California," I said. "Well, for the most part."

"What sign are you anyway, Adriana?"

"I'm Cancer, the crab. It's a water sign."

"I'm Aquarius, the water bearer," he said, with a smirk.

Looking at him, the song "The Dawning of the Age of Aquarius," from the hit musical Hair on Broadway, came to mind.

It turned out to be a spectacular sunset, and I was happy I'd gone along. When we got back to the house the electricity was back on, and life picked up where it had left off before the storm.

Saturday was the perfect day for an open house party. As the day progressed, there were brownies spiked with Mary Jane on the kitchen table. In the living room people were smoking hashish from water pipes, and some, including me, took MDA, better known as the Love drug. It all started out with music and dancing—not the kind where you dance together; more like dancing alone to the beat of your own drum.

There were so many different conversations going on, it was hard to make sense of any of them. People were laughing and crying, and some just stared straight ahead, lost in their own thoughts. This went on for hours, all day long. I was feeling a little unsettled. I thought that maybe it wasn't such a good atmosphere in which to be under the influence of a psychedelic—with so many strangers at the house. Romeo must have picked up on my feelings because he came over to me and asked if I was okay. I couldn't seem to get the words out, but shook my head. I knew he'd taken MDA with the rest of us, and wondered how he remained so together and calm.

In the middle of the living room I saw a girl who was totally out of it. God only knows what she was on. She was in some sort of a yoga position, with her ass in the air, rocking back and forth and moaning. Rocco, Casey's dog, was trying to sniff and lick her from behind. Everyone was staring at that weird and crazy scene. It was a good thing she was fully clothed.

I wanted to get out of that room and find somewhere peaceful, but I couldn't seem to move.

Romeo asked, "Do you have your own room?"

I still couldn't speak, but pointed in the direction of the hallway.

"Come on," he said, helping me up.

I led him through the hallway until I stopped in front of my room. He opened the door and we went inside. After he closed the door behind us, I immediately felt calm and could breathe again.

"Feel better now?" he asked.

I nodded.

"Just relax," he said, rubbing my shoulder.

We sat on my bed—a mattress on the floor. We were facing each other with our legs folded, as if we were going to meditate. I wished he would tell me a funny story, to get my head out of the weird space it was in. But instead we sat buzzing in silence for a long time.

I had left the window open in my room, and I could smell the cool, sweet, summer night air, and heard the water gurgling in the stream across the road. Romeo took my hand again and held it tight.

I said, "Can you hear it? I mean, the water from the stream across the road?"

"Yeah, I can hear it."

Again, we sat silently for a time. Then he began to tell me about his time in Vietnam—some of the things that had happened to him there; about the Vietnamese people he'd met, some of whom he'd made friends with. He told me some of them had been burned with napalm. Other soldiers in his troop he'd gotten close with, had been killed. Some of them were blown up right before his eyes.

I listened intently but didn't speak; I tenderly stroked his hand. I was happy that he felt comfortable enough to tell me these things. After a while, I got out of my own head and knew I was sharing in someone else's life. For some reason it made me feel good.

He said, "Nam left me with malaria, which causes periodic night sweats. For that, I receive a small monthly monetary compensation from the government." Then he gave a little half laugh and told me a funny story about a woman who all the guys had sex with there. He said, "She was an older Vietnamese woman who was really ugly, but she sure knew how to fuck."

We both began laughing. I wondered if Romeo had told Casey or Beach any of those stories, but I was glad he had told me.

Soon we were both overcome with a feeling of closeness, a connection that wasn't just physical attraction. It was deeper, like the mingling of souls. Psychedelic drugs had a way of doing that. It was getting dark outside, so I found matches and lit the candle on the end table next to my bed. We lay down on the mattress next to each other and stared up at the ceiling. Our bodies were still vibrating from the MDA. Everything seemed as if it was happening in slow motion. He took my hand in his and felt each one of my fingers individually. Then he moved the palm of his hand along my arm, caressing it softly. We turned our faces toward each other. He put his hand out, very slowly, and touched my face.

"The first time I laid eyes on you, I liked you," he said.

I didn't answer, but my mouth broke out in a big grin. Romeo leaned over and kissed me a few times, until he felt me kissing him back. His beard felt much softer against my skin than I had imagined it would. I grabbed hold of his hair and kissed him hard with my mouth open, and licked his lips with my tongue. He liked that a lot. We started taking off our clothes while trying to keep our lips connected, and when we couldn't, we began to laugh again. He moved his head all over my body, kissing me in various places. It was as if he was studying every inch of me and liking what he saw. Then he moved on top of me, and before I knew it, he was inside of me. It felt so good, almost like a religious experience. We stopped for a moment, just enjoying the sensation. Then we slowly rocked back and forth as one person, staring at each other. Soon, nothing else mattered but us.

One thing Romeo didn't tell me that night was that his time in Vietnam made him a junkie.

In the morning we walked to the kitchen together holding hands, looking to see if anyone was making breakfast. We found Max in the kitchen making waffles. Over breakfast, Max told us about a really cool place—the old abandoned Tuscarora Hotel, which he said was not far from the Yellow House. The hotel had a Native American name and was once a summer hot spot for vacationers. Romeo, Casey, and I wanted to see it and headed out with Max.

The hotel was in ruins, and we roamed through the empty rooms. In the shell of what once was the dining room, it was easy to imagine people laughing and talking over their food and cocktails. I thought about the life that once had gone on within those walls. It was definitely an eerie place though. The deserted cabins on the property surrounding the hotel were a real photo op. We spent part of the afternoon taking pictures of each other on the old, rickety wooden porches of the cabins. I have a great photo of Casey on the porch of one of the dilapidated cottages. He stood there barefoot in his overalls, his long strawberry blond hair cascading down his bare shoulders. He had the most innocent smile on his face, like an Appalachian teen being spied on.

As we got ready to leave I saw Maxwell Robinov skipping down the front steps of the Tuscarora Hotel with a large bouquet of wild flowers he'd collected to bring back to the Yellow House.

MAX AT THE TUSCARORA HOTEL.

On the ride back to the house, I told Romeo, "I have to go back to the city in a couple of days."

"Will you be at the house next weekend?"

"For sure," I said, "And I plan on staying for a while."

"Far out! I guess I'll be thinking about that all week."

I turned my face toward him and smiled.

The next evening, we all sat around the living room playing cards and talking. I looked at Romeo and felt a surge of desire for him. It was such a strong urge that I couldn't seem to shake it. Romeo looked up from his card game, and our eyes locked. He stood up and walked toward me, held his hand out, and I took it. He led me through the hallway to my room.

We went inside and closed the door. We stood there for a while. I wanted him more than just about anything at that moment. He grabbed me and kissed me hard. We lay down on the mattress and made love getting lost in each other. It was something I knew I would have a hard time forgetting.

When I got back to the city, I went directly to the apartment on West Lenox. Erik wasn't home from work yet. I started making us something for dinner, and the cats sat in the kitchen watching me. I was riddled with guilt and was hoping that it wasn't written all over my face. I didn't want to jump to any conclusions about what had happened upstate. I knew that I felt better on my own than I did with Erik. I loved him, but I didn't think I was in love anymore; that our special connection was gone. This seemed to be my pattern.

I heard his key in the front door, and soon he was standing in the kitchen. He pulled me to him, smiled, and gave me a big kiss. He said, "How was it upstate?"

"Great," I answered, acting as if nothing out of the ordinary had happened.

We had supper and then sat in the living room talking. I felt strange, as if I was hiding a secret, which I was. I decided, at that stage, it was best to keep it to myself.

Erik stopped talking and took my hand. I knew what he wanted. We walked into the bedroom, got undressed, and got in bed. I rationalized my actions by telling myself that I did still love Erik. After we made love, I felt confused. My life was in limbo—like that old song by Mary MacGregor, "Torn Between Two Lovers." Looking back, I would mark that up to "Youthful folly" (a common phrase referenced in the I Ching).

The next morning, all I wanted to do was go back upstate, but how could I bring that up to Erik? I had just been upstate for ten days straight. He knew I'd be living up there for most of the summer, and Erik wasn't going to give up his job at the bookstore. But I figured he was planning on going to the Yellow House with me on the next weekend, and that would be problematic.

As all this was running through my brain, Erik said, "I'm working late at the bookstore tonight, so figure out dinner for yourself." He slipped his suede jacket on, kissed me goodbye, and left. The cats stared at the door for a long time, expecting him to come back at any moment. After a while they gave up and went into the bedroom.

I figured I'd stay home and do some chores around the apartment. I was washing the breakfast dishes when the phone rang. It was Lonny Marcum. He was in the city too, teaching summer classes at the university on Staten Island. He said, "Romeo was asking about you, but knowing your situation, I wouldn't give him your phone number. He's staying in an apartment on Fourth Street in Greenwich Village we've been using in the city. He wants you to call him." Lonny gave me the phone number, which I jotted down on a pad we kept next to the phone in the kitchen.

I wondered why Romeo wanted me to contact him when we would be seeing each other on the weekend at the Yellow House. I stared at the piece of paper. I thought of my time upstate and those crazy nights that Romeo and I spent together. I picked up the paper and dialed the number.

Romeo answered the phone. When he heard it was me, he said, "I was hoping you'd call. I couldn't wait till the weekend."

"I've been thinking about you too," I said.

"Come down to the Village, and let's hang out."

"I'll meet you at the Café Reggio," I said.

I quickly took a shower and headed out the door. I walked to Sixth Avenue, through the tunnel, and took the subway downtown.

When I arrived at Café Reggio, I found Romeo sitting on one of the couches. My heart jumped when I saw his face. We ordered cappuccinos and Italian pastries. God, it felt so right, and there was definitely strong chemistry between us.

Greenwich Village was popping, with swarms of people walking in all directions. There was music streaming out of the underground clubs and people packed into just about every restaurant and outside café.

"Are you still planning on going to the Yellow House on the weekend?" I asked.

He smiled at me. "Yeah, I'll be there."

We began walking to Fourth Street, and although we didn't hold hands, I could feel an invisible vibrating string between us. Romeo stopped in front of an old brownstone with two potted geraniums on either side of the entrance. We walked up two flights of stairs, and he unlocked the door. Inside, it was a typical Greenwich Village apartment—very old and nothing special.

What the hell was I doing? This was a dangerous game I was playing, and I was plagued with guilt. Thoughts of Erik and the cats flashed through my mind, but I couldn't seem to stop myself. What exactly was I searching for? I didn't have any answers.

Romeo and I had one thing on our minds—making love—and we didn't waste any time. We took off our clothes and got right to it.

"That was crazy good," Romeo said.

Recklessly I asked, "Are you staying in the city tonight?"

He sat up, lit a joint, and said, "Just for tonight. I have to get back to Queens tomorrow." He passed the joint to me and seemed to be waiting for a response.

I took a toke and said, "My parents are expecting me for dinner at their apartment in the Bronx tonight." I had made up that story, but I figured that would quell any plans he had for me to stick around for the night. We left it that we would see each other upstate on the weekend. Romeo walked me to the train station. When I turned to leave him, he pulled me close and kissed me hard on the lips. He gave me a lingering gaze as I walked away.

I felt exhilarated, tingly, and filled with happiness on the subway ride uptown. As I approached my stop though, my feelings turned to guilt, confusion, and doubt. What was I going to do? Was it always going to be somewhere else, with someone else? I thought that I might be filling some lonely void deep inside of me that no one seemed to be able to fill. My stop came up, the doors of the train opened, and I rushed up the stairs to the street. I walked the few blocks to the apartment on West Lenox. During the ride up on the elevator I hoped Erik wasn't home, or at least wasn't sitting there waiting for me.

I opened the door and the cats were right there to greet me. I saw Erik's suede jacket on a chair in the kitchen, but there was no sign of him. I peeked in the bedroom and found him sound asleep. I took a shower and crawled into bed. I curled up next to him. He half woke up and pulled me toward him, spooning me. I fell asleep in his arms, with the cats settled at our feet. I was home—for now.

NINE

THE BEST-LAID
PLANS DISRUPTED

We should always smile whenever the press comes to
photograph or film us, even if they're dragging us off to jail.

—*Timothy Leary*

knew I had to tell Erik what was going on, but I didn't know how. I
dreaded the thought of another confrontation. I was sure he knew
something was up with me, because we were just going through the
motions of a relationship. The weekend was coming up, and I wanted
to go upstate, stay there, and never come back. Maybe I was running
away, but it seemed like the easiest and least painful thing to do—for me
anyway. I knew I was betraying him, even though I wasn't sure that what
I'd experienced with Romeo was real enough to last.

Erik came home from work; I was sitting on a chair in the kitchen. I
knew he could tell by my expression that something was wrong, perhaps
very wrong.

He sat down across from me reaching for my hand. "What's going on?
Talk to me."

I was working up the courage when he rubbed my hand.

I came straight out with it. "I met someone upstate."

"You mean a guy?"

"Yes." I didn't tell him that I had gone to bed with Romeo; I didn't want
to add insult to injury.

He was silent, but pulled his hand back.

"I need some time to think about us," I said. "I'm going upstate on Friday, and probably won't come back to the city for a while."

"I thought things were okay between us. For God's sake, why are you doing this?"

"I haven't been happy with our relationship, and I can't make believe anymore."

Erik looked angry and hurt all at the same time.

"You can stay here with the cats," I said.

The apartment was in my name, so I thought that would be a consolation.

"Say something. Please, say something!" I said.

Erik turned his face away from mine, but didn't say anything; I guessed he was digesting my words. Then he stood up, grabbed his suede jacket, and left the apartment without looking at me or saying another word.

The cats heard the door slam and sat there staring at it. When Erik didn't return they turned their gaze at me, as if I owed them an explanation. I began to cry uncontrollably. I had hurt someone very badly, someone I loved and who loved me.

I didn't know where Erik stayed that night, but he never came home. I tossed and turned waiting to hear his key in the door, but that didn't happen. The next day was Friday, and I wondered if I was going to leave without us talking again. I arranged for a ride upstate with Adam, who was in the city, and I began getting my things together. I figured Erik wouldn't come back to the apartment until he knew I was gone. Part of me was hoping for that.

During that episode with Erik and Romeo, I relived a painful time in my childhood. My mother had an affair with another man when I was a little girl. It affected my childhood, changed my relationship with her, and clouded my future relationships with men;

There was an Italian man, Dario, who had an import business in Manhattan. He would come to my mother's dress factory, and the women would buy imported cheese, olives, and homemade sausage from him. He was good-looking, dark, and dashing. He spoke mostly Italian but could carry on a conversation in English. He went to Italy often, and we always had the best Italian delicacies. My mother would light up when he walked into the factory, and he seemed to pay a lot of attention to her as well. Once in a while he would deliver to our home.

It was Saturday, my father's busiest day at the barbershop; we didn't expect him home until late. Dario came to our house with a box of goodies from Italy. I was in the living room but could hear my mother and Dario laughing and talking in the kitchen. When I didn't hear their voices anymore, I walked toward the kitchen to see why it was so quiet.

In the hallway hung a colored-pencil drawing my father had done. It was framed under glass, and in the reflection of the glass, I saw my mother kissing Dario. I was stunned. What the hell? I was only nine years old at the time, and I couldn't think straight. My eyes welled with tears, and I ran to my parents' bedroom and threw myself on the bed. I laid there in shock. I felt pain for my father. Eventually I heard the front door close, so I knew Dario had left. My mother found me crying on her bed and couldn't imagine what was wrong with me.

"I saw you kissing Dario!" She reached for me and tried to hug and kiss me, but I resisted her embrace. I screamed, "I hate you!"

"Adriana, I love you so much. Please don't hate me. Dario and I love each other. Someday, when you're older, you'll understand."

But I didn't understand at all. I couldn't even look at her. I felt pain and darkness surround me.

I don't know when my father found out about Dario, but he did. He'd refer to Dario as "The villain," as if we were living in an old black-and-white silent film. For a long time I slept with my mother in their bedroom, and my father slept on the Castro chair-bed in the living room. Eventually, my father got his own apartment, although I begged him not to leave.

My mother Vita's affair went on for years. Somewhere along the line, she found out that Dario had ties to the Mob, and stopped seeing him. My father forgave her; I never did. I now know it's possible to love two people at the same time, but as a child I understood none of that. I'd made a mess of things with Erik, and wondered if it was all for naught. Was what I experienced with Romeo something that could last? Was it love? I wasn't sure.

When I arrived upstate at the Yellow House I found everything exactly as I had left it the week before. I confided in Star and Suki, and they hugged me in support.

Star looked at me with sympathetic blue eyes and said, "Just go with your heart, with the flow of things, and stop beating yourself up."

Of course, that seemed to be my pattern, and how I got into these situations in the first place. I knew that my family and friends didn't think Erik was a good match for me, and I wondered if those outside influences had something to do with my change of heart. We don't live in the world all on our own. We live in families and communities, and their influence was definitely a factor for me.

Romeo, Beach, and Casey walked through the screen door into the living room. Romeo lit up when he saw me; he came straight over and gave me a kiss on the lips. Anyone who had been at the Yellow House on the previous weekend knew that we had a thing going on. Beach embraced Star, and I wondered if she'd said anything to him about my being in a relationship with someone else. I figured I should tell Romeo about Erik, but was waiting for the right time. At that moment we were just happy to see each other. Romeo wanted to take a walk across the road to the stream. He took my hand, and everything around me felt light, airy, and full of promise as we strolled out the front door.

As the summer progressed the parties continued. At times we all took note of strange bedfellows—some of the gay men were hooking up with the straight women, and some of the gay women were having sex with the straight men. Of course, I was no stranger to that situation. I had been nearly crucified for getting romantically involved with Adam Hirschfeld in the past. I noticed that Margot, one of the gay women, had a thing for Romeo. I kept a close eye on that woman.

There were orgies at the house, but I was not into that sort of thing. I had Romeo and was so in love with him that no one else interested me. Erik and the cats disappeared from my brain, save for a tinge of guilt now and then.

I was sitting in Romeo's lap on a chair in the kitchen watching Star make lunch. He pulled something silver out of his pocket and flashed it at me. It was a wide silver ring with two interlocking bands in a beautiful woven pattern. It was a fifteenth-century Renaissance design, something a woman would wear roaming around the halls of a castle.

He slipped it on my ring finger, gazed into my eyes, and smiled. "It's a friendship ring," he said. The ring had the power of love.

Max walked through the screen door at the back of the kitchen with a basket of fresh vegetables from the garden.

Romeo looked at me with a warm, contented smile. He searched for my lips and gave me a soft kiss. His soulful pale green eyes and soft face melted my heart.

"Isn't that a beautiful thing?" he asked.

"Us, the ring, or the vegetables?"

He laughed. "All that and more."

I nodded, not taking my eyes off his for a moment. I put my arms around his neck and kissed him slowly and passionately on the lips.

Star glanced at us, shook her head, and chuckled.

Romeo and I had been together for a few months, and I wanted him to meet my parents. Being half Italian, I figured he'd be a hit with my mother; after all, I'd never dated anyone even slightly Italian. We brought Casey, Beach, and Star along for support and drove into the city. We stayed at the apartment on Fourth Street in the village. I avoided my apartment on West Lenox completely. Erik and I had spoken since I left, but I didn't want to throw Romeo in his face. That would have been cruel.

The five of us filed into the vestibule of my parents' apartment house. I rang the bell and they buzzed us in. I had called them from upstate to let them know we'd be visiting. I greeted my mom and dad with hugs and kisses, then I introduced everyone. Romeo flashed that warm smile at my mother; how could she possibly resist that? Alfie the cat curled his tail around everyone's legs and sniffed. Romeo picked him up and started petting him. I think that won Vita over.

Sitting around the dining room table, my father jumped right into the conversation and didn't even ask anyone if they smelled gas. Star already knew of my father and his allergies, and I had prepared the others beforehand. My wonderful mother made the best dinner, and Romeo had her laughing in no time.

After dinner, I sat on the couch in the living room and put my feet up on the coffee table. Romeo sat next to me, and Alfie jumped in his lap. Casey sat at the far end of the couch.

My mother walked over to the couch and ran her hand along my bare leg. "Don't you shave your legs anymore?"

I shook my head. "I haven't in a long time."

Romeo chimed in. "It's okay with me. I sorta like it." He grinned running his hand along my other leg.

My mother shook her head in dismay as she walked to the kitchen to make coffee.

I was relying on Romeo for additional support because Casey was snickering.

Romeo said, "What do you expect from your mother? She sees you walk in with hairy legs like a Green Bay Packer!" He sure had a way with words. "Don't worry. I like it, and that's all that counts."

We went back to the table for dessert and coffee. My mother was impressed that the guys had been in the service; she admired that. She told the story of my father's enlisting in the service when they were first married. I'd seen photos of my dad and his brother Red, wearing their uniforms, with my mother standing between them. Then she said, "He never went into the service. They told him he was unfit physically and had flat feet."

I kicked Romeo under the table, hoping he wouldn't laugh. He didn't, but he had a big smile on his face.

It was a wonderful evening—my parents were so easy to love. When we left the apartment, there were hugs and smiles all around.

We stayed in the city on Fourth Street for another day doing city things. Star and I rummaged around the secondhand stores in Greenwich Village. We were looking for goodies to take back upstate. I found some beautifully embroidered patches that I wanted to sew on a pair of jeans.

Romeo wanted me to meet his parents, so we left the others at the apartment in the village, and took the train to the borough of Queens. They were very warm people, hard not to love. Romeo had a sister who had some health issues. She was thin and frail but very pretty. She and Romeo seemed to have a close relationship. While they were talking, I noticed a framed photo of Romeo in full paratrooper gear, displayed on a hall table. They were obviously proud of their son. I pictured him jumping out of an aircraft and parachuting into unknown territory in a foreign land, and was filled with admiration.

I was happy we'd spent time with our families, and how well it had gone. With our family obligations over, and some fun had in the city, we drove back upstate the next morning.

When we arrived at the Yellow House, we found Aiden, Sebastian, and Ivy sitting in rocking chairs on the front porch. Evelyn Moskowitz, a close friend of Aiden Wazansky's, insisted on being called Ivy. She was knitting something with different colored balls of yarn on her lap.

Max walked over from the garden to greet us. I called out, "Farmer John," and began laughing. He was wearing overalls and sporting a straw hat. Overalls had been his uniform for a while.

Romeo put his arm around my waist and grinned. "I have to get a pair of those!"

Within days, most of the men in the commune were wearing overalls. If they would've spent time in the garden like Max, I would've seen a reason for the overalls.

THE YELLOW HOUSE SUMMER, 1970.

Darius Blackwell, the landlord, came by and told us that the residents in town were beginning to complain to the state police about the goings on at the house. They were upset about their kids hanging out with us on weekends. At least Darius wasn't chewing on that damn cigar, but his words felt like a threat to me.

After he left, Romeo said he had a bad feeling about it. He said, "I heard Darius owns a lot of land in the county. He might be friends with the state police. I think we should pay attention to what he's saying."

Most of the others paid no heed to Darius' warning and had no intention of altering their lifestyles, but Romeo and I were troubled by his visit.

Life went on as usual at the Yellow House; the summer was half gone. During the first week of August, we heard about a big rock music festival, Strawberry Fields; happening in Ontario, Canada. A long list of rock bands would be performing, and the event was to go on for four days. Romeo and I wanted to go, but no one else in the commune was interested. We would have to hitchhike since the cars were needed at the house. Star Green remarked that she needed a break from Beach, and said she'd come with us. We left a day before the concert since we didn't know how long it would take us to hitchhike to Ontario. We grabbed our sleeping bags, some snacks, and had Max drop us off on the thruway going north.

On the side of the road, Star and I took note that Romeo was wearing water-striped bell-bottom jeans, a wife-beater T-shirt, and a beaded choker around his neck. The fact that he was over six feet tall and sported an Afro was also noted. We wondered who the hell would stop to pick us up. We decided that Star and I would stand on the road with our thumbs out—we were women dressed in ordinary shorts and tank tops. We told Romeo to hide behind the bushes. Star and I stuck out our thumbs and in no time a car stopped. We were on our way to Canada.

It was a long, grueling trip, in and out of cars, stopping at rest stops to eat and use the bathroom. At one point, we waited so long for a ride that Star lay down in the grass on the side of the road and took a nap. Finally, someone stopped for us, and, as luck would have it, they were on their way to Strawberry Fields as well. It took us about twelve hours to get there. The concert was held at a raceway park, which was a huge venue. It was still daylight when we arrived, so we looked for a good spot up on a hill with a great view of the stage. That evening the music started, so we stayed up all night.

While looking for food and beverages in the tents I lost Romeo in the crowd. Star and I went searching for him. I heard a familiar voice yell, "Hey Chica!" I turned around, and it was Romeo. I ran to him and wrapped my arms around him. He lifted me off the ground and said, "I love you, Chica!" From that day forward, *Chica* is what Romeo called me.

I remember one thing vividly from that weekend—after dark one night, Romeo and I made love in my sleeping bag, while Sly and the Family Stone was playing.

By the third day, we were feeling pretty ragged and decided to go home. We figured it was better to leave ahead of the crowds that would be leaving on the last day. We met someone at the festival who was heading back to New York City. He told us he'd drop us off on the thruway at route 28 near our town.

After three days in Canada, and a long ride home, we arrived at the Yellow House exhausted. The weekend was over, but there were still a lot of people hanging out at the Yellow House. Everyone wanted to drop acid, but I wasn't in the mood. Then I thought about the prospect of being the odd person out while everyone else was tripping. I decided to go along with everyone and swallowed a hit. It wasn't a batch of Max's patchouli blotters. Someone had brought the LSD to the house.

As soon as I felt the drug coming on I was overwhelmed with a negative feeling, and didn't want to be tripping. The Acid was extra strong, a double hit, or maybe I was fighting it. I couldn't wrap my head around how I was feeling, and began to panic. I tried to tell Romeo what was happening, but he didn't know what to do with me. I ran outside to the porch and sat in one of the rocking chairs, hoping for a change in perception. The row of flowers and bushes along the porch railing were melting right before my eyes. I began seeing strange visions, and hearing airplanes zooming around me.

Romeo must have sent Casey out to deal with me because the next thing I knew, he was sitting in the rocking chair next to mine holding my hand. Casey tried to calm me down. He kept saying, "Adriana, you're okay. You're okay. Just relax. You hear me? The feeling will soon pass." Whatever he was attempting to do wasn't working, and he knew it. Casey disappeared but soon returned with a glass of water and a capsule. "Adriana, take this; it'll help you." I swallowed the capsule without even knowing what it was. Within minutes (although I had no concept of time) everything changed. My head was brought down about two hundred levels. I was still tripping, but was out of danger. I smiled at Casey who was still sitting next to me holding my hand. He squeezed it saying, "You okay now?" I answered back, "I'm fine."

The next morning I looked for Casey.

"What did you give me yesterday?"

"Thorazine," he said.

"I thought that was horse tranquilizer."

Casey laughed. "It's a mood regulator. It worked, didn't it?"

After that experience, I was happy anti-psychotic drugs existed, but was terrified to take LSD again. My tripping days were over!

On the very next weekend, we had an open house party, and I was a little shocked to see Erik Eschweiler show up—and with a woman. I had already told Romeo about Erik so he wouldn't be in the dark. Erik looked beautiful with his shoulder-length, straight, blond hair, and he wasn't wearing glasses. He had on bell-bottom jeans and a Nehru shirt, with a long string of beads around his neck.

Romeo had never met him, so I nudged him and pointed out Erik. They walked over to us, and Erik introduced his lady friend. Her name escapes me, probably a mental block. Romeo and Erik checked each other out like two bulls in a pen waiting to rumble. To me, there didn't seem to be anything—at that point anyway—to be angry about. With a little conversation it all mellowed out.

Erik asked me, "Can we talk alone?"

We walked into the kitchen, leaving his lady friend talking with Romeo.

"I met her while I was hanging out at the Green House commune," he said.

"She seems nice."

"I think she looks like you a bit," he said.

I rolled my eyes.

"Things are okay with me. I wanted to let you know that I don't need the apartment on Lenox in the city anymore."

"I'll probably go back to work in the fall, so I want to keep it. What about the cats?" I asked.

"I gave them back to my friends."

"Erik, despite what happened between us, and how things changed, I did love you very much.

He half smiled but didn't respond.

"I'm glad to see you've moved on," I said.

It ended up being a very civil conversation, and at the end we hugged. I think he understood that these people were my friends—hell, they were my family. He had waited to come back to the Yellow House until he could make an entrance with a woman, and I understood that. The guilt I had felt for so long vanished, like a magic trick, in the party atmosphere around us.

I was well aware that Romeo, and a few others in the commune, were into heroin. I never witnessed them do it, but I could always tell when they had. Romeo told me that he, and lot of the other soldiers, got into it while they were in Vietnam. I knew that the poppy fields brought in big money in that part of the world. Southeast Asia and the Far East had been masters at the opium and heroin trade for centuries. I imagined that Romeo and the other guys had begun taking it to dull their senses to all the things they had seen and experienced.

It didn't change his behavior much, but I could tell when he was under the influence by looking into his eyes. He told me that there was a routine and a maintenance involved—he knew he couldn't do too much, or let it overtake him. Romeo said he only did heroin once in a while. For me though, after losing friends to heroin in the Bronx when I was a teenager, it was a death drug. I accepted this about him, not because I liked it, but when you love a man, you learn to live with all aspects of him.

When Romeo and I began staying at my apartment on West Lenox in the city, it bothered me to see his works sitting in the medicine cabinet. He needed smack for some reason I couldn't comprehend, and I wasn't going to judge him. Sometimes we'd be listening to music, and he'd disappear into the bathroom for a long time. I knew what he was doing. He'd come out very mellow, and sometimes want to make love. It was always very slow and satisfying for me. Sometimes he'd get fixated on a particular part of my body and pay detailed attention to it. Other times he would lay his head in my lap, and I'd stroke his face and run my fingers through his hair. It was a strangely comforting feeling, and in a weird way—God forgive me—I liked it.

September was right around the corner, and we wanted to take advantage of the last vestiges of summer. Romeo, Adam, Sebastian, and I, went for a hike up into the mountains, not far from the Yellow House. It was a beautiful hike through a forest, with the scent of pine permeating the air. The forest was like a canopy keeping the earth cool from the heat of the day. Little rays of sun peeped through the leaves as we walked along the path. The trees rustled in the breeze, and squeaked as the branches rubbed against each other. We didn't say much on the way up as we listened to the various sounds of the forest and the songs of different birds. We saw an owl peeping out of an opening high up in a large tree trunk. His eyes followed us suspiciously as we passed his tree. When we reached the top, the path opened to a field. We sat down and took out the nuts and various snacks we'd brought with us. Romeo and Sebastian were wearing overalls; Adam and I were in jeans and T-shirts.

We talked for a long time on top of the mountain. There was a great view of the surrounding county, and we were able to see far into the distance. We basked in the sun, and in the beauty of how our glorious summer had gone. We were appreciative of the harmony we all shared, and that we functioned well as a group despite our differences. At that point the communal experiment was a success, and we were thankful. The four of us put our arms around each other and smiled.

The hike back to the car was much quicker, and we descended in silence.

When we arrived back at the Yellow House in late afternoon, we could smell a wonderful dinner in the making. Everyone was settled into their groove around the house, doing whatever made them happy. I noticed that my friend Ross Grant was hanging out with Crystal, a California transplant. Crystal was strikingly beautiful—a tiny girl, with a huge head of kinky, blonde hair, pale blue eyes, and freckles. She always spoke with a very soft voice, but it commanded attention.

Suki Rosmond had already gone back home to California, and a newcomer, Marty Feinstein, was hanging out with us on the weekends. He was a friend of Ross's from the city. He had a wife and a basset hound. I wondered how they fit into our group. They were so straight, and none of us was married.

Romeo suggested we take a nap before dinner. We walked down the hallway to my bedroom holding hands. We got undressed. He lay down on the mattress and pulled me on top of him, and we made love. Then the strangest thing happened—his body odor began to repulse me and turn my stomach. I had a feeling I knew why, but I kept it to myself.

After we were finished, I lay next to him and rested my hand on his chest, lightly rubbing it back and forth. He was a beautiful creature, and I was so in love with him. He kissed me softly on the lips, and soon we fell asleep.

A knock on the door woke us up. It was Beach, letting us know that dinner was ready. It was a weekend, so there were too many of us to sit around the table; we ate buffet-style. The food was in large pots on the kitchen stove. We each filled a plate and sat on the living room floor. After dinner, I walked outside with Adam and Aiden to see the full moon. I thought about the moon landing that past year, and wondered what the earth looked like from up there.

When I walked back into the living room, Romeo took my hand and said, "Let's go to bed Chica."

I felt dreamy and warm all over, like a soft sweet butterscotch caramel, as we walked down the hallway to the bedroom.

I could hear Rocco barking wildly outside, which was unusual. It was so early in the morning that I was barely stirring. Romeo was sound asleep beside me. As I lay there, I felt as if someone was watching me. Then I heard a metallic clicking sound. I drowsily looked up, and standing at the foot of the bed was a state trooper with an assault rifle drawn and pointed at us. I nudged Romeo awake, and we both stared at him.

In a stern voice the trooper said, "Get up, get dressed, and get in the living room with everyone else."

We were in total shock. We were nude, and he made us get dressed in front of him. I was shaking like a leaf from head to toe, as the trooper stared at my nude body. Once dressed he escorted us, at gunpoint, into the living room, where we saw everyone sitting on the floor in a circle. There were a number of state troopers with their weapons pointed at us. Their faces were expressionless. We stole glances at one another, but none of us said a word. I wondered what the hell we had done to warrant the invasion.

One of the troopers—a fat, ugly one—came running in from outside shouting, "Whose damn dog is that out there? We're going to have to shoot him."

Casey pleaded, "Please, sir, don't shoot my dog. He's just trying to protect us. He's not a vicious dog."

We all chimed in pleading, "Please don't kill our dog." At that moment Rocco belonged to all of us.

The fat trooper escorted Casey outside and let him tie Rocco up. Back inside, Casey sat down and I overheard him whisper to Romeo, "There are three paddy wagons parked on the road, and a bunch of state troopers' cars."

We made up our minds that we hadn't done anything wrong, and these troopers, guns blazing, weren't going to scare or intimidate us.

We sat there for a long time while the troopers went through the house, ransacking everything room by room. We saw brown paper bags being taken outside, and wondered what was in them. After a while we began to feel brave, and there was chatter among us.

Ross Grant asked one of the troopers, "Hey man, can we at least play some music while you're trashing our house?"

The trooper talked to another one and said, "We don't have a problem with that, as long as you remain seated."

Jesse Bob Baker got up and put a record on the stereo. As soon as we heard the Rolling Stones' song "Gimme Shelter" blaring through the speakers, we began singing along. Soon we were all up on our feet, waving our arms and dancing in defiance.

After a few minutes of that, the trooper yelled, "Shut that shit down right now!"

We all sat down again in a circle but no longer silent or afraid. When the troopers were satisfied that they had gone through the house and got what they wanted, they led us outside one by one. We were carted off to jail in those three paddy wagons. I knew that the Stone's song "Gimmie Shelter," would forever remind me of that day—the day we conquered our fear, and were filled with defiance.

At the jail we had to fill out paperwork and show ID. The troopers seemed shocked that there were servicemen among us. As I was filling out my paperwork I overheard the guys being questioned. I heard Romeo say, "Matthew Romeola, US Army." Beach said, "Brent Beachwood, US Marines, sir."

I noticed Jesse Bob Baker's red fingernail polish as he was filling out his questionnaire. I couldn't imagine what the cops were thinking as they tried to piece our group together, and make some sort of sense out of us. I began to press the troopers with a barrage of questions. "Exactly what is it that we've done? What are we being charged with?"

An officer said, "You'll find out soon enough, ma'am."

We were separated—the men were put in one cell and the women in another, except for me. For some reason, I was put in a cell by myself. Was it because I had a big mouth and was asking questions? I didn't know.

It was a small building, and we were able to talk to each other through the open spaces between the walls. A matron came by my cell wheeling a cart filled with books. She said, "Here honey," handing me one to read.

I looked at the cover; it was a romance novel that exuded sex and intrigue. *As if I need any more of that in my life*, I thought. I handed the book back to her and lay down on the cot at the opposite end of the jail cell. I stared up at the yellow light bulb hanging from the ceiling, and had a hard time falling asleep.

In the morning, we were told that we each needed three hundred dollars cash for bail. I could hear through the walls that a kerfuffle was going on. The guys shouted, 'If we're held just one more day, they're going to shave our heads!" The girls yelled, "Get the guys out first!" We had no bail money, but word spread like wildfire through the county that the Yellow House commune had been raided, and that all of us had been taken to jail. Our friends at the

Green House commune, on the other side of town, tried to get some of the businesses in town to help us out. After all, these were businesses where we spent money every day. But no one would cash their checks or help us.

Someone made a phone call to Lonny Marcum, who was in the city with Sebastian Warren. They were setting up the student curriculum for the fall semester. The very next day, the two of them drove the three hours upstate with bail money for all of us. We made sure the guys were bailed out first [you know, the hair] and then the girls. We were told that we were being charged by room, according to what drugs and/or drug paraphernalia had been found in those particular rooms, each item being a separate count.

That sounded suspicious to me. We were seated on a bench, waiting to be released. I asked Romeo, "What was in our room?"

"Some hashish and a pipe."

We were told that the arrests and charges would be on our records for the rest of our lives. We all paid cash as we were released. Wow, they made a nice piece of change!

By the end of the next day, most of us were out of jail and back at the Yellow House, trying to put the place back together. I commented, "I'll bet Darius Blackwell had something to do with this." No one disagreed with me. Perhaps he was pressured by the town residents. At least Casey's dog Rocco was still alive, and we were all in one piece—and that was a blessing. As soon as the last person was released and we were all home safe and sound, we let out a big cheer and had a Get out of jail party.

The next morning, I wandered into the kitchen, leaving Romeo peacefully sleeping in bed. Someone had already made coffee and it smelled so good. I poured myself a cup, but when I took a sip it tasted funny and turned my stomach. One of my favorite things in life was a good cup of coffee, and now I couldn't even enjoy that. It confirmed what I previously suspected, but how would I tell Romeo?

Darius Blackwell came by a few days later and told us that the state troopers intended to raid us every month until we moved. He said the town residents wanted us out of their town.

None of us ever found that alleged arrest record they claimed we would have forever. But at age twenty-four, I had learned enough to know that there was no point in being where you were not wanted. It was almost September, and the search began for another house.

TEN

GOING TO CALIFORNIA- AGAIN

For a crowd is not company
Faces are but a gallery of pictures
And talk but a tinkling cymbal
Where there is no love

~ **Francis Bacon**, *English philosopher*

t was difficult to continue as we had been at the Yellow House, but we had each other, and we forged on. Romeo and I spent more time at my apartment in the city on West Lenox. We'd gotten closer, but I was still afraid to tell him I was pregnant. After missing two periods, I had to say something. On the Shoreline bus ride upstate, I planned on picking the opportune time.

When I told him, he stared at me silently. He hugged me, but his eyes couldn't hide the fear and uncertainly I saw in them. He'd told me about wanting to check out California, that his life after Vietnam was an experiment. How could I have been so careless, knowing I had been in this situation before? Once again, I thought of all the drugs we were doing, and the precariousness of our life style.

When he saw my worried expression, he flashed that smile and said, "Don't worry Chica. We'll figure it out."

As much as I loved him, and thought we belonged together, I knew neither one of us was ready for a child.

INK ON PAPER BARE TREE

It was the fall of 1970, and the leaves were already turning vibrant colors in Upstate New York. Soon the trees would be bare. There was no point in working in the garden any longer, and sadly, there would be no planting of winter vegetables. Once again, we relied on Lonny Marcum and Sebastian Warren to look for another house, they being the oldest and most stable among us. Their stats as professors looked good on applications.

On a rainy day, Max and Aiden were in the kitchen baking cookies, and a few of us were involved in a Hearts tournament on the living room floor. Two visitors from the Green House commune were playing guitar and singing songs. It was all very homey.

I noticed that Margot was laughing way too hard at Romeo's stories, and I caught her gazing longingly at him a few times. I didn't like being jealous; it made me feel weak and insecure. I knew jealousy was a useless emotion, yet I felt it. With all the things that had gone down in the past week, I chose to ignore it.

One of the girls said, "I know something that might get rid of your pregnancy naturally."

I said, "Really? I'm all ears."

"Drink a whole bottle of castor oil."

"Ugh, is that even be possible?"

"A doctor told me it causes an earthquake in the body."

"I'm skeptical but I'll try it."

"Mix it in something thick like a malted, and you won't even notice the castor oil," she said, in an informative tone.

I bought a bottle of castor oil at the pharmacy in town. The clerk behind the counter snickered, but I refused to react.

When I got back to the house, I told Romeo to make me a malted in the blender and throw in the contents of the entire bottle of castor oil.

He looked at me warily. "Chica, are you sure?"

"Just do it."

"I don't know about this Chica."

I grabbed the glass, held my nose—because the odor was unmistakable—and tossed as much of it down as I could. I gagged a little as my stomach turned, but I motioned for him to pour the rest of it in the glass. My body convulsed in disgust. We waited to see what would happen.

Pretty soon I had bad cramps, and ran to the bathroom hoping to see blood. I spent most of that evening on the toilet shitting my brains out. The next day, I was still pregnant, and Romeo's body odor still repulsed me.

On Monday, Romeo and I took the Shoreline bus into the city, and I went straight to the clinic. I told the doctor what I had done with the castor oil, and she laughed. I told her that I wanted to have an abortion. Without any judgment, she made an appointment with the hospital; abortion was now legal in New York State. The night before the procedure I tossed and turned, the whole gamut of emotions running through my brain. My belief, at that time, was that if a soul was trying to get to earth it would have to find another vessel. Perhaps that was a belief to dispel my guilt. I couldn't tell how Romeo felt, or what he was thinking. He seemed supportive and didn't try to dissuade me, so I figured that meant he would be relieved when it was all over.

On the day of the procedure Romeo went with me to the hospital, neither one of us saying much. It was a dangerous thing I was doing. There was always the chance that I might not be able to have children in the future, if and when I wanted them. We sat in the waiting room with so many other women, waiting my turn.

I asked, "What will you do while you're waiting for me?"

"Casey's on his way, and he'll hang out with me."

When my name was called we looked at each other. I got up and Romeo grabbed my hand and wouldn't let go. I turned to follow the nurse. I looked back, and he mouthed, *"I love you!"*

I lay on the table in a sterile room. A nurse put a needle in my arm and told me to count backward from one hundred. The last thing I remember was saying *ninety-seven*, and I descended into a swirling tunnel of darkness.

I awoke to the sound of a baby crying. I lay there confused for a while, trying to remember where I was. As I gained consciousness, I felt bad cramps—then I remembered I was in the hospital and why. But why was there a baby crying? *Oh God, please no! Oh God, no! Don't tell me they have me in the maternity ward.* I called out, "Nurse, where am I?"

"You're in the maternity recovery room," she said.

How cruel. It was gut-wrenching, gave me pause, and made me realize what I had done. I lay there motionless, choking back tears. What was this I was feeling? Remorse?

She said, "You'll be able to leave in an hour or so. The doctor just wants to make sure you're all right."

A little later, Romeo walked in with Casey. Romeo took my hand, kissed it, and said, "How do you feel Chica?"

I faced the wall and began sobbing and couldn't stop.

Casey looked uncomfortable. "I'll wait outside," he said, walking out of the room.

"What's wrong?" Romeo asked.

I didn't answer. I could still hear a baby crying.

"Why didn't you tell me how you felt?" he asked.

I had no answer for him. Romeo took my hand in his and comforted me as best he could. He whispered, "Everything's gonna be okay Chica. You'll see."

We left the hospital and took a cab back to my apartment. Romeo helped me into bed and then disappeared into the bathroom for a long time. I knew what he was doing, but figured it was his way of dealing with the pain of the day's event. When he came out, he lay next to me, and we held each other. He was very affectionate and petted me like one would pet a treasured kitten.

We were listening to the radio when an announcer broke into the normal programming to say, "Here's your top story for today, October 4, 1970. Janis Joplin was found dead in her apartment from a heroin overdose."

I turned toward Romeo with a troubled expression, but he just squeezed my hand and held on to me a little tighter. I said, "Wasn't it just a month ago that Jimi Hendrix died?"

Romeo shrugged.

"They were the same age—twenty-seven—and they had a thing for each other."

Romeo took my hand and kissed it. It all sounded so sad, and I was reminded of the precariousness of life. Somehow, I feared that what I had done would change us.

We stayed in the city at West Lenox for a week or so. I needed time to recover. We listened to music, read books, and Romeo did the cooking for a change. We both couldn't wait to get back upstate to the country. When it was time to go, Romeo borrowed his friend's car—we needed all the cars we could get for the Commune's big move to the new house.

We left the city and drove to the thruway. I had my hand at the back of Romeo's neck and was playing with his hair. After we had been driving for a while, Romeo said, "I'm so damn horny." He began caressing my hand.

I knew it would be weeks until we could have sex again. I began fumbling with the zipper of his pants.

"I think I know what you want."

I bent my head down below the steering wheel. He didn't object, so I kept going.

Romeo said, "Shit, the toll booths are coming up!"

I said, "Pull off the road!"

Romeo eased the car onto the shoulder of the thruway and parked. He grabbed the back of my hair and said, "God, don't stop now Chica." He finished with a sigh, composed himself, zipped up his pants, and eased the car back onto the thruway.

When we got to the toll booth, the toll collector asked, "How are you this morning sir?"

Romeo smiled. "Really good, sir, and you?"

The Yellow House was awhirl with packing and preparations for the move. A new house had been secured in the town of Hawk Dale, and we could move in on the first of the month. We'd already given notice to Darius Blackwell that we were leaving.

As soon as Margot saw Romeo she ran to him asking for help with something heavy. It was so obvious to me that she liked him. After the week I'd just had in the city, I wasn't going to make a mountain out of a molehill.

I jumped in and started helping with the packing. Later on, I took a break and sat in one of the rocking chairs on the porch. With the sound of the stream rushing across the road, I was suddenly overcome with emotion and sadness at leaving the old farmhouse.

Casey Cutler came out and sat on the rocker next to mine. He was quiet, but I felt one of his platitudes coming. "I can't know what you went through back in the city, but just know that you are loved."

I placed my hand over his and smiled. "But—"

"Look, you can't go through life looking over your shoulder," he said.

I thought, *How profound.* I turned and smiled at him.

We were all nostalgic about the summer we'd spent in the Yellow House, and realized that the experience we'd shared would never be repeated. Out of a world of struggle and strife we managed to find a bit of joy and happiness.

Looking back, I am so thankful to have been there. Life is fleeting, and we must grab each moment of joy.

It was moving day. As we loaded everything into the moving van, some of us were smiling, some were sad, but all of us were together. There were several cars in the driveway, ready to move all of us to the new house in Hawk Dale.

Aiden Wazansky nudged me. When I looked up I saw the sheriff's car on the road in front of the house. "What the hell is he doing here?" I remarked, sarcastically.

"Darius must have told him we were moving, and he wanted to see it for himself," Aiden answered.

The sheriff sat there in his car and wouldn't leave. When it was time to go, we all looked back at the old yellow farmhouse that had given us so much joy. We put our arms around each other, lingering there for a while. There were tears mixed with laughter as we all got into the cars. Romeo drove the moving van, with Casey riding shotgun; Rocco, Casey's dog, sat between them. I went in one of the cars with Adam, Aiden, and two of the cats. We began to drive out, a string of cars, with the moving van in the center of the caravan. We were escorted out of town by the sheriff himself. When we reached the county line, he pulled over, and we kept going.

Hawk Dale was a great house in a rural area. It was right on the road, but we knew that with the winter coming, that would be a blessing. The snow would get so high sometimes that the local roads became impassable, and we knew that our road would be plowed. There was some land in the back, and a forest across the road. Looking at the front porch, I pictured us sitting outside when spring arrived. Romeo and I chose a room on the second floor.

The summer was over, and some of us were living and working in the city, just coming up to Hawk Dale on weekends. Thanksgiving was coming, and we planned a big feast, inviting a lot of friends up for the long weekend. We had so much fun cooking and baking together in the kitchen. I'd made a pair of knee-high, lace-up, suede boots, and I wore them on Thanksgiving Day. Casey had been sick in bed for a week, but he wasn't missing Thanksgiving dinner. I remember him sitting at the dinner table wearing red-and-white striped long johns.

A rift developed between the gays and the straights in the commune, which intensified as the fall progressed. The straight guys were into heavy rock music, and there was some dissention brewing about the volume. It all came to a head one day when two of the gay guys, and a few of the women, were sitting on the front porch drinking tea, listening to classical music, and quietly chatting. When a group of the straight guys came home, they ignored everyone on the porch and walked into the house. They replaced the mellow classical record with Joe Cocker. There was a kerfuffle about it, but the straight guys dismissed the objections, referring to the group sitting on the porch as "a little tea party."

The politics of the day added fuel to the fire. Personally, I couldn't understand the whole thing. Just a few months back, everyone had been holding hands, and there was cross pollination. Suddenly, there was dissention and separation. What had changed? The whole situation seemed to spiral out of control that winter, and it intensified Romeo, Casey, and Beach's desire to leave. Romeo got on the let's-go-to-California bandwagon, which made me uneasy. The thought of leaving these people who had become my family and support system gave me nothing but angst.

Adam said, "Are you out of your mind? California has the Zodiac Killer! Crazy shit happens in that state."

Romeo laughed. "It will be fine, and if we're not happy, we can always come back."

After I stopped working, I gave up my apartment in the city to live in Hawk Dale full time. Romeo was supporting me with the cash he made from selling pot. The only peace around the house seemed to be during the week, when most of the group were in the city working. I treasured those days. Things were good between Romeo and me, but California was looming.

It was a cold winter morning with snow flurries. I bundled up and went out to drink my morning coffee on the front porch. I heard a hawk screech high up in the sky, and I watched it circle the house a few times. A family of deer wandered onto the lawn, foraging for greens. I sat in one of the rocking chairs, sipping the hot coffee, and felt like I was in a scene out of *National Geographic*.

At some point that winter the pipes froze, and we had no running water for days. We couldn't use the bathrooms, and were happy the forest was right across the road.

I loved Romeo in a way I hadn't loved other men; it was on a deeper level. Perhaps it was because of the epic summer we shared, the way we fit together, or just chemistry. (I have a theory that it's not so much how we love others, but the way they make us feel about ourselves.) I made up my mind that if he was going to California, I was going with him. I was tired of the politics in the commune, and the struggle with the cold weather. I began looking forward to the trip. Our plan was to meet up with Suki Rosmond and stay with her and her boyfriend Donny, in Glenn Cavern for a while. California was all the guys talked about, and despite my misgivings, that trip was already charted.

CASEY AND ROMEO HAWK DALE, 1970.

Adriana Bardolino

The guys bought the old Jeep Commando from Lonny, assuring Star and me that it would make it across the country again. The five of us—Romeo and I, Beach and Star, and Casey and his dog Rocco—were scheduled to leave a few days before Christmas. The night before we were to leave, there was a blizzard. Romeo and Casey were in New York City tying up loose ends before we left for the West Coast. Romeo called us from a public phone on the thruway, saying that there was no way they could get to the house; there was too much snow, and the local roads were closed. Star and I stayed up most of the night with Beach, who had stayed behind. Casey's dog Rocco sat on the floor staring at the door expecting Casey to walk in at any moment. Hours went by without a word from them, and there was no sign of the jeep. We heard a loud whirring sound, and a strong vibration shook the house. We ran to the windows and saw the snowplow barreling down our road clearing a path. Right behind the snowplow was the jeep!

I opened the front door as Romeo was shaking the snow off his boots. As soon as he saw me he put his arms around me and picked me up off the ground. He placed his cold hands under my plush mauve robe, and I could feel him shivering. His face was cold from the snow, but it felt so good against my warm skin. I was happy and relieved.

Over his shoulder I saw Casey walking up the porch steps with a strange woman on his arm. She was very beautiful in an exotic way, with long dark hair and jet black eyes. I was a little stunned.

Romeo said, "Oh, she's Casey's friend, and she's coming to California with us."

"Hi, I'm Valeria!" she said, in an annoyingly nasal tone.

Star and I glanced at each other with concern, and some annoyance. Beach grinned and started laughing. I wondered how the six of us, plus a dog, were going to navigate across the country in that old jeep in the heart of winter. But at that moment I was just happy they were home safe, and I had Romeo in my arms.

I was glad that Star Green, one of the women I was close with, was coming on the journey. We were both skeptical of Valeria, and thought she was just using Casey for a free ride to California. We also figured that Casey didn't want to be a fifth wheel on a trip with two couples, and was happy to have a beautiful woman on his arm. I saw nothing but trouble on the horizon with Valeria.

Casey kept bragging that he was friends with Peter Tork, one of the guys in the band the Monkees. He said, "I'm sure Peter will put us up for a while until we get settled in California." I figured he was just mouthing off to impress Valeria.

In preparation for the move to California, I had written a letter to the San Francisco Art Institute, and received an acceptance letter for the next semester. If nothing else, I knew for sure that art classes would give me purpose and joy as I navigated through uncertainty. I had neglected my art long enough. It was also a personal affirmation that I was not just going back to the West Coast on another boyfriend's joy ride, but that I was doing something positive for myself—at least that's what I told myself.

We began our journey very early the next morning. As we drove along the snowy road, I watched the Hawk Dale house fade from sight through the rear window of the jeep. I was going to miss everyone so much—all the friends I'd known for years, and my family. I was turning my life topsy-turvy again for a man. But I was hopelessly in love with Romeo; there was no denying it. Whatever the consequences, I was going to give love a chance. I had to see it through, so I was going to California—again.

The beginning of the trip was uneventful, even pleasant. Everyone was upbeat and talking away as Romeo drove. We did some shifting around at rest stops and changed drivers so no one got stiff or bored. Rocco seemed unaffected by it all; he was just happy to be with Casey. Our plan was to drive straight through, figuring on a three-or four-day journey.

At some point during the second day Romeo remarked, "There's something wrong with the gear shift; it keeps slipping. Does anyone have a belt?"

Beach handed him Casey's belt, and Romeo rigged the leather belt around the gear shift, pulled it tight once it was in gear, and secured it under his right hip. It seemed to hold, but I wondered for how long. In the back of the jeep Valeria was complaining about Rocco lying on her legs. She would yell at Casey, "Get your damn dog off my legs."

Star and I glanced at each other in affirmation of our first impression of her. Casey seemed frustrated that Valeria had absolutely no interest in him, emotionally or sexually, but just like a man, that made him even more hopeful and determined. She did take a liking to Romeo though, or was it just my imagination? Did I think everyone wanted him?

The cross-country trek seemed to be going smoothly, without incident, except for the gear shift. Luckily the belt seemed to be holding it in place.

As we approached Donner Pass in Truckee, Nevada, the weather was cold, although there was no snow. We pulled off the road and got out to stretch our legs and have a look. There was a great view from the top of the pass. We could see snow atop the mountains in the distance, and there were some white patches where we were standing. We knew that once we began going down the other side of Donner Pass, we would be close to our destination.

It was Christmas Eve and we wanted to celebrate with dinner at a restaurant. The only place we found open was a local western-style diner, which we thought was cool. It was already dark outside, and had turned very cold. As we entered the diner, the bell over the doorway jingled as each one of us passed through. There were only a few people in the diner. Being Christmas Eve, I imagined most people were snug at home with their families.

Valeria quickly took the seat next to Romeo, and I glared at her. I walked around to the other side of the table and took the seat across from him. Casey looked pissed off. I peered at Star who rolled her eyes. Romeo and Beach were looking at menus and were totally oblivious. We sat at the table waiting for the waitress.

The diner served a full-on turkey dinner with all the trimmings, but the mashed potatoes tasted as if they came out of a box; the gravy was tasteless and gooey; and the cranberry sauce came out of a can. None of us said much during dinner. I looked around and thought, *what a sad, dreary, lonely holiday this is.* I missed my friends and family. For some reason, even among these people I loved, I felt lonely. I searched around the room for a telephone but didn't see one. I asked the waitress, who pointed me in the right direction. I called Suki Rosmond and told her we were getting close and would probably reach their place by the next day. She said she couldn't wait to see us. My mood immediately lifted.

At midday the next day we rolled into California. Suki didn't think we'd find the house along the winding roads, so she told us to meet them at a popular garden center in Glenn Cavern. They were already there when we arrived. Star and I got out of the jeep and ran over to Suki. The three of us girls hugged. The three musketeers were back together again. After all the hugs and greetings, we got back into our vehicles and followed them to Donny's house. I sat in the front passenger seat next to Romeo, who was driving again.

"Thank God the belt held up through the whole trip. I had my doubts," I said.

Romeo smiled at me and put his hand on my thigh with a little love pat. "Chica, I'm feeling jazzed."

I looked out the window; we were passing hills with grazing sheep. I could smell the fragrant medicinal aroma of eucalyptus trees. It was a beautiful sunny day, and the air was fresh. For the first time, I felt positive about the trip.

We pulled into their driveway and parked right next to Suki's VW bus. There was a nice front yard and a deck off the side of the house. We were so happy to get out of the confines of the jeep after spending the past few days in it. Rocco was overjoyed too. He ran around the yard sniffing everything and peeing on every bush he passed. I walked into the house, which was very light and airy. Donny put a record on the stereo—Derek and the Dominos, and I heard "Layla." For years to come, that song would remind me of our good times, when we first arrived in California.

After lunch Romeo found a large straw chair on the deck and sat there in the sun reading a local periodical. I hung out with Suki and Star. Valeria did her own thing. There was a large bedroom in the front of the house, which Suki told me Romeo and I could have. I peeked in the room and saw a king-sized waterbed, something I'd only heard about but had never seen. I walked out to the deck to tell Romeo about the waterbed. He wanted to try it out immediately.

He grinned. "Chica, no one will hear us while the music is playing." He jumped out of the chair, took my hand, and we sheepishly walked past everyone in the living room. Romeo peeked in the bedroom and smiled at the waterbed.

"Do you really think we should do this?" I asked.

"Hell yeah!" Romeo said, locking the door behind us.

We sat on the waterbed, and it sloshed around like a raft in the middle of the ocean.

Romeo said, "Make believe we're on a magic carpet ride, and I'm a sultan."

I laughed loudly. He put his hand over my mouth, and then his lips. Soon, we were taking our clothes off, which proved quite a task on the waterbed. Just watching his facial expressions as he attempted to take off his jeans had me in stitches.

He leaned in and kissed me hard. "Chica, let's find out if sex is different on a waterbed."

We stayed at Donny's house for the better part of a week, but we needed to find a permanent place to live. We attempted to hit up Casey's friend, Peter Tork, the Monkee. We drove to his house, but we got the feeling that he was not agreeable to our staying there at all. The very next day, Suki told us she knew a couple who had a large house in northern Sonoma on Huntington Road, and they wanted to rent out half of it. She took us by to meet them and to see the house. We liked it, and there was enough room for all of us to live comfortably. It was a stucco house, with a covered front porch. The kitchen was very tiny with a Murphy table, and a foldout ironing board on the opposite side. Each couple had a room, but how that would work out for Casey and Valeria was anyone's guess. *Hell*, I thought, *Star and I could have clued Casey in on that situation, long before he dragged her on the trip out west with us.*

We had some crazy but fun times in those first weeks. We hiked in the mountains, and went to the old geysers and lay in the mineral baths. Suki turned us on to a Mexican restaurant called Juanita's. The patron, Juanita, a very rotund woman, was often seen reclining on her bed, while a waiter escorted us past her bedroom to our table. We went to the annual Renaissance Fair and saw crazy costumes and enjoyed early music. I always thought California was a unique and innovative place.

ROMEO IN THE REDWOODS.

Everything changed when I began art classes in San Francisco. There was no forethought, on my part, as to where we might be living in California. Soon, the distance between San Francisco and northern Sonoma became all too apparent.

My classes included painting, life drawing, and photography. I loved it all. The studios were open 24/7, and there wasn't much supervision by the instructors. I learned how to stretch my own canvas on a frame, and gesso the surface as a primer before painting. The school housed a very tight group of artists. There was very little structure, and the work choices were up to the artist. Art school soon became the only bright spot during that time.

Occasionally, Romeo would drive into San Francisco and stay overnight with me, and those times were really nice. We once stayed in an old Victorian in North Beach, owned by a friend of Suki's, and we had our own room. I did a photo shoot of Romeo in the nude—very artistic, not trashy. I didn't develop those photos until a year or so later, when I had my own darkroom.

But those times were rare, and I spent many a lonely night in San Francisco at anyone's house who was willing to put me up. I felt abandoned by Romeo, and had the feeling he resented my art, and the time I spent away from him. True, it was my choice to take art classes, but still, I felt no support from him. He punished me by becoming aloof and distant. We didn't seem to have that special connection any longer. Something was missing, and it was breaking me.

I didn't record much in my journal during that time, but I'd jot down lyrics from songs that mimicked my feelings. The Beatle's song "I'm looking through you" was one.

IN ART CLASS

Adriana Bardolino

When I was at the house on Huntington Road in Sonoma, there was dissention and bickering. I thought that was behind us when we left Hawk Dale in Upstate New York. Everyone was going in different directions, moving elsewhere, and it all felt unstable to me.

Valeria, who had no interest in Casey, developed a closeness with Romeo, which I resented.

Star said, "If you don't cut it out, you'll drive him to her," but I felt she was getting the attention that I should have had. Suddenly I developed a sense of morality! I hated her for going after my man. Valeria had a number of health issues, and at the time, I didn't see the connection with Romeo's sister. Perhaps it was why he related to her, and wanted to help her. I tried discussing my insecurities with Romeo, but he dismissed me as being ridiculous, and claimed I was making something out of nothing. I became the butt of jokes with the group when I talked about my feelings.

"Morality is simply the attitude we adopt towards people we personally dislike" ~ Oscar Wilde

Romeo would say, "You're making shit up! There's nothing going on between me and her. I just feel sorry for her." But that wasn't what my gut was telling me. Looking back, I think he was gaslighting me. Either way, I became jealous of the attention Valeria got, even though I knew jealousy was all about personal insecurity. Valeria was in the hospital for a bad infection at one point, and I observed Romeo washing her personal items in the sink. Instead of feeling sympathy for her, I felt anger at him.

At some point that jealousy became my obsession, and I couldn't shake it. I began a downward spiral. I was depressed and couldn't focus on my art or anything else. I didn't even want to finish the semester at the Art Institute. Everything around me seemed foreign and meaningless. I didn't feel it was my home. The summer of love was over, and I felt there was no love there for me. I wanted to go home, back to New York to the people who had become my family and support system. I was in a dark place, falling apart. I needed to make a change because I didn't like who I'd become.

I decided I would leave California and go back to the commune in New York. I'd felt apprehension even before we left for the West Coast. Something happened after I had the abortion. It was as if the ending of my pregnancy was the beginning of the death of my relationship with Romeo.

Perhaps I was projecting my feelings of guilt onto Romeo and was blaming him instead of myself.

When Romeo finally came to bed that night, I lay silent in the darkness for a while but then announced, "I've decided to go back to New York."

"Why? It's rough now, but things will get better."

"Things shouldn't be this hard. It just doesn't feel right, and I'm not happy here."

He sighed. "I don't understand what you want. Fuck, if that's what you want to do, do it."

"I've made up my mind."

"I guess there's no point in trying to talk you out of it, if you've already made up your mind." His words sounded empty and cold, like daggers in my heart.

"No, I guess not." I lay there silent again.

He said nothing to make me want to stay. He never said *I love you so much*, or *I don't want you to leave*. Lying there, I never wanted to love someone that much ever again, or feel the way I did at that moment.

Fear and Loathing in Limbo
—Hunter S. Thompson

It takes about a month to recover physically from a collapse of this magnitude, and at least a year to shake the memory. The only thing I can think of that compares to it, is that long, long moment of indescribably intense sadness that comes just before drowning at sea. Those last few seconds, when the body is still struggling, but the mind has given up.

I remember that day in the spring of 1971 as if it was yesterday. Casey drove to San Francisco International Airport, Romeo sat on the passenger side, and I sat between them. Romeo kept repeating, "I can't believe you're really leaving." I knew it was drastic, but I was in a very bad place and needed my sanity back. I always had a way of sabotaging my relationships, and this may have been no exception. The car radio was playing "Going to California" by Led Zeppelin. I thought of the promise and wonder we'd felt when we first arrived. I also flashed on my first days in Berkeley in the late sixties wandering around Haight-Ashbury in San Francisco with the joy of the peace-and-love movement. Driving to the airport, it all felt somewhat distant and lost to me. I had a knot in my stomach and a lump in my throat.

When we arrived at the airport they walked me into the terminal. Romeo had his arm around me. It crossed my mind that I was making a huge mistake, but I wasn't turning back. They came to the gate with me, which was possible in those days. The three of us were in a daze; none of us could believe I was leaving in a few minutes. I hugged and kissed Casey goodbye, and then turned to Romeo choking back tears. I loved him so much, but I couldn't continue on that way. I was afraid he'd end up hating me. Somewhere, I heard that when you lose respect for someone, you lose love. I thought that maybe, in some way, he'd lost respect for me, and didn't love me anymore. I hugged and kissed Romeo and said, "I love you so much."

"I promise I'll write to you Chica."

I walked away from them, down the ramp, onto the plane, and didn't look back.

From my journal:
It was a love so deep and fine, but I just had to go. Will we be together again, or grow further apart? I can only resist the end of love and beauty. I got lost along the way because you were lost to me.

ELEVEN

BACK IN THE FOLD

*Life shrinks or expands in proportion to one's own
courage Anais Nin ~ French writer*

I was on the Staten Island Ferry with Adam Hirschfeld once again. We glided past the Statue of Liberty in the harbor as the sun was setting right behind her torch. There was the strong, salty smell of the ocean as I watched the waves break on the side of the ferry. Seagulls had followed overhead, screeching and diving, ever since we'd left the dock in Manhattan.

ON THE STATEN ISLAND FERRY, 1971.

I felt as if I'd never left, as if it was all a bad dream. I was so low in California that I'd wanted to die, and I was scared. I was depressed over another love affair gone bad. I thought of Noah and how I'd left him in Berkeley when things got rough. I had seen terror in his eyes and knew he was falling apart. I knew now how he must have felt.

I think we all go through the many ranges of emotions in life. It seems only fair.

Back on the East Coast I felt as if I was with my people, my family, and it felt good. Adam walked to the railing and put his arm around me and I was home.

He said, "Geez, you're racking up more miles than Kissinger." I smiled. Then he said, "You know, with that troubled frown on your face, you look like that Italian actress, Anna Magnani."

That got a snicker out of me. "Mount Etna just erupted in Sicily, and I think I'm about to blow too!"

Adam laughed and stared down at the murky water being churned up by the ferry.

"See any Coney Island white fish (condoms)?"

"No," I laughed. "That's about the only fish that can survive in this polluted water."

He was taking me to the house the commune was using in the city on Hilltop Avenue in the Saint George area of Staten Island. The house wasn't far from the ferry terminal, so we went there straightaway.

We walked up the front steps and into the kitchen. I saw Ivy and a few other familiar faces, and I could breathe again. There were shelves in front of the kitchen window with an assortment of colored-glass bottles of various sizes and shapes, which looked heavenly with the afternoon sun shining through. Ivy was sitting on a chair crocheting something—she loved doing that. She introduced me to her new beau, Darby, a very tall, dark, and quiet type.

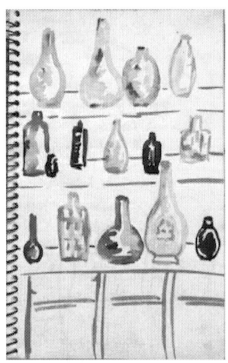

WATERCOLOR OF BOTTLES

Adam said, "We haven't been living here long. Someone just moved out, so you could have their room." Adam walked up the stairs with me and put my things down on the floor inside the empty room, save for a bed. I knew I could rummage around the secondhand stores and fill that room in no time. He took my hand and said, "It's going to be all right you know. You have to go through the valleys to get to the peaks!"

I forced a smile. "I know."

The very first night I slept in the house on Hilltop Avenue I dreamt of Romeo. My hands were outstretched trying to touch him, but I couldn't quite reach. I wanted to hold him, kiss his lips, and feel his weight on me. I awoke convinced he was next to me. It was so real that I turned my head to face him, but I was alone.

A few days later, I took the train up to the Bronx from the ferry terminal at the tip of Manhattan. I needed to see my parents and feel their unconditional love. As soon as I hugged my mother, she comforted me as if I were a small child again. She let me cry it out.

I was blithering, "You meet someone, you fall in love, and you know you're perfect for each other. It all turns out to be a rotten lie and a miserable turn of events."

My mother hesitated to answer, as if she was thinking of the loves in her own life. Then she said, "Sometimes, we love a person, but they're not good for us, and we have to cut them loose. We cut them out of our lives so we can live, breathe, feel at peace, and be happy again. Even if you think of him for the rest of your life, leave it. In time you will forget, and others will take his place."

I stopped crying and looked at her. I realized that she knew exactly what I was going through, that she had been there. In that moment I understood that the same things that bring us joy can also bring us sorrow. For the first time I saw my mother as a woman, not just as my mother. I took the train back to Lower Manhattan and walked around the city for a while before taking the ferry back to Staten Island. On the ferry ride, Elvis's song "How's The World Treating You," kept playing over and over in my head.

It was April 1971, and the first really nice spring day. Just about all of us from the Hilltop Avenue house headed upstate to Hawk Dale in the country for the weekend. The air was fresh and balmy with the perfume from spring blossoms. The last time I had been at the Hawk Dale house there was snow everywhere. In the afternoon Adam and I took a walk in the woods, just like old times. I could hear the water from the brook in the forest across the road. Adam took my hand and we started running across the meadow toward the barn. We rolled over each other in the grass, laughing and kissing like two children.

Earlier that day we walked to town to meet Aiden's bus, but Aiden never showed up. Then we went to the post office. I was expecting a letter from Romeo any day, but there was none. We both felt sad, lonely, and deserted by the people we loved. We walked home feeling empty. So there we were, rolling in the grass, trying to forget our disappointments. We made love in the meadow near the barn, filling each other up. That evening, the sunset was like a Baroque painting. I stood on the porch expecting to hear trumpets. I went to my old room—the room I'd shared with Romeo— and consulted the I Ching for its wisdom.

I Ching; **Return**

After the time of decay comes the turning point. The transformation of the old becomes easy. Societies of people sharing the same views are formed."

In the morning, I drank my coffee on the porch. I noticed deer grazing next to the barn; they seemed unfazed by me. When the sun came up over the barn, they flicked and fluffed their tails and scampered off. I glanced down the road and saw Adam picking dandelions. The spring baby dandelions are always the most tender. I walked onto the road. The sky was turning gray, as if it was getting ready to rain, and the air became heavy. I was finally at peace.

From my journal:
I walked outside and it felt strange. The wind blowing through the trees, a soothing, warm, moist, wind. The sky is thick with clouds and it smells like rain. Everything is still except for the buzzing of bees and the cicadas in the trees. I stood very still letting the breeze blow my skirt. I can see you down the road. I smile at you and you wave. Spring is definitely here.

Crystal mentioned that Star Green had called and was coming for a visit at the end of the month. That was interesting, since I'd just left her and Beach in California. I checked the post office every day for a letter from Romeo. Then one evening, he called.

His rap was filled with uplifting stories about what he was up to, as if I was missing it all. His sentences were filled with phrases like, "It was far out, I was really jazzed, and it was crazy good." He made it all sound as if I should be there sharing it with him. But all I felt was the distance between us, and none of the closeness we once had. I wondered if our love affair was just part of our summer of love in the Yellow House. I attempted to write Romeo a letter many times but just tore them up. I thought of the song "Nights in White Satin" by the Moody Blues, and the words expressed what I felt inside. The truth was that despite everything that went down, I was still in love with him.

I looked forward to Star's visit hoping she'd clue me in as to where Romeo's head was at back in California. It was good to see her again, but she had nothing to share with me about Romeo. Whatever I asked about him resulted in a vague, tight-lipped response. Star voiced some platitudes regarding women's duties, which I didn't quite get. It crossed my mind that perhaps she knew something about Romeo and didn't want to hurt me. After she left, I knew nothing more than when she arrived.

> From my journal:
> Your visit was strange, and your rap was filled with the same old illusions and pipedreams about love and women's duties. You told me I should be satisfied with the crumbs he might throw my way. I love you still but hate your naiveté. Your man needs you Lady Jane. Learn to love yourself as much as you love him, maybe even more. Just speaking from one woman to another.

After our weekend upstate at the house in Hawk Dale, back in the in the city on Staten Island the search for a job began. I was sitting at the kitchen table in the house on the hill, combing the classifieds, with the wall phone at the ready. Someone was playing Tracy Nelson's "Down So Low" on the stereo in the living room.

One particular classified ad caught my attention. It was with a research company that was partnering with a major TV station, looking for participants in the National Violence Study. I dialed the number and made an appointment for an interview.

I took the ferry into Manhattan and walked to the address on the ad. An older woman interviewed me. They were looking for people with good recall to watch family-hour TV programming, and discuss issues concerning violence. I met the requirements for memory retention, and I, along with three men, got the job.

Each day during the two-hour break between TV programming, I wandered around the city. There is always a feeling that anything could happen at any moment, and usually did. At times the City evoked a turbulence, an excitement, and at other times, it sparked revulsion or confusion. But there certainly was never a dull moment. Casey Cutler always said that New York City was "The church of what's happening now!" Funny thing is, after working on the National Violence Study project for a year and a half, the three men and I agreed that we had become desensitized to the violence.

On a weekend upstate at the house in Hawk Dale, there was a thunderstorm, and the landscape surrounding the house resembled the

English countryside. We hung out indoors playing various card games like Hearts, and the dice game Yahtzee. Adam had gotten me into meditation again, and it was helping me find inner peace.

The sun finally peaked through the clouds creating a huge rainbow that settled right over the house. Someone yelled, "Hurry! Come outside and see it." We all rushed out through the front door. It was glorious until the rain began coming down hard again. We all stood out there letting the rain pour over us.

Ross whispered, "There's a present for you inside."

I went inside, fetched a towel from the bathroom and dried myself off. Ross, Crystal, and a few others were sitting on the couch in the living room. On the coffee table was a round blue mirror with neat little rows of white powder and a short straw. I knew what it was; I had tried cocaine before. I snorted up a whole row of the powder and passed the mirror to the person sitting next to me. "Sweet cousin cocaine." It's a strange drug. It makes you feel invincible, as if you could do anything. Of course, it has a lot to do with who you are with, and I was with everyone I loved.

That evening, I was upstairs taking a bath by candlelight. I heard a knock at the door. Margot stuck her head in, "Mind if I join you?"

I smiled. "Come on in."

She took her clothes off and got in the tub with me. Since I returned from the West Coast we'd become close friends. We sat in the tub talking about anything that popped into our heads.

She asked, "Do you miss Romeo?"

"So much." I knew she had a thing for him, but I didn't go there.

She said, "Don't worry; you'll see him again. Love doesn't really ever go away. It just changes sometimes."

I knew I'd always love him, in a way. I remembered my mother's words, and they gave me strength.

Since I'd returned from California, that weekend was the first time I missed drawing and painting, and I felt a creative surge. It was something I hadn't felt since I left the art school in California. The lyrics from a Bob Dylan song popped into my head. "She's got everything she needs, she's an artist, she don't look back."

From my journal:
I feel a rebirth in the arts, an energy of expression which fulfills me greatly. I feel productive. Forms take

shape flowing out of me through the paint brush onto the canvas, charcoal onto paper. Lightly colored lines and bold statements. I was asleep for a while, but now awakened to the life force within me. It's all so beautiful and has lifted my spirit. I believe meditation had a hand in it.

Our friends from the Green House commune came by to hang out with us for a day of music and good times. There were guitars, flutes, kazoos, harmonicas, tambourines, and voices in harmony. Aiden Wazansky's friend played and sang the blues so fine, and I enjoyed singing with her. We had an incredible thing going on the front porch. People driving on the road past our house stopped, got out of their cars, and hung out to listen. It was a great day, which flowed into a great night.

I am not sure how Erik Eschweiler came to the house in Hawk Dale, maybe with the Green House people. He had been dating one of the women from that commune at one time. I knew what he wanted. He'd probably heard through the grapevine that I'd left Romeo in California. There was some awkward conversation between us. When I finally went up to my bedroom, I found Erik sleeping in my bed. I stared down at him, turned around, and went back downstairs. I didn't want to get involved with him again.

There were still a few stragglers left in the living room quietly talking. Aiden's friend was playing a bluesy version of a Janis Joplin song on her guitar. I began singing with her, and it put me in a soulful state of mind. After the song was finished we hugged each other.

I said, "I'm so happy you came by today."

"Me too! We should do this more often." She said.

Then she packed her guitar away in the case and left.

Crystal and I were the only ones left in the living room. She stared at me as I settled on the couch. Ross had already gone up to bed. She looked at me and spoke in that soft, reflective voice of hers.

"Whenever I see you get into music, I see Romeo. It was almost as if he was here."

"I felt it too, as if he was here with us," I said. But inside, I felt like a piece of me was missing.

She stood up, leaned over, and stared into my face as if she was about to say something profound. She must have seen tears in my eyes, because she placed her hand softly on my shoulder, turned away, and silently walked upstairs.

Because Erik was sleeping in my room I curled up on the couch and fell asleep. Sometime during the night I awoke with a start from the strangest dream. I recorded the dream in my journal:

> I dreamt that I received a letter from Romeo, and all the letter said was I love you, I love you, I love you, over and over again, so many times that it filled half the page. Funny thing was, that the writing was all crossed out with a big X. At the bottom of the page was written, Are you coming back to our little nest or not, Love Romeo. That had been crossed out as well.

I lay there in the dark wondering what that dream meant. A beam of moonlight shone through the window and onto my face. I lay there for a while thinking about that crazy dream. Then I closed my eyes and fell back to sleep. Erik probably left with the Green House people because when I woke up in the morning he was gone.

The summer was on the horizon, and we wanted to do something totally different. There was a brief discussion of a trip to Jamaica. Everyone was abuzz with ideas of where we should go.

Sebastian Warren said, "I have a brilliant idea—something totally outside of our comfort zone! Colombia, South America."

Lonny added, "Those attending classes at the university can get credits for the trip."

I was downright scared. It might be 1971 in America, but I'd heard that Colombia was a third-world country. On the other hand, we would all be traveling together, and it could be the experience of a lifetime. There was a lot of back-and-forth on the subject, but in the end we all agreed we were on our way to spend three months in Colombia. I went to my room and immediately got out the I Ching. I tossed the three Chinese coins for insight and guidance. I cleared my mind of everything but our impending trip. The resulting trigram spoke of "Feasting in the temple of the ancient ancestors." I thought, *Now what the hell could that mean?*

After a bon voyage dinner at my parents' apartment in the Bronx, we rented two cars and headed to the thruway going south from New York to Miami on I-95. We figured it would take us a few days to get to Florida. We had plane tickets to fly from Miami to the coastal town of Barranquilla, Colombia, South America.

It was my first trip along the Atlantic Seaboard states. Once we began driving through the South, we saw lots of tobacco, cotton, and tall fields of corn. The Carolinas were very hot and muggy. The air was heavy, and my skin felt like it was coated with moisture. On the car radio we were able to pick up local radio stations that touted Jesus, who died for our filthy sins, and they played lots of Elvis and the blues. Going through Georgia we stopped at a fruit stand. We bought a bag of Georgia peaches and a watermelon. I only hoped that Jesus hadn't died in vain.

We arrived in Miami very early in the morning; the beaches were deserted. We stopped at a street stand for a "Bullet"—a tiny shot of very strong Cuban espresso. There were no gloomy faces; it was a city of smiling faces. All we could see for miles was sandy beach, blue ocean, and palm trees. We got into our bathing suits and hit the beach. We had an overnight flight to Colombia, but for the rest of the day, we enjoyed the sun and the sand. As we frolicked in the ocean, we were totally oblivious to the wild adventure on which we were about to embark.

We arrived at the airport for our 3:00 a.m. flight. After checking in we walked to the gate. I looked through the glass wall and commented, "I think that's our plane." It was nothing like an American air carrier; it seemed rickety and unsafe. It was a double-prop-engine plane.

Ross Grant joked, "We're boarding Aero Crash," and everyone laughed except me. All twelve of us flowed through the gate onto the aircraft and took our seats—although the seats were basically metal chairs. I buckled up for what I figured would be a few hours of a rough ride. I had flown quite a few times, but this gave me pause. A group of Colombian patriots were sitting in the rear of the plane. They kept ordering more drinks as the flight progressed. When they were thoroughly inebriated, they began singing songs. With the little bit of Spanish I knew, I thought they sounded like patriotic songs. For some reason, the relaxed and jovial atmosphere put me at ease. I closed my eyes and fell into a deep sleep.

I was awakened by the voice of a stewardess, announcing something in Spanish. I looked out the window. We were descending through the clouds. I could see the sun rising over the Andes Mountains. A feeling of excitement overwhelmed me, and I wondered what experiences we were going to have in this foreign country. It was a bumpy landing, but as the plane came to a stop we all breathed a sigh of relief. The patriotic group of Colombians began clapping. They apparently were happy to be home—or just happy we landed. We grabbed our sacks and packs and strolled off the plane into a strange land.

TWELVE

THE RIVER

The distant bells they call out to me
They speak of peace and fulfillment from a place filled
with incense, where dwells calmness and serenity
For a moment they awaken a sleeping part of me,
outgrown and forgotten
The young years of innocence and simplicity
I try to grasp, but cannot reach, the bells once so near,
now far away

anding in Barranquilla, Colombia was a culture shock we were not prepared for. It's an industrial seaport town with not many modern conveniences. Even though it was June of 1971, I felt as if I had passed through a time machine back 150 years in the past. It was like leaving the civilization we'd known, and entering a wild and savage one. There were no paved roads, only dirt streets and wooden buildings. I saw no cars, only donkeys and horses for transport. Women walked very easily with large baskets balanced atop their heads. The air was oppressively hot and muggy, and it was only nine o'clock in the morning.

PHOTOGRAPH OF OUTSIDE MARKET

We looked for the bus depot where we were to pick up a bus to Santa Marta, a resort town farther along the coast. Luckily we had Aiden Wazansky with us, who spoke Spanish, so we easily found our way around. We were such a large group of freaky American hippies that our presence seemed to disrupt the whole town. We were hard to miss, since most of the men towered over the locals. Crystal looked like she'd just stepped off a Hollywood movie set, with her mass of kinky blonde hair, her tiny but curvy figure, and pale blue eyes. Ross paraded her around like she was Jean Harlow. The locals followed us wherever we went with innocent curiosity. They'd often follow our back-and-forth conversations from one face to another, as if they were watching a ping-pong match.

On our way to the bus depot, the wonderful aroma of strong coffee drew us into a storefront; we hadn't had coffee since Miami. When we reached the depot, the transport was an old American school bus. As we boarded, there was Spanish music blaring from a radio where the bus driver sat, and I saw red pom-poms draped across the top of the windshield. There were statues of the Madonna, Jesus, and other religious icons on the dashboard, and a big crucifix hung in the center. The interior of the bus was plastered with posters of Che Guevara and Topo Gigio, the Italian mouse puppet, who was some sort of a cult hero in Colombia. I knew we were in for a wild ride.

It was a long, dusty ride over dirt roads, with obstacles such as large rocks and tree roots that the bus driver had to navigate past. We were jiggled around like dirty laundry in a washing machine, but the scenery outside the windows was a feast for the eyes. We passed a desert-like landscape with adobe houses here and there, and grass huts with corrugated tin roofs in colors of turquoise, red, and pink. Every house had banana plants in the yard, and a stone fireplace for cooking. We passed swampland with houses on stilts, and grazing white Brahman cows with long floppy ears and humps on their backs. The livestock looked half-starved, and many of the people standing outside weren't wearing shoes.

As hippies we had very little, but I felt rich in comparison. The bus route went along roads that took us high up into the mountains and down through the depths of the jungle. The road was so narrow that I found myself holding my breath and avoided looking down. There were no guardrails. When a transport approached from the opposite direction, we cringed as the bus moved over to let it pass. Occasionally, we got a glimpse of the ocean.

Whenever we passed through a town, the residents would swarm the bus selling their wares—anything from ponchos and wrist watches, to fruits and cooked food piled high on trays. On one of the stops I had to use the bathroom, so the bus driver told me he'd wait. I walked into the crowd of locals and asked a woman where *el baño* was. She took me by the hand and led me behind a house where there were a few holes in a wooden plank on the ground. She lifted her skirt and peed in one hole, so I just squatted over the hole next to her and did the same thing.

When the bus boarded a ferry, these entrepreneurs jumped off just as the boat was leaving the dock. I learned to haggle the prices pretty quickly, while keeping in mind that what I was haggling over cost eight pesos, roughly forty cents in American money. The year of Spanish I'd taken in high school was coming back to me.

We finally arrived in the resort town of Santa Marta, which was right on the ocean snuggled between mountains. Aiden asked one of the locals in Spanish if there were other people like us in town. The man told us that there were hippies living in the mountains, very poor, just living off the land. But we were tired and figured we'd investigate the next day. We found a small boutique hotel for the night. The hotel reminded me of the movie *Casablanca*, with an enclosed garden and café, and I remember a monkey in the courtyard. As we sat drinking a coffee in the café, I expected Peter Lorre or Humphrey Bogart to walk in at any moment.

After we got settled, we cruised around the area, looking for a place to eat. We were walking past a house with a large picnic table in the front yard, when the husband and wife invited us in for supper. I sat at the table with chickens and roosters running on the ground around my feet. Dinner was fried potatoes, rice, fresh avocados, and meat—I didn't ask what kind of meat. We paid them for the meal, and they invited us back for breakfast. After supper, Lonny Marcum and Sebastian Warren disappeared for a couple of hours. When they returned, they had managed to pick up a large coffee can full of marijuana really cheap. It was enough to last the whole summer—at least that's what we thought at the time.

In the morning, we returned to the same house for breakfast. They served fried eggs, which I assumed were fresh from the chickens running underfoot, and a very plain bread called *pan*, which means bread in Spanish. People in Colombia drank hot chocolate instead of coffee with breakfast. They told us to check out the village of Taganga in the surrounding mountains if we wanted to connect with other hippies. Tomorrow was another day, so we headed for the beach to go swimming. In town that evening, we searched for a place to watch the sunset. We found a café on the ocean and drank local beer, a popular brand called Aguila. We were beginning to get adjusted. I was falling in love with the place, and strangely feeling at home.

SUNSET IN SANTA MARTA

The next day after breakfast we looked for the transport to Taganga. When we got there the transport was a large truck with racks in the back—something one would use on a hayride, only there was no hay. We climbed aboard and stood up in the back. We held on for dear life as the truck wound its way up the mountain road along the cliffs. As we turned a corner of the mountain, we saw a town below with a beautiful beach. There were palm trees, dark-blue water, and pebbles instead of sand. Dark-skinned men were in ab grassy field under a tree sanding the bottom of a large boat. It was a very primitive village, with pigs and donkeys running everywhere.

We made friends with some of the local guys—hippie wannabes—and hung out with them for the day. Sebastian shared some pot with them, which they really liked. They warned us not to go too far out in the ocean because there were sea urchins, which Aiden translated from Spanish as "Black porcupines of the sea."

"You step on one of those, and you'll be sorry," said one of the boys. What a place it was; I didn't want to leave. We never did run into the hippies who were supposedly living in the mountains. We took our clothes off and waded nude in the ocean, but stuck close to the shore to avoid the urchins. Some of the town's elders rushed down to the beach yelling at us in Spanish.

Our friends translated: "You have to leave. Go now. You will bring us bad luck."

The young guys explained that the fishermen were religious and very superstitious. They believed that if we swam nude in the ocean, the fish would not come to their village. So basically, we were chased out of town. It's good to remember to be respectful of other people's cultures and customs, but we were not.

That night I felt very alone. I lay awake feeling empty. Everything in my past seemed so distant, almost as if it had been a dream. Was I really in love with someone? Did someone really love me? Will it ever happen again?

After a few days in Santa Marta, we were on our way to Cartagena. By now, we'd even learned to bargain for the price of the bus. En route to Cartagena the countryside was not dry at all. We passed lush, green mountainsides, lakes, and streams. This was more like what I had imagined Colombia to be. We passed *fincas* (farms) with cattle and horses. It rained hard, and when the sun reappeared the air smelled fresh and sweet.

Cartagena was a walled city, an old medieval fortress. We found a really nice hotel and settled in. I grabbed my Pentax camera and decided to have a look around by myself and take some photographs. I walked along the narrow, winding streets and saw beautiful pastel buildings. There were endless balconies with wrought-iron railings, hidden courtyards, and huge carved doors, not unlike one would see at the entrance to a castle. I heard church bells ringing in the distance and walked in their direction. As I approached the church, I could hear guitars and a choir singing, and realized there was a Spanish mass in progress.

I walked up the steps and stood inside the doorway, listening quietly. With the aroma of Frankincense, a feeling of calmness, peace, and serenity came over me. It was all so beautiful. For a moment I was sad that there was no one to share it with. I walked outside and down the church steps. My sadness turned to joy and excitement for the unknown yet to come. In that moment, I knew that God would not abandon me.

From Cartagena, we traveled inland to Bogota, the capital city of Colombia. I was not expecting such a bustling metropolis. Bogota is set nine thousand feet high in the Andes Mountains. Walking through the streets, we saw lots of hippie freaks, and were hoping to make friends with other like-minded young people. We met up with Mitchell Dosky, Lonny's boyfriend, who had been living in Colombia for months. He really knew his way around and had connections. It crossed my mind that Mitchell might have been a big motivation for Lonny wanting to explore Colombia.

We found an adequate hotel in the heart of the city. Walking along the corridors one evening, I wandered into the basement. I saw women scrubbing linens by hand in big stone vats, and sheets hanging on lines to dry. I guessed there were no washing machines. The hotel was not far from the American embassy, which we frequented on a regular basis. There was something comforting about being there while in a foreign country. Perhaps it gave us a feeling of security. The toilets in our hotel had no toilet seats, which was another reason we liked to visit the American embassy.

While wandering through the streets near the hotel, we befriended a skinny street dog. He was riddled with mange and had sad eyes. We gave him scraps from our meals. Locals laughed when we petted him. It was sad. We affectionately called him The Mange:

From my journal:
It must be hard going through your brief life with mange
Kicked from place to place for just wanting some food

Craving a little love and sympathy
I found you cute and loveable
But there is no love or sympathy for a small helpless dog
Rotting away on the streets of paradise

The weather was cold and cloudy in the city, and it rained just about every day—not surprising, as Bogota is virtually in the clouds. We found a great place for breakfast, Santiago's. Over breakfast the next day, Mitchell Dosky told us about a camp on a river a little way outside of Bogota. It was run by a couple who set up huts alongside the river. Getting to the camp required a seven-kilometer hike (about ten miles) through the jungle, but he assured us it was a paradise and well worth the effort. He also said we would need hammocks because of the torrential rains, and we'd want to sleep up off the ground.

It was my twenty-fifth birthday, but I had forgotten about it, with all the excitement of the trip. Back in the hotel room I was surprised with a birthday cake, candles and all. I was thankful that my special day was remembered. We went to a popular restaurant, where the specialty was Argentinian steak, cooked right outside the restaurant on big grills. We noticed a group of young children watching us from the entrance. We asked the waiter what they wanted. He told us that they lived on the streets, and would take whatever food we had left when we were done. When we finished our meal, we motioned for the children to come in. They grabbed the scraps that were left on our plates.

Walking back to the hotel we noticed families hunkered down to sleep on the sidewalks. They just covered themselves with newspapers to keep warm. I'd never seen such poverty. I definitely felt like a rich American that day.

We took a side trip to a town called La Dorada. A group of cows were sleeping in the town center under the shade of a large tree. The streets were all dirt, and once again we found ourselves in an early western-style town. We aimlessly walked around for a bit, looking for shade as the sun blazed down. Our throats were dry from the heat and the dirt kicked up by horses. We came across a saloon and walked up the wooden steps and through the swinging doors. We ordered *cervesas* (beers) all around. We had a fun afternoon, but the time ran away from us, and we missed the bus—the only one leaving town that day. The local *policia* insisted that we would not be safe in the town after dark. They escorted us to the local jail where we spent the night behind bars to keep us out of danger—we were sure *not* miss the bus back to Bogota the next day.

Only a few months back I'd been depressed, heartbroken, and had wanted to die. In Colombia, South America I was full of life, adventure and happiness. Something was happening to me.

I woke up a little groggy the next morning. I looked around and everyone was still sleeping, except for Adam, who was reading. I looked out the window to see what the weather was like, and saw armored tanks and soldiers in the street outside the hotel.

I yelled, "Wake up! Something's happening out in the street."

Everyone got up and ran to the windows. There was a communal cry of, "Oh, shit!"

Sebastian said, "I don't think we should go anywhere today."

"No kidding," I said. "I don't think we should even try to get to the American embassy."

By that evening the tanks were gone, and we felt it was safe to venture out into the streets. Mitchell heard that Carlos Santana was giving a concert at a large stadium at the edge of the city, and we all decided to go. There were so many people flowing through the gates that at one point I was literally carried by the crowd. For a while, my feet didn't even touch the ground, and I was scared. I kept telling myself, *For God's sake, don't fall down because you'll be trampled to death.* There were soldiers everywhere with automatic weapons to keep the crowds under control. I wondered if the tanks we'd seen in the streets that morning had something to do with the concert. Perhaps in the past there had been unrest or riots.

It was a great concert and definitely an experience I would not forget. When we got back to our hotel we ran into some American hippies in the lobby. They told us that Jim Morrison, the lead vocalist of the Doors, had been found dead in his bathtub in Paris.

It was July 4, American Independence Day, and a small group of us headed out on our adventure to spend a week at the camp by the river. We were such a large group, and attracted so much attention, that we often split up to travel. A bus dropped us off at mile marker 30, and we began our trek through the jungle along a well-traveled path. Mitchell had been there before and knew the way. It was oppressively hot and sticky and was a very long hike. The jungle was alive with wildlife and strange sounds. The first thing I noticed was that as we got deeper into the jungle, the trees began to look prehistoric—much larger, with hairy moss all over them. There were parrots screeching and flying from tree to tree over our heads. Along the path we came across a strange man who was sitting in a clump of bushes. He was half naked with his legs crossed meditating. As we passed him, he never even looked up. I loved the wildness of Colombia, and was feeling exhilarated.

Eventually we reached the camp, which was a group of bamboo huts in the middle of a banana grove. It was very well set up, with a large fire pit, a makeshift stove, and a generator. We picked our huts and slung our hammocks. The camp was filled with American, European, and Colombian hippies. The couple who ran the camp were Don Manuel and Doña Gabriella. The heat was truly oppressive during the day, which is probably why everyone took a siesta; it was difficult to function. Your brain turns to mush, and you have to lie down.

That first evening, someone at the camp had a guitar. I picked it up and played as we sat around the fire. Don Manuel and Doña Gabriella seemed very pleased. Dinner consisted of rice, beans, potatoes, and fried plantains—no meat. I didn't mind, not after seeing the bloody animal carcasses hanging in the outside markets crawling with flies. I avoided meat for the rest of our trip. During the night it rained torrentially, and I was happy to be suspended in a hammock. I looked down at the ground, and by the light of the candles, I watched the water flow through the hut right under me.

The next day we walked along the river and explored the surrounding area of the jungle. We walked through a field with Brahman cows and saw mushrooms growing in the cow pies. We picked some and put them in a sac to take back to the camp. Adam suggested that the river was the perfect place to take magic mushrooms. Later that evening, we all ate them together so we'd be in the same frame of mind. We took off our clothes and swam nude in the river as the sun was setting.

As the effect of the mushrooms came on, I was floating on the surface of the river, looking up at the gentle banana leaves dancing in the evening breeze. The jungle plants and flowers along the riverbank had a golden glow. This was truly a magical place, and I felt so peaceful and happy.

Adam, who was floating next to me, remarked "Isn't it glorious?"

"Adam, I'm in heaven."

He splashed my face, sighed and said, "Me too."

The sun was baking me bronze, so much so that my hair was light brown, and my eyes were golden. The river was truly filled with heavenly bliss. I didn't want to leave the river, I never wanted to leave Colombia.

That night after we retired to our huts and were snug in our hammocks, we heard horses and gunshots. A group of crazy, drunk campesinos (rural natives) rode into the camp looking for fun. We women were afraid of getting harmed or raped—there was no law in the jungle. Men rode around on horses like cowboys, with machetes and guns, and that was the law.

The campesinos were playing Mexican music, which was very popular in Colombia. They drank more and more beer and tequila, tossing the bottles all over the place. Don Manuel and Doña Gabriella hung out with them until four in the morning. They kept the campesinos occupied, making sure we were all safe, and that nothing in the camp got destroyed. I had the impression that it wasn't the first time this had happened. Finally, we heard the clopping of horses' hooves, a few gunshots in the air, and the campesinos rode out of the camp the same way they rode in.

We were up as the roosters crowed, a little off-key on our last morning. We were going back to Bogota after a glorious week by the river. Javier, a young teenager, had befriended us. He went out of his way to help and protect us. He noticed that I wrote in my journal each day. He took the journal out of my hand and wrote a passage in it. Roughly translated into English by Aiden, part of it said that loving is never having to apologize. He asked why the soul was born of the flesh, when the flesh was the death of the soul. I thought that was very profound for such a young man. It made me sad that he thought that way about the soul and the human body. Perhaps it was a religious influence.

He'd accompany us out of the jungle, and I was thankful for that. After breakfast, we were off at daybreak. Although Mitchell Dosky knew the way, he let Javier lead us through the fields. It was quite a walk to meet the milk truck, with whom we were hitching a ride back to mile marker 30. It was a bumpy ride out to the main road standing in the back of the milk truck. By now, we seemed to be used to this mode of transportation. My time at the river proved to be a spiritual experience.

After our camping trip at the river, I couldn't wait to have *huevos pericos* (scrambled eggs) and a hot chocolate at Santiago's. When we arrived at the restaurant it was very crowded so we had to share a table with strangers. Some might say that was an ordinary occurrence, but I felt fate had a hand in it.

At the table was a young man who told us he was an art student from Brazil, visiting Colombia for the summer break. He was an Inca, originally from Peru, and spoke three languages—Spanish, Portuguese, and Quechua {the ancient language of the Incas}. He was rather good-looking, with dark hair and cocoa skin, but his eyes were steel grey. There were freckles across his nose and cheeks. He introduced himself as Lucas Antonio Castanera, but said to call him Luka. I felt an immediate connection to this Inca, and we began talking. He seemed to know a lot of people, so I wondered if he was telling the truth about being an art student from Brazil, but I was just there for the summer and didn't care. He spoke a little English, and I spoke a little Spanish, and it seemed to work just fine.

I left our group at Santiago's after breakfast and toured Bogota with Luka, who knew where everything was and everyone on the street. He looked out for me, and protected me from some of the pickpockets and opportunists that hung out on the streets of the city. We walked for what seemed like miles and stopped in a shabby storefront, where he said campesinos ate on a regular basis, and the food was authentic. We danced through the aisles of a local bodega looking for snacks. Many of the stores had piped in music. We were having such a fun day; half the fun was trying to communicate with each other.

He took me to a friend's house in a nice neighborhood, and she invited us in for coffee. She was older than me and had two children. One was a teenager, to whom Luka seemed to be a mentor. Perhaps she was divorced. I had the impression she liked Luka more than a friend. When we left her apartment Luka took my hand in his and we strolled away from her down the street. When I turned to wave goodbye she was still watching him, and I wondered what their real relationship was.

Walking along the city streets we passed a café where local men were playing their guitars and singing. Luka reached for my hand and held me tightly to his body. "I teach you the Cumbia, mos' popula' dence in Colombia," he said, with a wildly attractive expression. I felt a thrill, and I wasn't objecting.

Afterward, we sat down and had a cold local beer called Costenia. He explained to me, in his broken English, that he was a Bolivian revolutionary. I had been more radical myself at one time. He seemed very old-fashioned for a young guy, but I liked it. We walked to the American embassy, where I was hoping to pick up a package with rolls of film. I'd asked my mother to send it, as film was very expensive in Colombia.

Luka walked me back to the hotel, and we made plans to meet for breakfast at Santiago's the next morning. Walking up to the room I thought of how different he was than other men I'd known, and how different I was with him.

When I got back to the hotel room, Lonny was combing the classifieds of a local newspaper for a house we could rent for the whole month of August.

Mitchell said, "I ran into some Colombian guys today, and they invited us to a party."

I said, "We should definitely go."

That evening we took a taxi, and as we approached the address Mitchell had written on a piece of paper, we noticed very expensive cars parked on the street. The party was wilder than we were expecting, and there was cocaine on every table. Cocaine was very cheap in Colombia, and we did a lot of it. These were rich Colombian kids, and it was like a frat party, which was not our scene. We stayed for a short while, did some coke, and left.

The next morning Lonny put down the newspaper he was reading, "I found us a four-bedroom *finca* we could rent for the whole month of August. Should we take it?"

We all squealed with delight.

Lonny read out loud, "It's in a town four hours outside of Bogota, with five surrounding acres. A husband and wife live on the property as caretakers."

I enjoyed the city, but it would be nice to cook our own meals; besides, Colombia is a big country, and we wanted to see more of it. The finca could serve as our home base.

There was still more than a week before the end of July, and we were determined not to let the time go to waste. Over breakfast at Santiago's the next morning, Luka told us about a festival going on in a town not far from Bogota. Only a few in our group were interested in another trip so soon, but I wanted to go.

Six of us—Ivy and Darby, Ross and Crystal, Luka and me—left for a short adventure. When we arrived in the town, the festivities were already happening. I could have sworn I heard gunshots, but hoped they were firecrackers. We roamed around the town all day long. Later on, Luka and I broke ranks with the group. I assured everyone they needn't worry about me, that I'd be safe with him.

Luka and I wandered through the festival and stopped to eat at a stand that had local food and beer. After dark, the culmination of the evening was a fireworks display and local music. Everyone was dancing the Cumbia. Luka began swaying his hips to the music and held his hand out to me. I took his hand and we glided around the floor with a rhythm that was very sensual. He held me tightly, and our bodies swayed together to the music. I looked in those steel-grey eyes and got lost in a dreamland. I was living in a movie, and that's how the night progressed.

We left the festival and walked through the streets of the town, Luka with his arm around me. I knew what I wanted, and I knew he wanted it too. We saw a saloon, went through the swinging doors, and stood at the bar. Luka ordered us two whiskeys. Our eyes connected for an extended time; then we both smiled. I turned my gaze away as I felt a shiver of desire run through me. We noticed that there were rooms above the saloon, so we walked to the desk. Luka got us a room for the night. As he was talking to the clerk in Spanish, I imagined that I was one of those saloon girls in the 1800s getting ready to take her cowboy upstairs to her room. We walked up a beautiful, wide, well-polished, wooden staircase. The rooms upstairs were divided with very flimsy walls, as if they had been offices at one time.

It was a tiny room with a full-sized bed, a sink, and a dresser. The bathroom was down the hall. Luka kissed me with those full lips, and I kissed him back. We got undressed and lay on the bed. We began to make love, and I felt as if I was making love to myself—or maybe learning to love myself. There were no expectations about a relationship, just the moment. The timeless act felt pure and sacred.

In the past it had taken me a while to relax enough with the man I was involved with to actually enjoy the sex and be satisfied. But with Luka, it was the natural end to an ancient act. When we were finished, Luka kissed me and rolled off. We lay there next to each other for a while. After a prolonged silence I said, "Teach me something in your native Quechua."

He said, "*Api ami.*"

"What does it mean?"

He said, "It means, I love you!" He began kissing me all over, moving his head lower on my body. I tugged at his hair, and he smiled up at me. I saw the freckles across his nose and cheeks. I thought to myself, *God, he's so damn beautiful.*

He pulled himself up, put his arms on either side of the pillow, got on top of me, and we made love again. He looked at my face while we were doing it. It was so very hot, yet sweet. Afterward, I fell into a dreamy sleep.

The next day we reconnected with the others at the place we'd agreed to meet. We shared our experiences-though not all of our experiences-on our bus ride back to Bogota. Something was definitely happening to me in Colombia-something wonderful!

I wrote in my journal:

> It was nice to make love to an ancient Inca. Made me want to go to Peru and do it again in a temple above Cusco. The heat of the sun shining on an altar to the gods. I want to tell you how you make me feel, but we don't speak the same language. Words aren't necessary for what we did.

THIRTEEN

THE HOUSE OF EL CAPITAN MORALES

Ere I had finished this reply, my soul began to expand, to
exult, with the strangest sense of freedom, of triumph, I
ever felt. It seemed as if an invincible bond had burst, and
that I had struggled out into unhoped-for liberty.

—*Charlotte Brontë, Jane Eyre*

hen we returned to Bogota from our side trip, we were greeted with
the news that Mitchell Dosky had been diagnosed with hepatitis,
and we were all afraid that we had been exposed. We visited a local
doctor, and luckily we were all clean. We did have to get gamma globulin
shots as a precaution. When Ross Grant saw the size of the needle—and it
was freakishly large—he fainted dead away. Sebastian and Lonny had to
pick him up off the floor. I will admit that the injection really hurt, but I
had been through a lot worse in my young life.

We looked forward to moving to the finca where we would be able to
prepare our own meals, and Mitchell Dosky would have a place to rest and
recover. I had begun reading *A Separate Reality* by Carlos Castaneda, and
the events at the finca would soon reflect aspects of the book.

We all boarded the bus that was to take us to the small town where the
house of El Capitan Morales was located. All of us plus one—Luka. What
an asset he turned out to be for me, in more ways than one. As expected,
the bus was crowded with locals going to various towns along the way, some

holding small livestock. We saw a line of people forming and rushed toward the front to be assured of a seat. We knew it would be a four-hour journey. Luka sat by the window, and I sat next to him on the aisle. A woman was standing in the aisle carrying a large live chicken, which she held upside down by its feet. Every time the bus made a turn, the chicken's beak came very close to my nose, and I found myself eye to eye with it.

When we arrived in the town, Aiden asked some locals, in Spanish, where the house of El Capitan Morales was. Their expressions changed immediately from frowns to smiles just at the mention of the place. They happily pointed us to the road that led to the finca. It was obvious that El Capitan was a well-known—and perhaps well-liked—resident. We walked past a fountain in the center of town and noticed there was an alligator tied up. People taunted it, and threw cigarettes at it. I quickly walked past the scene, not wanting to give credence to it.

As we approached the finca, we saw a gate in the middle of a tall wall that surrounded the property. We rang the bell. A young woman came to the gate to let us in. She spoke English and welcomed us into the house.

She said, "My name is Isabella Esperanza. My husband and I live in a cottage on the property, and we are available to help you in any way we can."

I learned later on that she had three children and was just about my age. I thought she spoke English very well.

"My husband works in other towns and is away a lot," she said, "But I will be here always to assist you."

We walked around examining the house which far exceeded our expectations. The kitchen was very primitive, with a small gas stove, a large sink, a butcher-block table against the wall, and a single chair. There was a solo light bulb hanging from the ceiling. I tugged at Luka's arm directing his eyes to the lime tree outside the kitchen window. Some of the branches jutted through the bars into the kitchen over the sink—the windows in the house had no glass, only wrought-iron bars, although some of the rooms had sliding screen doors. There was a large room in the center of the house that served as a living room/dining room, with a large table where we could eat our meals.

The property was filled with fruit trees—banana, papaya, coconut palms, avocado, and mango. Right off the living room was a sliding screen door through which I could see a hammock swinging between two palm trees on the lawn. The vista was spectacular. The house was set on top of a cliff, two thousand feet high, overlooking the Bogota River; we could see the Andes

Mountains in the distance. Below in the valley were green pastures with white Brahman cows. I wondered if Isabella and her husband had horses, but I didn't see any around the property. There was a large swimming pool off the side of the house, which I was sure we'd make good use of. We were all very pleased and began settling into our home for our last month in Colombia.

I felt centered and powerful in Colombia, as if restraints were lifted from me; maybe it was the raw wildness of the country. My past melted away like a stick of butter left out in the hot sun—butter being a rare commodity in Colombia. I was at total peace, an inner peace that I hadn't felt anywhere else. I could spend an hour in the hammock gazing at the Andes Mountains. I took a nap and got lost somewhere in time.

When I awoke Luka wasn't next to me. I slid out of the hammock and searched for him. I found him in the kitchen preparing supper. He didn't notice me, so I stood in the doorway and watched him at the butcher block. He had a towel wrapped around him from the waist down. He looked like he had just stepped out of the shower. I stared at his body—smooth, dark, hairless, and strong. He grabbed the machete and began chopping up yucca for a soup he was making, and I saw his muscles tense. Watching him in that primitive kitchen was like being in the year 1492. I walked up behind him and put my arms around his waist and my face in the back of his neck. The ringlets of his dark hair were damp at the base of his neck, and he smelled good. He turned only his face to kiss me, and then went back to his work.

PHOTOGRAPH OF SUNDAY MARKET IN COLOMBIA

On Sundays, there was a large open market in town. I'd get up as soon as I heard the church bells ring, and I'd reach over and wake Luka. Mitchell, Luka, and I would walk into town very early, while it was still fairly cool. Eggs were expensive for the locals, one peso each, but we could afford them. The milk was intolerable, so I avoided it completely, as well as a drink they made called *aguapanela*—basically brown sugar boiled in water. There was only one cheese, and it was kept in a display case labeled *queso*, which means cheese in Spanish. The vegetables were riddled with amoebas and had to be washed thoroughly and boiled before eating, as did the water. Most of us had dysentery for a while. I often made a large pot of German potato salad with olive oil, onions and bacon. Ross and I would sit on the floor with the pot between us eating as much as we could to keep the weight on. Still, I lost twelve pounds. Ross lost thirty.

In the evenings, if it was hot in the finca, Luka and I would walk into town. We loved to sit in the café where the locals were playing their guitars and singing songs. We'd start with beer and progress to tequila. We'd get pretty drunk, and sometimes stupid. Luka would take my hand and pull me out of my chair to dance. The men in the café would give us wolf whistles, as if they were calling their cattle. We'd often stay at the café until the wee hours of the morning. I felt totally uninhibited in Colombia.

A little black dog appeared outside the front gate of the house. We let her in and gave her scraps. She was not skinny but had no collar. Isabella told us her name was Tabasco. I imagined she hung around whenever there were people staying at the house.

Luka and I were hot and dusty from our trip to the market, so we ran out to the pool, got naked and jumped in. Adam and Aiden had just returned from a trip to Bogota, and while there they'd picked up our mail from the American embassy. They also had a tale to tell about some hippies who went on a camping trip in the mountains around Bogota who were robbed by bandits. Adam said, "Everything was stolen from them—their backpacks, money, and jewelry. The robbers cut the backpacks right off their backs with machetes." It was disturbing to hear, considering we were thinking of another backpacking trip through the jungle. We had to rethink our plans.

Ross befriended a Colombian guy, Tobias Ibarra, who hung out at the house with us. There was a large German population that defected to South

America after the Second World War. We met many people with Spanish first names and German surnames, and vice versa. Tobias gave me a beaded necklace he made himself with Colombian beads, which he claimed had special power.

Tobias said, "The Indians have a sacred ceremony for a baby when it's born. They wrap the strands of beads around the baby's wrist or neck, but they never take them off."

Luka nodded in confirmation.

Tobias had some strong marijuana that he said was of a magical nature. We all smoked some, and it was quite psychedelic. We were talking and telling stories when my mind began to drift into a world of fantasy. I stared at Luka, who was sitting across from me intently listening to Tobias's stories. They spoke to each other in Spanish, and even though I didn't catch everything they were saying, I enjoyed watching their exchange.

Luka was attractive in an exotic way, this descendant of the Incas. I pictured him in a temple of the gods on a mountaintop in an ancient city, his face painted with war symbols and feathers adorning a headband. He had the high cheekbones of the Peruvian ancestral tribes—a civilization built high above the clouds in the mysterious Andes Mountains. I pictured us making love, and was overcome with an intense desire for him.

My fantasy was rudely interrupted when I heard Ivy ask, "Did you pick up potatoes at the market this morning?"

And just like that, the spell was broken, and my fantasy evaporated into the humid air.

I searched everywhere but couldn't find my undergarments one morning, and I wondered where I'd left them. I passed by the kitchen and saw Isabella washing them in the sink.

"Isabella, what are you doing?" I asked.

"Oh, señorita, it's my job."

I was a little shocked, but I didn't want to embarrass her or make her feel bad, so I just let her do it. The pool water was looking very green, so Sebastian asked her to empty the pool and fill it with fresh water—apparently, there was no chlorine in that town. That night we noticed a dancing light inside the swimming pool, and couldn't figure out what it was. I walked out to the pool with Aiden. There was Isabella, inside the empty pool with her daughter holding candles, scrubbing the pool by hand.

Aiden said, "Isabella, you don't have to do that."

"Please, señor," she said, "I have done this before. It's part of my chores around the finca."

We were discussing the work that Isabella was expected to do around the property, when Tobias said, "Sometimes when people are very poor, they actually sell one of their children."

I listened in disbelief. Then I remembered that when we were in the resort town of Santa Marta, we met an older man in a café. He owned one of the yachts in the harbor and spoke English. He had a very young boy with him. We could tell the boy was his personal servant, and I wondered what else he did for the man. It was a side of poverty I had never thought about.

Ivy, Crystal, and I were sunbathing in the nude outside on the grass. There were tall walls around the house but not on the grassy cliff side that overlooked the river. We had just been swimming in the pool, and the sun felt so good on our naked bodies. We heard a donkey braying in the distance and laughed at the sound.

I was writing in my journal, something about Crystal resembling Eve in the Garden of Eden, when I had an eerie feeling that someone was watching us. I looked up and saw someone's eyes through the bushes—eyes like a wild animal. I alerted the girls, and we sat up and covered ourselves. Even when the man realized that we'd seen him, he continued staring and wouldn't leave. He must have climbed up the side of the mountain to get to where he was.

In the book I was reading, *A Separate Reality*, it spoke of allies and special people who existed between worlds. There was some talk among us that this man might be one of them. I walked into the house and told the guys that the Peeping Tom, or as I referred to him, Peeping Juan, was back again. The guys came out and chased him. I didn't think he was harmful or dangerous, but it was strange.

We were feeling restless and wanted to see more of Colombia. At the dinner table that evening we discussed a trip to Cali, and Indian towns farther south. We heard that the Pan American Games were going on in Cali and figured that people would be there from all over the globe. Adam and some of the others in the gay contingent decided to go to Ecuador. There definitely was a widening wedge continuing in the commune between the gays and the straights. I was sad to leave the finca, even though it was only for a short trip.

Cali was an unexpectedly beautiful city. It reminded me of Montreal,

Canada, with bridges, cobblestone streets, and elaborate cathedrals. We ate and drank a lot over the two days we spent there. The city was teaming with people from all over the world who came to participate in, and observe the Pan American Games in the summer of 1971. On one of the days we were there, thousands of bicycles were everywhere you looked. They raced over the bridge we were standing on—so exciting to watch.

We found rooms in a nice hotel. Luka and I were happy to be alone. I woke up the next morning and slipped out of bed to open the shutters. The room had very high ceilings and tall, narrow windows. I looked out over the city. I could hear church bells ringing calling people to daily mass. I glanced over at the bed, and Luka had his eyes open; he'd been silently watching me. He motioned for me to come to him, and I did. He took my hand, and I sat down on the bed. He lay his head in my lap looking up at me, and I bent down and kissed him on the lips. I was wearing one of his white T-shirts. He lifted the front of the shirt and began kissing my body, fondling my breasts, and sucking on the nipples. Then he began playing with my cucci, first with his fingers, then with his tongue. After that went on for a while, I grabbed him by the hair and held his head down there.

That night, all six of us went to a café for dinner and discussed our plans for the next few days.

Ivy told us about something terrible that had happened to her that day;

"I was walking on one of the narrow cobblestone streets and stopped to rest my back against a window. A woman inside reached through the bars and clutched my hair. She was banging my head against the bars, yelling in Spanish, '"My home is not a zoo!"' She pulled out some of my hair. Luckily, someone stopped to help me, and got my hair loose from her grip."

I said, "You're traumatized, I'm ordering you a tequila."

If Luka had been with her it never would have happened.

Luka told us that the most efficient way to get to Popayán, the next city on our list, was by train, and that we could pick up the tickets at the train station.

When musicians walked into the café, the other two couples left, but Luka and I stayed. We were high on tequila and high on life. We danced with the heat and humidity surrounding us. It was all so strange, me and the Bolivian revolutionary as he liked to call himself. We were like two refugees from another life or another time. We connected even though our worlds were so different. I felt free and natural with Luka. I was lost in the moment without a past or a future, and I liked it. My time in Colombia achieved what years of meditation couldn't—be in the present!

IN CALI, COLUMBIA, 1971.

In the morning, we all left the hotel together after breakfast, and went straight to the train station. As we boarded the train for Popayán Ivy said, "Today is Friday the thirteenth," and I wondered if it was really necessary for me to know that.

It was the craziest train ride I'd ever been on. It was an old train, like something out of one of those *Orient Express* mystery movies. Our seats were in the dining car, which had a grill to cook food. Porters were running to and fro carrying trays. The train had an amazing route. It climbed high into the Andes Mountains giving us breathtaking views. We could look down in the valleys and see waterfalls flowing down the length of the mountains. Then it descended into a thick jungle and through a coffee bean plantation. Luka and I sat opposite Ivy and Darby. Ross and Crystal were on the other side of the aisle. We were all talking and laughing when suddenly the train began to grate along the tracks, and everything came to a screeching halt. We were nearly tossed out of our seats.

The engineer was saying something over the speaker.

I asked Luka, "What is he saying?"

"Da engine go off da track," he said.

We're in the middle of the freaking jungle, I thought.

I noticed some of the locals quickly gather their belongings and rush off the train. Perhaps they lived in one of the little towns between stations and decided to walk home. Then I saw porters jump off the train with machetes and start chopping wood in the surrounding jungle. I figured it was for the grill. There was plenty of food on board, and they began giving it away, along with beer and sodas. Luka got word from the engineer that we'd be stuck for many hours, until another engine was brought from the next town.

Hours went by. We stayed in our seats not knowing what to do. I noticed that Ross was trying to get my attention. His eyes were very wide and seemed to be signaling me of danger. I looked up to see men board the train. They looked like banditos or maybe *federales*. They were dressed like Pancho Villa, with black hats and magazines of bullets across their chests, and they were carrying guns.

Maybe that's why the locals got off the train right away, I thought. We sat very still so as to not draw attention to ourselves. They stormed through the dining car, took a quick look at us, and just passed us by and walked to the next car. Maybe they thought, *what money or jewels could those hippies have?* Actually, I was looking like a native. I was bronze, and my hair had grown really wild and almost reached my waist. I was able to carry on a simple conversation in Spanish. Besides, I was with Luka.

After we felt the danger had passed, we got up and walked through the cars and eventually got off the train. We weren't brave enough to venture too far. When it got dark we slept in our seats— it was a very restless sleep.

As soon as the sun was up, some of the porters jumped off the train, got their machetes out and ravaged the jungle in the immediate area. They were climbing trees and chopping off fruits. I doubted that even a wild chicken was safe. A short while later they returned with bananas, avocados, papayas, coconuts, and plantains to fry. We were lucky to have such industrious men on board, which resulted in a hearty breakfast. Twenty hours later we heard the chug-chug-chug of an engine coming. So goes transportation in a banana republic on Friday the thirteenth.

The farther south we traveled, the more Indians we encountered. I bought a beautiful embroidered skirt in an outside market in Pasto. We took a day trip to an Indian village called Sibundoy, where we were invited into a hut to see how the indigenous people wove blankets and belts. Watching the women working on the looms was yet another scene right out of 1492.

Luka said, "People in this village dress da same way for hundreds years."

Ross was having a private conversation with the man who took us to the indigenous huts. Ross said, "The man is a shaman—an Indian *brujo*. He administers Yage (pronounced YA HAY) in his home."

Luka widened his eyes.

I understood *yage* (also known as ayahuasca) to be a natural psychedelic, very physical, and that the brujo stayed with you and guided you through the experience.

Ross said, "Crystal and I are following him to his house to try yage. We'll catch up with you guys tomorrow."

Luka nodded, and we agreed on a place to meet.

Ivy and I had the impression that Crystal wasn't as keen about taking Yage as much as Ross was.

"She'll do whatever Ross tells her to," Ivy remarked.

That night Darby said, "I heard there's snow in Tulcan."

I said, "I'm already cold in Pasto, and I don't want to go any farther south. I want to return to the finca."

Ivy nodded in agreement.

In less than two weeks my summer in Colombia would be over, and I wanted to spend it at the house of El Capitan Morales. We stayed overnight in Pasto at a hotel that had rooms off a courtyard. It was very cold. I was feeling nostalgic, almost as if I didn't want to go home. I loved the wildness of Colombia and its people. I was enjoying the primitive existence, as if I were writing my own history. I think Luka wanted to come to America with me, but I wondered how that would work. Would I feel the same way about him if we were not in this magical place?

We all met in the lobby of the hotel in the morning for breakfast. It was a long bus ride back to the finca, maybe nine hours, but Ross kept us entertained with the crazy story about their yage experience.

Ross said, "When Crystal and I arrived at the shaman's house, it had no windows or doors." Ross turned to Luka and said, "The brujo and I checked each other out for a few minutes. He spoke Quechua but also English."

I saw a smile break out on Luka's face at the mention of his native language.

Ross said "I formally asked the shaman if he had yage, and he said yes, that he could accommodate us. Before anything could happen, though, I had to pay off his debt at the local bodega."

Hearing this, we all busted out laughing.

Ross continued, "In the bodega he made me buy Aguardiente, the local alcohol. He also added chocolate and all the necessary items needed for the preparation leading up to the taking of yage. The shaman was exceedingly gracious and put us both at ease. It was quite physical at the onset. Crystal and I both threw up a few times. Then the shaman told us—Ross lowered his voice to mimic the brujo—"'Now you are both ready for the doors of perception!'" I began to hallucinate. It was more like magic mushrooms than LSD. I felt no fear, and the best part of the experience was a feeling of well-being afterward, which the shaman told me would last for a few days. I'll never forget the feeling of oneness I had with the universe."

Upon our return to the finca, we heard a troubling story from Sebastian. He and Aiden had met two local guys in town who they'd approached about buying some pot—that big can of marijuana they bought when we first arrived in Colombia didn't last as long as expected. The locals led them to a desolate area and robbed them of their money and jewelry. Sebastian said "They took my watch, and when they couldn't get my ring off, they were going to chop my finger off with a machete. I twisted that sucker off as fast as I could."

On our second day back there was a big drama. Sebastian came running out of one of the bathrooms yelling, "There's a snake in the toilet!"

Of course, everyone ran into the bathroom to see it for themselves. As soon as the snake's head appeared over the rim of the toilet, there was a mass exodus out of the bathroom. It was like a scene from an old Marx Brothers movie—everyone trying to get through the doorway at the same time. We searched for Isabella but found her husband instead. He told us to boil a pot of water and dump it in the toilet. The boiling water acted as only a temporary fix, and when we least expected it, the snake would appear again. We were very cautious before sitting down on the toilets. Eventually her husband made a snake sling, caught the snake the next time it appeared, and chopped its head off.

On a particularly beautiful day, Mitchell, Luka, and I hiked down the side of the mountain, all the way to the Bogota River below in the valley. There was no swimming in the river because there were alligators in the water. We also got a closer look at the white Brahman cows in the field. A natural by-product of the cows are magic mushrooms. Since it had rained a lot over the past few days, there were mushrooms everywhere growing out of the cow pies. The cows warily watched us as we collected mushrooms. We hung out by the river until late afternoon, almost till sunset. Then we hiked back up the mountain to the house.

It was our last week in the house of El Capitan Morales. It was time to eat the magic mushrooms we'd gathered in the field by the River. We played music and waited for the effect to come on. Luka and I stripped down nude and jumped in the pool. Time seemed suspended, and I felt suspended in it. It was all like a beautiful movie I never wanted to end. I had made a wreath of leaves the day before, which was at the edge of the pool. I placed it on Luka's head, my Incan warrior. I wanted to tell him how I felt about him and how he made me feel about myself, but the words wouldn't come. He held me up as I floated on the surface, with the sun reigning down on us.

We got out of the pool, dried ourselves off, and went inside. Everyone was sitting around peacefully in their own worlds. It was a day of introspection, and I was examining aspects of my life. I wondered why I felt such freedom in Colombia. I enjoyed painting in my journal, and there were paints out on the dining room table. Luka reached for some paint and began painting my face with Indian symbols. He put on a headband and tucked a feather in it, as if he somehow saw himself in the dream I had. I was wearing the embroidered Indian skirt that I'd purchased at the market in Pasto. Luka wore a simple woven fabric wrapped around and tucked in at the waist. As he was painting my face I felt beautiful, sacred, and alive. I was going to remember that feeling for a very long time, maybe forever.

The summer was over and most of us were leaving at the end of August. Mitchell Dosky was remaining in Colombia. He told us he had no desire to return to the States. Adam and Aiden were still in Ecuador. I was already enrolled in fall classes at the university on Staten Island. Our return flights were to Miami from Barranquilla, so we had to make our way back to that industrial seaport town. Luka took that long, crazy bus ride with us and came to the airport. I didn't want to leave Colombia. I didn't want to leave him. I was lost in his eyes, and in the person I had become. I was afraid that as soon as I stepped off the plane in Miami, *the ME I'd become in Colombia*, South America, would be lost forever.

Luka promised he'd write to me, and told me he wanted to come to

America. I still wasn't sure if we would be the same in America. I told him that I looked forward to it. We embraced and kissed. Luka smiled when I said, "Api ami." I turned and followed the others down the ramp and onto the plane, looking back a few times.

I had a window seat. It was raining hard as the prop plane took off. I watched Luka standing alone behind that big window on the observation deck, watching me fly away.

FOURTEEN

INDEPENDENT WOMEN

"Deeper down than we are rich or poor,
black or white, we are he or she"

The Hard and he Soft, *by Roszak*

n uneasy feeling came over me as we drove up I-95 from Miami to
New York City. I was sad throughout the entire flight back to Miami
from Barranquilla, Colombia. My mind's eye kept replaying the
scene of Luka standing alone on the observation deck watching our plane
take off in the rain. I had the urge to jump up and yell that I had changed
my mind and wanted to stay in Colombia. Of course I didn't do that, but
I was afraid I was leaving that feeling of joy, total freedom, contentment,
and self-love behind. Why was I forever leaving what I wanted? As we
drove through the South with Georgia peaches, pecan pie, and the home
of evangelist ministries rushing past the window at fifty miles an hour, I
was detached.

Once back in Staten Island I looked forward to starting classes. I was
majoring in Women's Studies and wondering where the subject would take
me. My life, thus far, had been sectioned off by the men I was involved with,
and I'd learned something from each one of them. Recently, I had become
interested in women's rights and their contributions to society and history,
much of which I was finding out was left out of text books. It was 1971, and
women in Switzerland just had been granted the right to vote.

I was given an extensive list of reference books to read such as *Mothers* and Amazons, *The Infancy of Medicine*, *The Origin of the Family, Private Property and the State*, and *Wayward Servants*, to name a few. And there was the usual list of novels written by women such as *The Bell Jar* by Sylvia Plath, *A Room of One's Own* by Virginia Woolf, *Diary of a Mad Housewife* by Sue Kaufman, and *The Autobiography of Alice B. Toklas* by Gertrude Stein.

For one of my classes I wrote a paper on women in prisons. My research stated that Forty-eight percent of women had been incarcerated for victimless crimes. The largest group was for lewd soliciting. Eighty-four percent of the women were in for drug addiction or alcohol abuse. Unfortunately, most of the women were not even aware of their rights. Many of the textbooks I was reading exposed women as mere commodities in most cultures, virginity being a must for marriage selection.

I remembered a funny story my mother told me about women in Italy. In the old days, she'd heard there was a custom of hanging the bloody sheets on the clothesline in the yard after the honeymoon night for public inspection. Women who weren't virgins would kill a chicken, sprinkle the blood on the sheets, and hang it outside for the neighbors to see. Family crisis averted!

—Redstockings, **Redstocking Manifesto**

Women are an oppressed class. Our oppression is total, affecting every facet of our lives. We are exploited as sex objects, breeders, domestic servants, and cheap labor. We're considered inferior beings, and our prescribed behavior is enforced by the threat of physical violence.

The gay women in our commune were becoming very radical. One of the women, Jade, had a partner named Slade, who was a tough character. I felt safe around them though. Jade was sitting at the table while I was making a cup of tea.

She said, "If a man ever says to you, "'I invented you,'" you should answer, "'I didn't even know you existed.'"

"That sounds reasonable," I commented, while sipping my sassafras tea.

"And never forget we have witch power!"

I nodded but didn't respond. I thought of a passage from a book I'd read:

Witches have always been women who dared to be: Groovy, courageous, aggressive, intelligent, non-conformist, explorative and curious, independent, sexually liberated, and revolutionary. This may explain why nine million women have been burned as witches.
The New Women "**Witch Power**"

Growing up in the Bronx you had to be tough and street-savvy. When I was in elementary school, a clique of tough girls waited for me after class, grabbed my books and shoved me around. After they did it a few times, I went home whining to my mother. Vita said, "Adriana, you have to show those girls you're not afraid of them." The next time they were waiting for me after class, I came in swinging right at the leader of their pack. She was shocked, but after that day she respected me and looked out for me. We even became friends.

I was on my way to the university when Jade and Slade offered me a ride. The university was within walking distance, but I figured, *Why not?* We all got in the front seat of Slade's car, with me sitting between them. At a stop sign, the guys in the car in front cut us off. Slade stopped the car, ran to the trunk and pulled out a baseball bat. She ran after their car swinging the bat. I was motionless and speechless. The guys drove off. Slade calmly walked back to our car, tossed the bat in the back seat, and drove off.

After an uncomfortable silence, she turned to me, "Now, *that's* how you handle it, honey!"

When we reached the steps of the university I got out of the car, looked back and said in a sarcastic tone, "Thanks for the ride."

The radical politics at the house on the hill was getting on my nerves, which added to the negative things rolling around my brain from the past few years. I had a great room on the third floor though, and I adopted a black cat and named her Sabrina; she was a love and curled up with me at night. On dense nights I could hear the forlorn sound of the foghorns from the boats in the harbor, and could smell the sea air. Staten Island is a unique part of New York. You're not in the city, but just a short ferry ride away.

Ivy walked into the kitchen with a large manila envelope and handed it to me. It was from Lucas Antonio Castanera in Colombia, South America. Inside, there was a letter written in crude English. An electric current moved up my spine. He said sweet things about missing me, how he felt about me, and that nothing was the same after I left. He closed the letter with "Api ami, Luka." The envelope also contained paperwork for me to look over—papers that would enable him to come to America. I froze, and looked up at Ivy.

She asked, "What does he say?"

"Oh, he misses me, and he wants to come to America."

"And how do you think him being here would work out?"

I shrugged my shoulders. I had no answer. I was already living in a different world, a world that I didn't think he'd fit into. Maybe I was rationalizing my decision to leave Luka and Colombia behind. I took the manila envelope and set it aside. I took his letter out from time to time and read it, but I didn't respond.

We hadn't seen much of Judd Thatcher since our summer of love at the Yellow House. He was back on the scene, and in one of Lonny Marcum's classes at the university. Judd knew a guy named Jeremiah Murphy, who had built a cabin in the wilderness—far north in Upstate New York. A few of us went up for the weekend. It was the fall of 1971 but more like winter that far north.

It was so good to be in the wilderness again. The weather was brisk, and there were snow flurries. Sitting around the fireplace was a joy; in fact, we all slept in a loft above it huddled together in our sleeping bags. The fall colors of the trees were psychedelic as we took a walk in the woods behind the cabin. I felt much more alive in the country than I did in the city.

There was a really nice guy there whom I'd never seen before. He introduced himself as Troy Bloom. We struck up a conversation, and interestingly, he lived in the Bronx. He told me that he edited movies for a TV station. He was tall, well built, and very attractive. He had wide cat's eyes that were a speckled shade of green. His hair was a kinky dirty blond, and there was a lot of it, which he wore in a ponytail. All marks of a true Leo in every way. We really connected, and made plans to keep in touch when we were back in the city.

Not long after that weekend I received a call from Troy Bloom asking me to meet him in the city for a movie. He told me that he went to the movies at least four times a week, which I thought was odd; then again, he was in the film-editing business. I took the ferry into Manhattan and met him at a movie theater on Second Avenue. Afterward, we went to a bar and had a few drinks. I wasn't planning on getting involved with anyone, but he was such a great guy.

It had only been a few months since I'd left Luka in Colombia, and I was trying to put that behind me. I convinced myself that Luka would be totally out of place in America, and that he'd be lost in my world, which would make me terribly sad.

I invited Troy to the Hilltop Avenue house. His visit to the commune got mixed reviews. I am not sure what the objections were; maybe he was too macho. He did give the impression of a knight in shining armor and all that goes with it—armor being hard, shiny, and cold. He had a brassy exterior, but underneath I found him to be warm and sweet. Anyway, I liked him.

Looking back, he could be aloof at times. He might have needed to be worshipped, and I wasn't that type of woman. Still, I began dating Troy Bloom, and pretty soon he was hanging out at the house on the hill, and spending weekends with me at the house upstate in Hawk Dale. After one such weekend upstate, I sat down and wrote a letter to Luka, telling him that I'd met someone else. At the time I thought I was doing the best thing for both of us.

From my journal:

Walking up the hill toward our house
The sun reflects off the window of our room
The attic room on the top floor
Makes me warm inside
Two cats laying on the bed in our room
Of Persian rugs and hanging robes
Candles, flowers and jewels of love
Tenderness for both
Hair like a lion's mane soft and warm
Looking outside
I can see the hill covered with snow
Waiting for spring
After we make love
We all sleep together in purring delight

Months had gone by when I sensed hushed chatter in the commune, and although I couldn't put my finger on what was going on, I knew it involved me. I approached Adam, since he and I were friends the longest, had been so close, and through so many changes together.

"What's going on?" I asked. "I can feel something is wrong, and I know it has something to do with me."

Aiden came into my room, closed the door, and sat on my bed next to Adam. I knew Aiden was nervous because he began to stutter, saying, "Sssstay calm; we need to ttttell you something."

As I waited, I became more agitated.

Adam said, "Troy talked to us because he was afraid to tell you that he slept with a woman he works with at the TV station."

I sat there in disbelief at such a betrayal—to tell my friends and not me. Everyone in the commune knew about it except me. I was humiliated and incensed. I said, "I'd like it if you both left."

Adam said, "We can stay with you, if you want."

"No, I want to think about this alone."

As soon as they left the room I shut the door and went slightly crazy. I became a madwoman tearing down everything—the tie-dyed sheet behind the bed, the curtains, pictures, everything. Even my cat Sabrina hid under the dresser. True, he'd never said we were committed, but we were practically living together. I thought we were in a monogamous relationship. I wondered what was going through his mind at that moment. He didn't come to the house for days, but he did call, saying that we needed to talk. We met at a bar in the city and I let him do the talking.

He used all the old clichés like, "She didn't mean anything to me; it just happened. We work closely together."

He left out the part where she worships him, I thought. "Troy, it bothered me more that you couldn't tell me about it, and that you confided in everyone else but me."

He shrugged sheepishly.

I should have taken that incident as an omen, but I didn't. I kept seeing Troy, though not as often.

I was reading *Sleeper,* a comic book series by Ed Brubaker, and I copied the following into my journal:

> Now everyone is acting. Everything is props. The world is
> engaged in a gigantic benign conspiracy to force you to
> be what you are. Every night all the people you will speak
> to on the morrow, hold a secret informal rehearsal. All is

theater. Everything is bathed in stage lights. You yourself
are an actor. If you muff a line, so what. All situations are
scenes, all places are sets, and all objects are props.

I found a part-time job in Manhattan in the coding department at a
market research company, the same company at which some of my friends
worked. The days and hours were flexible, and I needed the money to pay
for my classes. On the ferry ride to work each day, I'd observe the seagulls
following the ferry in majestic flight, with their artful plunges into the
water. Looking down at the foamy, greenish-gray water being churned up
by the boat, I always wondered if anything in that polluted water was still
alive.

I took a break from Troy Bloom and concentrated on my job and my
classes. At the house on the hill there were meetings—lots of gay versus
straight rhetoric. I wondered where it would lead. I had the feeling that
something had to give, and I'd be the odd one out.

I wrote this in my journal:

Where has it gone, the high times we all shared? So, you
don't like who I'm sleeping with? Why has it come to this
bullshit? I don't give a damn who you sleep with, never
did, never will. Be happy with who you are, and don't put
me up against the wall.

Between my classes at the university, the politics at the Hilltop Avenue
house, weekends in the country at Hawk Dale, and work in Manhattan,
I was adrift in a rough sea. During the day my mind often returned to
Colombia. My thoughts drifted back to the prehistoric rainforest we'd
trekked through to get to the camp on the river, and the endless fields
of sugar cane. My mind's eye saw the finca on the cliff overlooking the
Bogota River, with the Andes Mountains in the distance. My mouth
watered for a *jugo de maracuya*—passion fruit juice. I missed the thrill of
the torrential rains. I missed watching the sun go down, and listening to
the buzz of the *chicharas* (cicadas) calling each other from tree to tree. I
missed the wildness of the country, but most of all, I missed Luka, and the
uncomplicated love we shared, our connection, and the contentment I'd
experienced there.

I felt that I was missing something, as if I'd been slighted. I was craving
self-affirmation. I did have love for Troy Bloom, but there was something

missing. We didn't have a deep connection, and our sex life never got off the first floor. I'd been with other men, and I knew what it could be like.

I met someone who lived in our neighborhood not far from the house on the hill. He was in a relationship too. I guess we both were looking to even a score. I ran into him on the avenue. We struck up a conversation over coffee. He told me his girlfriend was out of town. We walked to his house in the rain. I don't remember anything about him; I can't even remember his name. We had sex at his house, in their bed. Afterward, I walked home alone with a smile on my face, but not feeling much of anything.

I wrote in my journal:

> Beautiful rainy day, rain some life into my soul. I'm flowing with the water off the roof. He loved me so hard I got weak in the knees. I got my period today, washing all opportunity from the womb. Someone is playing Jimmy Reed on the stereo in the living room. The sound is so mellow, but the drum beats to my soul. "Ain't that lovin' you baby; ain't that lovin' you babe, ain't that lovin' you baby, and ya don't even know my name."

A memory popped into my head. I remembered my mother wanting to wipe me, to see the blood, the first time I got my period. Maybe it was an Old Italian custom, but I thought it was weird and wouldn't let her. I didn't feel close to her at the age of twelve. Looking back, I wished I had.

It was late fall, and a few of us spent the weekend at Jeremiah Murphy's cabin. It was bitterly cold—ten degrees below zero up on that mountain with the wind chill factor. There were a few dogs there that weekend. They were excited about the snow and refused to stay indoors. I watched them through the window, romping, biting the snow, and rolling in it. Troy Bloom was there; we had friends in common. His mustache froze and we laughed about it. I was on good terms with him, and wondered if we had a future. For some stupid reason I remained forever hopeful that things could change.

In one of my women's study groups, we had an interactive meeting— women telling stories of how men affected our lives. We discussed how we felt and acted differently with women when there were no men around.

One of the women said, "I don't think men are comfortable with or like strong, independent women."

Another woman said, "Sometimes it seems like we're two different species." We all laughed.

I said, "I think women are bound to the earth, and men are of the sky. Maybe they fly around until they meet a special woman and become grounded." In reality, I was the one flying around.

After the meeting, we formed a circle, locked arms and swayed. At home that night, I described it in my journal:

> There she was, beautiful, long red hair, sensitive and quiet. All of a sudden she was pouring her guts out to us, mere strangers. But women are not strangers; a lifetime of pain and shit-eating grins unite us. For the first time in my life I loved women. I am them. Women swaying, bodies together screaming to be free. Women, untapped sources of creativity. All of us freaking out, crawling toward the center, the womb. Pulling it all out, crying and wailing in pain. Stamping our feet in disgust, helplessness, and frustration. Strength replaced weakness, and all the women flowed into one woman.

I was spending hours in the darkroom at the university, and the winter was flying by. I was dating Troy again, and things were okay between us. I wouldn't say it was an intense relationship, because Troy Bloom had an armor around him which he never let me get through. Perhaps we didn't have the right chemistry. My mother, on the other hand, loved Troy and thought he was a fabulous catch. He was good-looking, smart, and had a great job. It was true; he was an all-around nice guy. I never discussed any of our personal problems, or the sexual issues in our relationship with her. She seemed so happy about our union; I didn't want to burst her bubble.

In the spring of 1972 I was still enjoying my Women's Studies classes at the university and was happy to hear that Ruth Bader Ginsburg was the first woman to be tenured as a faculty member at Colombia Law School in New York City. Progress was happening for women. I was enjoying our weekends at the house in Hawk Dale. There was much less discord and politics when we were all in the country.

As the summer approached, Troy and I got it in our heads to walk the northeastern portion of the Appalachian Trail. It was quite a feat we were taking on. I was out of the university for the summer, and Troy's TV shows were on a summer hiatus. I had some money saved from my job at the marketing company. Troy, his best friend Christian, and I embarked on a long trek across the northeast. Our plan was to walk the Appalachian Trail, starting in Massachusetts, through Vermont, to the end of the trail in Maine. We took a Greyhound bus to a small town in Massachusetts, where we were to pick up the trail. We got off the bus with all our gear and wandered through the town looking for signs to the Appalachian Trail. The most difficult part of the trip for me was getting used to carrying a twenty-five-pound pack on my back. I felt like one of the Santini brothers moving a television from New Hampshire to Vermont. The guys were always helping me with something, and I was forever trailing behind them feeling inadequate.

I wrote in my journal:

> Rain and storms last night. It was very windy at the top of Prospect Mountain in Vermont. Massachusetts was beautiful, although the path was very muddy. The wind was blowing, and the trees and bushes were swaying wildly. The clouds and rain gave everything a luminescent quality. There was glittering silver on the leaves and a spray of mist on our faces as we passed by windblown trees.

The Appalachian Trail passes through towns. I imagined the early settlers making this same trip on horseback or on foot. As we'd come through the woods into a clearing we could see the next town below us in the valley. There was a good sense of how we had walked over the mountain, where we were coming from, and where we were headed, like a living map. There was a lot of rain, and every time we passed through a town, we'd go straight to a laundromat to dry our clothes.

We didn't encounter many women on the trail, and I understood why. We went days without a hot shower, and had to wash in cold streams. I didn't realize how strenuous the trip was going to be. We did meet some great people on the trail. It was nice to hear about where they'd come from, and why they were walking the Appalachian Trail.

After seven days in flimsy tents we came across a great cabin next to a lake in Vermont. It was part of a larger campground with recreational facilities. We saw canoes leaning against a building. We dropped our gear and went canoeing. It was the first really fun day we'd had in a while. We stayed in that camp for a few days. We hiked in the surrounding forest the next day. When we returned to the cabin we found a family of porcupines in our bunk beds. They were not intimidated by us in the least. They made the strangest sound, like the sound of a boomerang. They eventually climbed down off the bunks but they took their time. There wasn't much sex on the Appalachian Trail. I felt grubby, and sometimes annoyed. We did have sex on occasion, but it wasn't memorable, with Christian sleeping a few feet away.

I wrote in my journal:

> Griffith Lake, after a nine-and-a-half-mile hike over hill and dale, through fog and gnats. We quickly dumped our packs, tore everything off, and literally "jumped in the lake." It's really nice here, not too buggy, and the sun is shining brightly. The mosquitos were so bad in some places, we had to lift our mosquito nets to take a bite of food. Heavy rain is predicted for tomorrow. Troy is sitting close to the fire patching his shirt. Christian and I are playing cards. We left our names and comments in the log book in the cabin.

The very next day brought hurricane-force winds and more rain. Luckily, there was a shelter at the camp, and we were not the only travelers stuck there. A group of hikers were nice enough to share their K-rations and hot cocoa with us. I went to fetch fresh water, which required a three-tenths-of-a-mile hike through the drenched forest, along a very muddy trail. There wasn't much to do on days like that, so I read from the book I'd brought on the trip, *The Bell Jar* by Sylvia Plath. The next day the weather cleared a bit, and we continued on the trail.

Further along we were hit with yet another big storm. At that point, three weeks in, we were tired of fighting the elements. We were wet most of the time, slipping and sliding along muddy trails and stumbling over wet rocks. Some nights, even the tent wouldn't hold back the rain.

The trail opened onto a large field, and we found ourselves walking along an old stagecoach trail. We could see the grooves in the earth made by the wagon wheels. I could almost hear the squeak of the wooden wheels as they must have gone into the grooves, perhaps on just such a rainy day, except it had been more than two hundred years in the past. I pictured women sitting inside covered wagons with checkered bonnets, and the men sitting up front driving the wagons, sporting dusty derby hats, holding the reins and guiding the horses. The thought of it gave me a thrill. When we made camp that night, I threw the I Ching. The trigrams I received spoke of deliverance and the desert. I laughed and thought, *What the hell can that possibly mean?*

The next day the trail took us through a really nice town, Darby, in Rutland, Vermont. In the center of town there was an old stone house that was converted into a museum. We meandered through the rooms looking at everything. Afterward, Troy and I sat on a large, old-fashioned swing on the front porch. It was a nice break from the trauma of the two storms we had just been through. We dreaded getting back on the trail.

When Christian caught up with us on the porch we grabbed our gear and began walking through town looking for a sign to the Appalachian Trail. A Greyhound bus sat in a parking lot with the information ticker flashing NEW YORK CITY. The three of us looked at each other and hopped on.

FIFTEEN

MAKING LOVE IN
A MEMORY

"When one is in love, one always begins by deceiving oneself, and one always ends by deceiving others. That is what the world calls romance"

~ Oscar Wilde

W E needed to dry out after almost a month on the Appalachian Trail. We were back in New York City for only a few days. Troy and I didn't tell our families that we had left the trail, and we stayed at his friend Harry's house. We thought, what better place to dry out than the Grand Canyon?

We rented a car and headed southwest on Route 80. The first break was at a truck stop we'd heard was famous for their homemade apple pie. That night we slept in our sleeping bags at a rest stop. Nebraska was flat, flat, flat, with such an expanse of sky—more sky than you could ever imagine. We saw Black Angus cattle lining the plains. I pictured them as buffalo with Native Americans riding their horses alongside the car.

We picked up two hitchhikers who told us that there was a happening going on at Strawberry Lake in Colorado, which they referred to as a "Gathering of tribes." I didn't know what that meant, but it sounded interesting. We dropped them off on a ramp before leaving the thruway. We stopped to get groceries, and the whole town was abuzz with talk of the festival. We overheard someone say that there were probably twenty thousand people in attendance. We stocked up on food and followed all the cars to the festival.

We came upon a large open field next to a lake. Cars were parked haphazardly, VW buses with psychedelic paintings, and there were quite a few teepees. Thousands of freaky people were walking around, some of them nude, building fires and banging on drums. We parked the car where we hoped we wouldn't get blocked in.

People were stripping down and going into a big hut at the edge of the lake. There were hot rocks in a fire pit, which were doused with water to make steam. We took our clothes off and did the same as everyone else. People rubbed mud all over each other's bodies. A man and a woman held tree branches which they would softly whip across our bodies for a massaging effect. People chanted and laughed. When the heat of the sauna was overwhelming, everyone jumped in the cold lake, squealing and splashing with joy.

Soon, people made circles, and that's when it became tribal. A guy saw me writing in my journal and grabbed it away from me. He drew two nude stick figures in the pages of my journal with the letters OM everywhere.

There were strange cloud formations overhead and a fire-red sunset that evening. We slept there in the field that night. When it got dark we made love in our double sleeping bag to the sound of tribal drums and people's chatter. In the morning we were awakened by horses racing past us chased by dogs and children. It was hot and sunny when I sat up yawning. In the distance were the snowcapped Rocky Mountains, an awesome sight. The whole experience was rejuvenating and spiritual.

We left the festival and drove along the Colorado River until evening, and camped there that night. We were able to reach Aspen the next day.

I didn't see much in the way of fresh produce in any of the food markets we shopped at. We drove twelve thousand feet up to a mountain pass and stood on the Continental Divide. We could see the mountain range that goes all the way from Canada to South America. We began to pass more cabins on our way farther west. There certainly was a lot of land, and we were forever driving past expansive ranches with cattle, horses, and sheep.

Troy pointed to a sliver of a river, and said, "According to this map, that's the Rio Grande."

"Well, it's not that grand today," I commented.

When we arrived in New Mexico we stopped at an outside market where Native American women were selling their pottery. I bought a tiny bowl painted with tribal symbols. Walking through the marketplace I heard Mexican music. The smell of beans cooking, and the heat of the chili sauce evoked a flashback of Colombia. I felt an ache and saw Luka and me dancing in that café in Cali. There, I'd been so happy and alive.

There was no release from the memories as we entered the town of Santa Clara which reminded me of Taganga. I felt a tinge of desire for South America. It's amazing what memories Mexican music, the smell of beans cooking, and some hot sauce can evoke. A feeling of sadness came over me because I didn't feel that way with Troy Bloom. I did love him, but not in that intense way, where I was surrounded by magic whenever I was with that one person.

When we got into the car Troy reached for my hand and asked, "What's wrong?"

"Nothing really," I answered, "just some old memories."

We needed to find a laundromat in town because just about every piece of clothing we had was dirty. While we were doing our laundry, we met Mr. and Mrs. Gonzales. They were so friendly, and we talked to them for a long time. They took a liking to us and invited us to their hacienda at the end of town for an evening meal.

That evening we followed their directions to the edge of town, and looked for a dirt road to the right of a large tree. We found the house easily; it was quite a large compound. There were dogs of varying sizes running everywhere. As we got out of the car a bunch of children surrounded us and walked us to the house.

The walls of the adobe were filled with saints and Mexican art work. Mr. Gonzales said, "Three generations live in this house."

"Wow, that's wonderful," Troy said.

Mrs. Gonzales prepared the most wonderful meal of lamb, potatoes, yucca, and beans. I prayed that the meal wouldn't evoke more memories of Lucas Antonio Castanera, or Colombia.

Mrs. Gonzales began slicing a few limes, and with their aroma I saw Luka standing in that primitive kitchen in the house of El Capitan Morales chopping yucca with a machete. I'd grab a lime from the branch that came through the bars into the kitchen window, and give it to him to slice. I thought of the way he turned and looked at me, and the thrill I felt. The memory was interrupted when Mr. Gonzales laughed loudly as he put more hot sauce on my plate.

After supper, we thanked them for their hospitality, and as we were leaving Mr. Gonzales said, "Always remember, when you are in town our home is your home!"

We slept in a camp in Gallup, New Mexico that night. In the morning we returned the car to the rental agency, and hitched a ride to the Grand Canyon. The sight took my breath away. The canyon looked like an ocean that had been drained of water, and I pictured large dead fish lying at the bottom. But what was at the bottom of the canyon was the Colorado River. It was a beautiful shade of turquoise glistening in the sun. We stood there turning our heads 360 degrees—it was almost too much to take in. After regaining our composure, our plan was to hike down to the base camp at the bottom of the canyon, and stay for a week. We slept at a campsite we found up at the top that night.

We found a place to have breakfast the next day, then began the hike down into the canyon. It was hotter than hell, and after walking for hours we were still circling the rim. We stopped to rest and drank some water. I began to wonder if we'd brought enough water with us. We knew there were springs and waterfalls we could drink from at the bottom, and we intended to reach the base camp before it got dark. Parts of the trail were in disarray with rock slides rendering the path unclear. I feared that we might have taken a wrong turn. The sun was going down, so we decided to sleep right there on the trail, and continue when the sun came up. We lay down right where we were, and stared up at the stars which were numerous and sparkling. We fell asleep from exhaustion, and the next thing I knew, it was almost daylight.

When I opened my eyes I saw a little mouse sitting on a rock staring at me. I sat up and woke Troy. We were both hungry and thirsty.

Troy said, "We should save the little bit of water we have left in case we went the wrong way."

"Good idea," I said.

I took two oranges from my backpack, and Troy cut them up with his trusty Swiss Army knife. Troy spit his section out, "Tastes like pure sugar." Neither of us could eat the oranges, so I left the sections on the trail for the mouse. I was thirsty and a little scared.

"Troy, what if we went the wrong way?"

"Let's just walk a little further and see what we see."

We began walking swiftly. We hadn't walked even half an hour when we saw a wooden sign with a pointing finger that read "Base Camp 1 1/2 miles." Our spirits lightened immediately. We drank the water we had left and began walking more leisurely along the trail. Obviously the trail went along the rim for most of the way, until the last two miles where it descended straight down.

When we reached the bottom, hot and thirsty, I saw water and ran toward it. I tossed off my pack, lay in the water, and drank it at the same time. The bottom of the canyon was lush with patches of greenery and a number of cascading waterfalls. We found a pool that had been created by a rock formation. We took off our clothes and dove in. We swam there every day while in the canyon.

BOTTOM OF THE GRAND CANYON.

A group of people had been staying at the base camp for the entire summer. They had an elaborate campsite set up with many conveniences, including an old iron stove—God only knows how it got down there. The oven worked so well that they even baked a cake in it. It operated on burning wood and coal. I watched one of the women fill a cake pan with batter, cover it with another cake pan, slip it between the burning wood and coals, and, *voila*, cake!

Troy and I walked to the Colorado River, which was about a half mile from the base camp. There were swift running rapids in the river, and we often saw rafters go by. On one of those days, a group of rafters come very close to the shore. They signaled us to approach. They had beers tied with ropes along the sides of the raft dangling in the water to keep them cold. They tossed us a six-pack, and we hurried back to the camp to share the frosty treasure.

There was a girl stuck at the camp for weeks because she'd hiked into the canyon with sandals instead of proper hiking shoes. She'd lost two toenails, and her feet were damaged. She told us she couldn't hike back up until they healed. I figured she'd probably have to be taken out by helicopter.

We were sitting around the campfire, and Rusty, the guy who seemed to be the leader of the group, said, "There are Indian villages in remote parts of the canyon that most people don't even know about. Over the summer I've seen Indians ride out on horses and mules, and return with supplies. When you guys hike back out of the canyon, I'll hike out with you. We need supplies for the camp."

"When is the best time?" I asked.

"In this heat? Best time to walk out is late afternoon as the sun is setting. We'll bring lanterns for the rest of the trip up in the dark."

This was a brilliant idea, since on the day we hiked out of the canyon the temperature was 114 degrees.

After a light supper on the day we decided to leave, we began our hike out of the canyon in late afternoon. It quickly went to dusk and soon was dark. The lanterns worked well. I got the shakes a few times and thought I would pass out, but I didn't. We got as far up as the Santa Maria Springs which had a shelter. We camped on that plateau for the night. Early the next morning, we continued and beat the sun up to the top. The Grand Canyon was incredible, but I could never do it again.

We hiked out of the canyon with Maya and Crow, a couple we met at the base camp. They Mentioned having a cabin in the woods in Flagstaff, Arizona, and invited us to spend some time with them. The four of us said our goodbyes to Rusty and headed to the highway. We put our thumbs out and hitchhiked to Flagstaff.

Their cabin was outside of town, nestled in the mountains, surrounded by pine trees. It had a wood-burning stove and electricity but no running water. Crow told us we could take showers at their friend's house down the road.

After supper I took a walk to their friend's house for a badly needed shower. Walking back to the cabin the sky turned dark. I could tell there was a storm brewing, so I quickened my step. I came across a girl riding a horse. She gave me a ride back to the cabin. That was the first time I'd ridden bareback on a horse. It was the most remarkable sensation.

We had to find a way back to New York, so I went into Flagstaff with Maya to find a car rental agency. I was able to reserve a car out of Phoenix for our trip home. Maya took me to a local supermarket. She seemed to know how to work the system there pretty well. She had me wait in the car. She soon returned with a large box filled with groceries they'd given her for free. I used some of the ingredients to make a lentil soup for dinner.

We were hit with a thunderstorm and lost electricity. Crow lit a storm lamp, and we sat around the wood-burning stove, played music and told stories while lightning and thunder shook the cabin.

It was over one hundred degrees when Maya and Crow dropped us off at the car rental agency in Phoenix. We hugged and said our goodbyes, thanking them for putting us up. Troy and I found a place to have lunch, and then headed out on the highway back to New York City.

That night we slept at a rest stop where two wild donkeys hung around our car. I imagined people fed them on a regular basis. We gave them apples. We passed some beautiful areas through Arizona, and strange land formations in Utah. We stopped at a Lookout over Navajo Lake when the car overheated.

I was feeling distant from Troy but didn't want to get into it until I had some time to think about my feelings. Looking back, staying busy that summer might have been a way to avoid dealing with the problems in our relationship. We arrived back in New York City in no time.

In the middle of August a friend told us about a string of lakes in Nova Scotia. We embarked on a short trip with Troy's friend Harry and his dog, Sydney, a rather large Newfoundland. We drove to Bar Harbor, Maine, and took a ferry to Yarmouth, Nova Scotia. We waited for quite a long time to drive onto the ferry. I observed a freighter leaving port after it loaded its cargo. It passed under a bridge, through the harbor gates, and out to the open sea. The scene sparked a daydream.

I remarked, "I'd like to be on that ship going somewhere, to some far-off place strange and different."

Troy and Harry stared at me but didn't say anything.

"Let the salty air blow my thoughts clean," I said. "We'd bob around for days, weeks, maybe even months, drifting timelessly somewhere under the sun and moon."

"That's weird," Troy said. "You're strange sometimes!"

I didn't answer. What was the point?

Our ride was turbulent, and the ferry bobbed around like a cork in the middle of the ocean. Troy and Harry spent the whole three hours chucking their guts up in the bathroom below deck, while I fooled around with the slot machines in the casino room.

A lighthouse keeper in Yarmouth Nova Scotia gave us directions to a great place to camp, which we found easily. We camped in a perfect spot at the edge of one of the lakes. There were bushes of blueberries, as well as wapato, an edible aquatic plant, growing in the reeds in shallow water. We swam nude, ate fresh-caught fish, and told stories around the campfire. There was an incident with a black bear, but Sydney's barking scared him off. We spent two glorious weeks there and never saw another person, well, except for that one day a guy motored past us in his boat. He waved at us, and we waved back.

Leaving Canada, we stopped at a tavern for refreshments. The three of us sat at the bar and ordered beers. The bartender ignored me and served Troy and Harry. He said, "Miss, if you want to be served you'll have to sit at a table. We do not serve women at the bar."

I was shocked and threw a fit. "If I can't have a damn beer here at the bar, I don't want one." I stormed out, expecting Troy and Harry to follow me.

But no, they stayed in the tavern and drank their beers. I sat in Harry's car, pissed off, with Sydney drooling all over the back seat.

The guys were snickering, but I didn't say much on the drive back to

New York City. I flashed on an excerpt from a Victorian saga I'd read "Mrs. Satin," by Johanna Johnson;

> Victoria and Tennessee walked into Delmonico's on Fourteenth Street by themselves and seated themselves at a table. The flustered waiter reminded them of the ruling. They asked to see their friend, the owner. But he too, though he admired the sisters and valued their patronage, was firm. Ladies alone could not be served at this hour. Brushing aside his apologies, Tennie Rose went to the door, opened it and waved to the cab man who was waiting for them in the carriage outside. "Come down off your box and come in here" she called. When the red-faced and embarrassed cab man was finally pushed in with his knees under the tablecloth, Tennie ordered "Tomato soup for three"

As we drove over the Verrazano Narrows Bridge into Staten Island, I was feeling ambivalent about being back at the Hilltop Avenue house after being gone all summer. I wondered if things had changed, or even worse, if things were the same. I hadn't been happy with the living situation for a while, but didn't want to break with the commune. As we pulled up to the house on the hill, my attention turned to my cat Sabrina—I couldn't wait to hug her.

In early fall Ross Grant was hanging out at the house on the hill. We were sitting in the kitchen listening to Jade talk about the IRA and the ongoing conflict in Ireland. After being gone all summer, I was out of the political loop.

When Jade left the room, Ross said in hushed tones, "I heard about an old Victorian for rent on Waverly Street. It's not far from here."

I nodded. "I'm definitely interested."

Even though I loved everyone, I was fed up with the gay-versus-straight politics, and was open to the idea of living somewhere else.

"Come on," Ross said. "I'll take you to see the house."

As soon as we walked through the front door I liked it. It had that early 1900s feel.

Ross said, "There's something special about the place, but I don't want to sway your decision."

"I don't know what the hell you're talking about," I said.

There was no front porch; rather, it was a front stoop. Off to the right of the steps there were rose bushes under a large bay window. The kitchen was in the back, which opened to a yard where I pictured growing herbs and tomatoes.

There were enough rooms for all of us and any significant others. Whitney Kennedy, who was in some of my Women's Studies classes, wanted to live with us. Whitney was a very tall, pretty redhead, with a great sense of humor. She was romantically involved with Troy's friend Harry. Then there was Marty Feinstein, Ross's friend, who was part of the Yellow House commune toward the end of that magical summer. His wife divorced him and took the basset hound with her. Crystal left Ross and moved back to California after we returned from South America, so he was single again. It all moved along like Siddhartha's river, ever flowing and changing, but still the same river.

We moved into the Waverly Street house, and I was relieved not to be living with discord—not yet anyway. Since Troy and I were the only couple we picked the front master bedroom on the second floor. It was a large room with a bay window. The Victorian was perfect—or so I thought.

There was something weird about the house, but I couldn't put my finger on it. The very first night we stayed in the house, Troy and I went upstairs to our bedroom, closed the door, and finally had some decent sex. I was so tired from moving and unpacking that I fell asleep soon after. I woke up during the night feeling very cold and tugged at the covers thinking Troy had them. I soon realized that I was covered, yet the bedroom was very cold—unnaturally cold. I sat up and touched my face which was as cold as a tray of ice cubes.

I woke Troy. "Do you feel that?" I asked.

"Feel what?"

"How cold it is in here."

Troy sat up and was still for a moment. Then he said, "Yeah, freaky cold; it's totally weird!"

I tried not to dwell on it, but I had my suspicions.

There was a large ornately carved table in the dining room that came with the house. It was not unlike a table one would see in the great hall of a castle. We were all playing cards when I heard someone in the kitchen going through the silverware drawer; then the sound stopped.

I said to Ross, "Did you hear that?"

"Hear what?" He got up and walked into the kitchen and yelled back, "I don't see anything."

"Maybe there was a mouse walking through the silverware drawer," I said.

Ross looked at me sheepishly, and quickly changed the subject. "Suki is on her way from California to stay with us for a while."

I was surprised at how quickly and easily Crystal was being replaced with his former paramour, Suki. Then again, I was happy that my Virgo sister was coming to stay with us.

On Saturday afternoon the guys were at the pool hall down the street. A national pool tournament was going on, and there were pool sharks competing from all over the country. Whitney was at the university, and I was alone in the house. I was sitting in the living room by the bay window reading when the sky began to darken, and I knew rain was coming. I walked up the stairs to see if I'd left our bedroom windows open. As I was walking up the staircase someone grabbed my arm. I turned around with a start, but there was no one there. I ran up the stairs to close any open windows, grabbed my jacket and got the hell out of there.

I walked down the street and into the crowded pool hall. I spotted the guys at a pool table and ran over to tell them what had just happened.

Ross said, "That's what I didn't want to tell you—the house has a ghost! I didn't say anything because I was afraid you wouldn't want to rent the house."

"Well, I know now, don't I?"

Ross laughed with a devious expression on his face.

Whitney Kennedy went to the Staten Island Hall of Records to search for some history about the Victorian. She found an article in an old newspaper about a murder that was committed in the house. It was headlined as a terrible tragedy. Whitney got a copy of the article, which she read to us at the dinner table that evening. "A mother was murdered by her son in the front upstairs bedroom," she read—the very bedroom Troy and I had chosen to sleep in.

"Yikes," I said, "That's really heavy."

We thought we'd look in the basement for clues, but there was a padlock on the door. We finally found the right key on the key ring we were given when we rented the house. We walked down the steps into darkness with a flashlight until we found the light switch, and snooped around for anything of interest. Oddly enough, we found old photographs; one photo in particular we imagined was the son. We also found surgical instruments, all very weird and creepy. When we were satisfied that there was nothing else to make sense of down there, we walked up the stairs, shut the basement door, and locked it with the padlock.

We discussed the situation over supper that night. We took the man's photo we'd found in the basement, and stood it up on the mantel of the fireplace. We wanted to convey the message that we were aware of him and meant him no harm. We were hoping he would give us a sign—maybe by moving the photograph. Looking back, I am not sure why we assumed the ghost was a man.

That night after we had all gone to bed we were woken from a dead sleep by furious pounding and tugging on the cellar door. One by one, we came out of our rooms and peered over the bannister, down the staircase toward the cellar. We all were terrified, and none of us had the guts to go downstairs. We locked ourselves in our bedrooms and waited until morning. Before breakfast we checked the basement door, which was still locked with the padlock. We figured that the ghost was disturbed about our having moved personal items around in the basement.

Days went by and the photo was still on the mantel just as we'd left it. I called my mother in the Bronx and told her the story, who in turn relayed it to my father.

She said, "Your father says to stand a crucifix on the mantel where the photo is."

I stood a crucifix inside of a wine glass, and placed it on the mantel next to the photograph. Oddly enough, the ghost never bothered us again.

We had some crazy Friday-night poker games. Everyone came to the Waverly Street house to play cards. There were so many people that sometimes the dealer and the two people to the right of the dealer had to stay out of each round. The poker games often went on all night with a steady supply of cocaine.

We loved Judd Thatcher, but he was the worst sore loser. If he won he was all smiles, but if he lost there was no reasoning with him. I lost count of how many times he stormed out pissed off as if the games were rigged, and we had it all planned to steal his money. Of course, he was always back the following Friday.

One Friday night Judd showed up with his jaw broken and his head swollen and purple. It was easy to see, because the top of his head was bald, with straggly blond hair at the base. He had mouthed off to a woman who was cleaning the tables in the university cafeteria. Later that day her husband and four sons were waiting outside for him. They worked Judd over pretty good. His jaw was wired shut and he had to drink through a straw.

That night the card game went on till the wee hours of the morning. I gazed at the bay window and it was getting light. Troy was winning, but a number of people had already gone home. Marty Feinstein threw his cards down, leaned back in his chair and said, "I'm out. I think I've lost enough for one night!"

Ross asked, "I know it's early, but do you think the bagel factory is open?"

Whitney said, "Hot bagels with butter and cream cheese sounds really good right now."

"I won big tonight so I'll buy," Troy said.

"I'll fly if you buy," Marty said.

Troy and Marty left the table and headed out the door.

There was a very small attic room at the top of the Victorian which I converted into a darkroom. I had tons of black-and-white negatives that I'd carried around for years. Imagine my joy as the negatives came to life on the photo paper as I dropped them in the developing bath. There were some beautiful shots of people that I'd forgotten I'd taken. I would gasp, sometimes laugh, and sometimes cry, as the images appeared. The darkroom was a creative saving grace for me during that period.

> Photography is a way of feeling, of touching, of loving. What you have caught on film is captured forever. It remembers little things, long after you have forgotten everything ~ Aaron Siskind ~ American photographer

It was after New Year's in 1973 that Troy and I stopped having sex. We began sleeping separately, hoping that it might ease us into a different relationship. We liked and loved each other, but that intimate part of our relationship had faded—it had never been that intense to begin with. It was a strange time; we were more like friends than lovers. I guess you'd say we were comfortable with each other.

I continued with my Women's Studies classes at the university and was happy to hear that the US Supreme Court overturned the states' bans on abortions in *Roe v. Wade*, maintaining a woman's right over her own body. I was sitting in the cafeteria reading one of the reference books on my suggestion list:

> It is clear that women have had few, if any rights under the law. Most women throughout history being considered appendages of their husbands. According to historical doctrine, the women lost their legal existence upon marriage. She not only lost her name, but also the right to sue, sign a contract, or manage her property. —Ann Garfinkle and Carol Lefcourt, **Women's Servitude Under Law**

On TV that night, the news was all about the Senate hearings on the Watergate scandal. A lot was happening in the world. Most of the talk in the hallways of the university was about the United States ending its involvement in Vietnam, with Nixon signing the Paris Peace Accords.

Wandering through the halls of the university that week, I passed an art class. Through the open door the scent of turpentine and paint wafted into the hallway taking me back to the art school I'd attended in San Francisco. I thought of my love for Romeo, and felt a pang of sorrow and regret at the way we ended. I remembered how my artistic inspiration was crushed when I decided to leave Romeo and California. For some reason I began having strong flashbacks of Romeo and our summer of love in that old yellow farmhouse. How in love I was with him; how well we fit together.

A few weeks later Adam Hirschfeld called from the Hilltop Avenue house to tell me that Matthew Romeola, a.k.a. Romeo, had telephoned from California and was coming for a visit. I can't explain the feeling that came over me. Troy knew about Romeo. I'd told him the whole sordid tale about the fiasco in California, and how I'd left there a broken woman.

The very next week we got word that Romeo was on his way over, so we all walked to the house on the hill. We sat on the floor around the low coffee table in the living room waiting for him to show up. It had been about a year and a half since I'd seen him, and I wondered how I was going to feel. I heard that he and his new girlfriend, Jenna Maplewood, had just gotten back from a trip to South America. I imagined there were some tales to tell.

Suddenly there he was walking into the room. We all stood up. He looked at me, and when I saw his face I wanted to die. I knew right then and there that I was never really in love with Troy Bloom. We all hugged and kissed, and it was all so warm and fuzzy. He gave me a special lingering hug, even though Troy was standing next to me. Romeo and Troy checked each other out, the way guys do, stomping and digging their feet in the dirt and snorting. I was very uncomfortable when the two of them were talking.

Someone asked, "Where's Jenna?"

Romeo answered, "She's coming next week."

Great, another hurdle to get over—meeting Jenna Maplewood, I thought. *What the hell kind of a name is that anyway?*

Romeo was his usual upbeat and funny self, and I was smitten all over again. I thought of how everyone used to say we were so similar. Star said we were the male and female version of the same person. Maybe we were too much alike. Pretty soon we were all laughing at his funny gestures and stories, and I began to relax.

I was involved in a conversation with Adam, when through the chatter I heard Romeo yell, "Hey, Chica." My head snapped in his direction and I stared at him. I wanted to kill him, but just melted instead. *Oh, if he only knew what that did to me.*

We could hear the rain on the roof rushing off the skylight, and saw flashes of lightning in the sky. It was strange having Romeo around again, and it threw me for a loop. I was sneaking over to the Hilltop Avenue house to see him, and we made the most of the week before Jenna arrived. We made love in the attic room every chance we got. Perhaps it was making love inside of a memory. We reminisced about our summer of love in the Yellow House, and how we would listen to the rain against the roof, just like we were doing again.

It seemed so intense, and I tried to block what I was feeling. I kept wondering what made me still want this man who basically abandoned me and fucked me over. Why did I still love him and want him? It all seemed so crazy. I wondered what was going through Romeo's mind. What was he feeling? He seemed so into me and so loving. I didn't know. Maybe he didn't know either. It was strange how we connected as if we'd never been apart.

I knew this was only temporary. I knew that as quickly as Romeo appeared, that was how quickly he would disappear. I'd felt his presence before he even arrived, like a premonition. There we were again, lying together as we had done so many times before. I felt as if I'd been struck by lightning, and a bolt of love went straight to my heart.

Jenna Maplewood finally arrived. Her hair was all gray, and she was older than me. She was into health food, and talked about Romeo as if he were a potted plant. She described to us how she nurtured him, and it seemed motherly to me. She reeked of patchouli, which I'd loved when Adam used to wear it. She was a big woman, and insisted on referring to me as a "Little mama." She wore a nose ring and walked around with a joint dangling from her lips. Every sentence she spoke was animated.

I was so jealous of her that I could taste it because she had what I wanted. I was hanging out at the house on the hill a lot during those two weeks because Romeo was there. I'm sure Jenna picked up on it. A woman can sense these things. She was clever enough to let Romeo have his space. How does the saying go? "The only way to tame a bird is to let it fly!" It was true that I had left Romeo, but he abandoned me emotionally long before I left him in California. He probably hadn't the slightest idea about any of this, and I thought I would go mad. I kept telling myself he'd be gone in a few days—and in a few days he was gone.

It was the spring of 1973, and I was going on twenty-six years old. We were notified that the Victorian on Waverly Street was being sold out from under us. Some of the members of the original commune, mainly the gay contingent, purchased seventeen acres in northwestern New York State. They planned on building houses on the land. I didn't know what I wanted. They were keeping the Hilltop Avenue house as a city home, so staying there was always a possibility. I knew I couldn't live with Troy anymore.

Judd Thatcher and my friend Kelly Cooke were a couple now. They told me they knew of a house in the Hudson River Valley in Upstate New York that was coming up for rent. It was an old farmhouse on ninety-five acres of land, complete with an apple orchard, a stream, and a barn. They were planning on renting it, and wanted to know if I was interested in moving up there with them. Judd said it would be available in late June, and that we could be there just in time for the summer. Judd referred to it as Deer Creek.

SIXTEEN

A FORCE OF NATURE

Find a little bit of land somewhere, plant a carrot seed. Now sit down and watch it grow. When it is fully grown, pull it up and eat it!

—*Stephen Gaskin, self-proclaimed hippie and cofounder of "The Farm," on a formula for how to slow down*

The plan was to move to the old farmhouse in the Hudson River Valley in June, but for now, I was still at the Waverly Street house on Staten Island. Troy Bloom was there too, and it was awkward. He began sleeping in our room again, but we were not intimate anymore.

On the weekend, Judd took Kelly, Whitney, and me up to see the farmhouse. It was a long drive, but we enthusiastically discussed our plans all the way there.

My first impression driving along the Hudson River Valley, was that it resembled a Pieter Bruegel painting, with rolling hills, farms, cows, haystacks, and horses. We found the house—an old two-story federal-style; very austere, with no porches but lots of trees. I saw two chimneys, one on either side of the house. This meant that there likely were four fireplaces. We walked around the grounds. As far as the eye could see, the land on both sides of Deer Creek Road would belong to us. On the opposite side of the road was an old barn, but I didn't see any cows. We walked around the back of the house, and I could hear swift-running water. I walked down to a bridge over a fast-moving stream along the back of the property. I pictured myself swimming there in summer. Up on a hill beyond the stream was an apple orchard. There were still a few apple blossoms floating in the air on a light breeze, even though spring was nearly over. I knew there would be apples in the fall.

I noticed a small gated area with gravestones. Judd said, "Those are the graves of the Dutch immigrants who built this house in 1880. I guess they wanted to be buried on the land."

That was a little sinister, but I loved how the place reeked of history. Walking back to the house I noticed patches of wild blueberries and black raspberries, and thought of homemade jam. The kitchen had a fireplace with a Dutch oven on the side, neither of which seemed to be in working order. I was entranced by the place and took solace in the fact that soon we'd be living there.

Back on Staten Island, I was finishing my last semester at the university, and making as much money as I could at the market research company in Manhattan. I had no idea what type of work, if any, I'd be able to find upstate in the country. That spring, the weather was as hot as summer. We hung out outside on the stoop at the Waverly Street house with tall glasses of alcohol filled with lots of ice. All that was missing were men in white suits and women fanning themselves, and we'd have had the makings of a Tennessee Williams play. The smell of the rose bushes in the front of the house was sublime.

It was a Sunday afternoon when Amber and Kelly dropped by with some friends. They were women I met in my Women's studies classes. We had done a photo shoot the previous week, for which we dressed up as Native Americans and pioneer women. I developed the black-and-white photos in my darkroom.

PHOTO SHOOT, STATEN ISLAND, NY.

Walking up the steps behind Amber was a guy she introduced as Bobby Becker. As he sauntered up the steps I noticed he was wearing a pair of well-worn jeans, a thick brown leather belt, and a jeans jacket with no shirt. I thought, *that's interesting.*

Bobby was a British transplant going to our university, and I wondered how the hell I hadn't run into him before. I loved his English accent, and he had an infectious laugh that exposed dimples. I liked him in every way.

Amber sat down on the step next to me, and Bobby stood in front of us. Ross asked Bobby if he wanted a drink. He said, "Gin and tonic—Tanqueray if you have it." When Bobby reached for the drink Ross handed him, his jeans jacket opened revealing his smooth, hairless chest. He wore his dark frizzy hair in an Afro style, and had brown puppy dog eyes. I wasn't sure what his connection to Amber was, but I definitely planned on finding out when she and I were in class together. I sat on the front steps enjoying the afternoon sun, the smell of the roses, and feeling the intoxicating effect of the alcohol. It prompted me to write this poem:

> I could sit here soaking up the sun forever
> The roses too, all around me
> Feeling their red-velvet softness inside of me
> I will put rose oil all over me
> So I could be a rose in the garden

In class a few days later, I asked Amber about Bobby.

"You mean that crazy Bobby Becker?" Be careful, he gets around. He can't be tied down to any one woman."

Kelly told me the same thing that first day he came to the house with Amber. But I couldn't get Bobby out of my mind and hoped I'd see him again. I was walking down the hall to another class, when I heard someone call out, "Adriana!"—it was Bobby Becker.

There he was in that same jeans jacket, only he was wearing a shirt underneath. He said in that lovely English accent, "Hey, we should get together."

"I'd love that," I said. It was a very short conversation since we were both hurrying to classes.

He said, "I'll come by Waverly Street and pick you up on the weekend. We'll drive to the bay."

"Sounds good to me," I said.

We exchanged numbers.

Troy wanted me to feel things that I just didn't feel for him anymore—some things I'd never felt. He was saying things to me that he should have said a long time ago, so his words no longer mattered. I was looking forward to moving upstate and getting out of the city for a while.

From my journal:

> I thought about standing on top of a hill in a long skirt, walking along a country road, smelling the woods and farms. I want to run barefoot, shouting through a grassy field. I want to swim nude in a stream and feel the water rushing around me, with little fish nibbling at my toes. I want to be an animal again, part of the earth and run it through my fingers, smelling the dirt. I want to see the mountains breath at night, with trees swaying in the wind. I want to look up and see the sun through the forest. That's what I want.

Bobby came to pick me up on Saturday. He was driving an old green pickup truck and looked really hot behind the wheel. There was a large, scruffy dog in the back. Bobby said, "That's Ziggy." I gave the dog a pat on the head and jumped into the passenger seat. The plan was to drive to the water, and Staten Island had plenty of that. Bobby said that Ziggy needed a good run. We drove for a while, and talked the whole time. He was sweet, and his dimples, accent, and laughter were disarming. I wasn't nervous and conversation came easily. I felt as if I'd known him in another life, and it wasn't the first time I'd felt that way about someone.

We found a nice stretch of beach, and as soon as the truck came to a stop, Ziggy jumped out of the back and took off running. Bobby and I took our shoes off and walked along the sand. He said, "I came to this country from England to go to school, and to experience America." He probably was a few years younger than me, because I had returned to finish my second two years of college after a break to experience the real world.

He said, "You told me you have your own darkroom. That's cool; I dig that."

"I can get lost in there for hours."

"You seem to be an independent woman. Most of the women I know back in England are a little more traditional."

I smiled but didn't say anything.

We found some interesting seashells along the beach and gathered them to take back with us. I felt the waves roll over my feet as we walked, and I let the water cleanse my soul. Walking along the beach my thoughts flew back to Santa Marta, when I'd first arrived in Colombia, South America, thousands of miles away. I remembered stopping at a local fish market where the fishermen were selling the fish and clams they had just fished from the ocean. In contrast, on Staten Island, there was the skyline of New York City, with overpasses and bridges on the horizon.

On the drive back to Waverly Street Bobby said, "I want to see more of you."

I smiled. "I was hoping you would."

Bobby was a force of nature who came into my life at the perfect time. I felt starved for love and affection. I don't mean the surface kind; I mean the deep, meaningful kind—a mingling of souls. Throughout my life I'd always had the feeling that there was a master plan somewhere. I felt as if I was sharing feelings and experiences with certain people—people who were special because they were meant for me, and I was meant for them. Bobby and I had not been intimate, but I wondered when that would happen—because I knew it would.

On Sunday Bobby Becker called to say he was on his way over. When I saw his green truck pull up to the house I ran outside and jumped in. He was wearing a bandana in an attempt to tame his wild hair; sort of a Jimi Hendrix look.

He said, "I know of a pond where we can go skinny-dipping."

It was a really hot afternoon, and beads of sweat rolled down the side of his face. He had to feed Ziggy and water his plants, so we stopped at his house. I found it very homey for a guy's house. He lived alone in the small apartment of a private home. There was a nice porch at the front entrance covered by trees and shrubs, which gave it a secluded feeling. He sat on the couch and rolled two joints to take with us. I took a quick peek in his bedroom and saw a double bed. He caught me but looked away.

The pond he'd mentioned was in a very out-of-the-way place, down a dirt road.

I said, "I'm a little reluctant to take my clothes off."

"Bobby laughed, "Don't worry; no one ever comes here." He fired up a joint, took a toke, and passed it to me.

We undressed and jumped in. The cool water gave me a rush. For some reason I felt a little shy, but Bobby swam over to me and put his arms around me. We bobbed in the water, our bodies close together—close enough that I could feel every bit of him, and he could feel every bit of me. He looked in my eyes and gently kissed me on my lips, parting them. I could tell he wanted to do more, but he said, "Let's go back to my place."

We dried off and walked back to the truck. He took my hand and caressed my fingers during the ride back. We stopped at a small roadside restaurant for beer and raw oysters. I wasn't fond of oysters, but I gagged a couple down.

When we arrived at his place it was still steamy, even though it was getting dark. He said, "Sit on the porch. I'll go make us Tanqueray and tonics." (Bobby Becker is the one who got me into Tanqueray and tonic, which is still my favorite cocktail.)

We sat there leisurely on the porch chairs, and, somehow, I didn't feel the need to talk. I listened to the locusts buzzing in the trees and prayed for a breeze.

"You can't escape from the heat on still nights like this," he said.

"Yeah, the clouds are just hanging with moisture. Damn, I wish the rain would just come down and cool everything off," I said.

He turned to me. "I know how I can cool you off." He sauntered over to my chair, bent down, and kissed me on the lips. I put my arms around his neck, which was still damp from the pond. The sweetness of his smell intoxicated me—well, there was also the gin.

He said, "Let's go inside." He walked me to his bedroom. We embraced, kissed and began getting undressed. I lay down on the bed, and he lay on top of me. He was a little wild in bed, not exactly rough, but all over the place. It was different, but I liked it.

Afterward, he said, "Don't go home tonight."

I smiled and kissed him.

During the night we made love again. He pulled me close and put his arm over my chest. I felt safe with Bobby. He made me feel warm all over, and as soft as crushed velvet.

The next day was Monday, and I had no classes but Bobby had to work at the plant nursery. He dropped me off at the Waverly Street house, and we gazed at each other as he drove away. Troy saw me come in but didn't say anything, and I felt a tinge of guilt. Over the next few days, all I could think about was Bobby Becker.

There was a movie in town that Bobby wanted to see, *Last Tango in Paris*, with Marlon Brando, and he suggested we see it together. When he came by the house to pick me up, the guys all gave me a funny look. I didn't care; I just floated out the front door and down the steps, jumped in the truck, and off we went. We both loved the movie, and we discussed it at length at his place that night. I wanted to get drunk, but Bobby had something else in mind. After he made us Tanqueray and tonics, he took out a tiny plastic bag and dumped the contents onto a mirror. I watched him chop the white powder and divide it into neat little lines.

I stroked his leg, which he really liked, because he gasped. Bobby said, "That Brando—he's really something!"

"I know, I related to Brando much more than I related to Maria Schneider's character. To me, he seemed so real, and she seemed so bubbly and empty-headed."

"Yeah, when he told her about the pettiness of looking for security in another person," Bobby said.

"And the way he didn't want to know her name or anything about her. That the two of them should just be in that time and space, without knowing anything else. I didn't understand why she was there, or why she went back again and again."

Bobby took another swig of his Tanqueray and tonic. He said, "I loved the way Brando told her that the only place she'd get good lovin was in that room, in his bed. Then Bobby turned to me and said, "Just like you're gonna get right here in my bed tonight."

The way he looked at me sent a thrill through my body, and I took another sip of gin to calm down.

We were wide awake on liquor and coke, so not much sleep would happen that night. Bobby had an old-fashioned claw-foot bathtub. He said, "Let's take a bath."

I thought of the scene in the movie when Brando washes Schneider in the tub with such tenderness, as if she were a child.

Bobby ran the water and went looking for candles, leaving me sitting on the edge of the tub, nude. It seemed very romantic, a bath by candlelight. I thought it might have something to do with his being British. I didn't know any American guys who ever wanted to do that sort of thing. We hung out talking in the bath for a long time with the candles burning. Eventually, we dried off and walked to his bedroom. He lay me down on the bed, got on top of me, and pushed my legs open with his. We made really sensual love.

Suddenly, he stopped and said, "Hear that?"

I could hear heavy rain beating down on the roof of the house, and I didn't know which was more thrilling—Bobby Becker or the sound of the rain. Finally, there was a release from the heat in more ways than one.

During the week I ran into Amber in class, and she questioned me about Bobby. She seemed jealous, and I got the impression that maybe they had a thing at one time; maybe still did. Kelly's words—that Bobby slept around—reverberated in my head, and I didn't want to get too attached to him. I also knew that I'd be moving soon. I hoped Bobby would come to Deer Creek to visit me, but I had no way of knowing if he would. Maybe Bobby Becker was just what I needed in that moment in time, and I should just enjoy the time we had together, like in *Last Tango in Paris*.

I spent a lot of time in my darkroom when I was at home. It was a refuge from the reality around me. Our move to the Hudson River Valley was coming up in a month, so I began putting things aside to take to the new house. I was leaving Troy Bloom all the furniture we'd collected together. The farmhouse had some furniture, and I wanted to start fresh.

I heard a knock at the door. I peeped through the lace curtains at the bay window and saw Bobby Becker. When I opened the door he handed me a bunch of violets and lilies of the valley that were hidden behind his back. He presented the bouquet like a magician with a magic trick. "I picked these from the garden behind the nursery where I work."

"I love them," I said.

Bobby always put a smile on my face. I was alone in the house, so after I put the flowers in water, I took Bobby up to my darkroom to show him the photos I was working on. I got the contact sheets out, and we looked them over with a magnifying glass. He liked the two photos I'd taken of him.

The American photographer, Berenice Abbott, said, "Photography can only represent the present. Once photographed, the subject becomes part of the past."

I didn't feel that way about photographs!

"I want to remember you always," I said. "You don't mind, do you?"

Bobby shook his head. I actually think he was flattered.

"You're the most real person I know," he remarked.

I smiled rolling my eyes. I wanted him to know that whatever happened with us when I moved upstate, it was okay. I wanted to tell him how happy and alive he made me feel when I really needed someone like him in my life, but I didn't say anything.

We went up to my bedroom and made love. I prayed that Troy wouldn't come home early from work. Whatever issues Troy and I had between us, I still loved him and wouldn't want to hurt him. Of course in reality, it was a little late for that! After we were finished, I took Bobby to the backyard off the kitchen. There still was some shade out there, and we hung out for a while. We spent the day together, and then walked to the University for Test Results, as it was the end of the semester.

When Bobby dropped me off at the Waverly Street house, everyone was already home and discussing dinner.

Troy came flying down the stairs glaring at me. "What the hell happened in our room?"

I glanced at Whitney, who had a big grin on her face. "I was packing and throwing stuff around," I answered. The truth was that Bobby Becker always wrecked the room when we made love.

In the weeks to come I felt Bobby pulling away from me, but I didn't know why. There was a change in his behavior. We continued seeing each other, but it wasn't every night. It was almost the end of June, and I wondered if his distancing himself had something to do with me moving upstate. Maybe he needed to break the close attachment we'd developed. I wanted it to continue, but maybe it wasn't going to work for him. Not everyone can deal with a long-distance relationship. I chose not to confront him about it because I wanted us to part on good terms.

I said goodbye to Bobby Becker outside on the steps of one of the university buildings, because I didn't want it to be in an intimate setting, heavy and emotional.

He kissed and hugged me. "I'll miss you, but I promise to come up to Deer Creek to visit."

When I got home, I wrote this poem in my journal:

I have to let it flow
I have to let you go
To where you want to be
Like a bird, I set you free
You are beauty, you are life, if only for a little while
I saw you today, maybe for the last time
I'll never forget your face
You'll always be part of me

It was the end of June, and we were already living upstate at Deer Creek in the Hudson River Valley. I consulted the I Ching and threw the three Chinese coins. The hexagram that resulted was "Grace."

The house and our land was so much more than I had imagined. Kelly Cooke and I turned the earth for a garden behind the kitchen, with the generous help of Marty Feinstein. We added cow shit from the farmer who rented part of the land from the owner. I sat in the dirt and ran my fingers through it. I watched Kelly shoveling bare-breasted., and was in hog heaven!

Big Thunder Wabanaki, Algonquin

"The Great Spirit is in all things. He is in the air we breathe. The Great Spirit is our father, but the earth is our mother. She nourishes us….That which we put into the ground she returns to us."

Earlier that day, Kelly and I walked through the apple orchard, up to the top of the hill. We picked some fresh spearmint, with the intention of drying the leaves for tea. Later on, we walked across the road to the old barn, which was deserted. There were old chicken coops but no chickens. I saw wildflowers everywhere. I stared at the old barn door, inspecting it with intense interest, and had a creative brain surge. I wanted it as the headboard for my bed. I just had to figure out how to get it loose, across the road, and up to my bedroom on the second floor.

There must have been a shortage of women in the valley because a plethora of men, who were hanging around Deer Creek, were interested in me. I had no sexual interest in any of them. I did make use of the situation though. I asked a couple of the guys to help me unleash the barn door across the road and haul it up to my bedroom. Geordie, one of our neighbors, and a couple of his friends offered to help. I had that barn door behind my bed in no time. I adorned the nooks and crannies of the door with dried wildflowers, photos, and candles. It was quite a spectacle. Everyone was amazed at my barn-door headboard.

I remained devoid of feelings of tenderness toward anyone, and remained suspended in an emotional limbo. There was so much love lost in my young life, that I became afraid to feel anything. Every time I got close to a man and thought he was the one, or that things were getting serious, it would trigger something in me to change. As a child I felt abandoned when my father moved out and got his own apartment. Looking back, I think I sabotaged my romantic relationships with men, figuring they were going to leave me anyway. Even if things were going well, an inevitable end always plagued my thoughts.

I was working in the garden with Kelly and watching Whitney build a doghouse. Kelly had the family dog. Her parents figured he'd be happier with us in the country. Afterward, the three of us went swimming in the stream behind the house. When we got back, Jeremiah Murphy and his girlfriend, Daisy Holmes, were sitting in the kitchen. Daisy Holmes was much younger than Jeremiah, but they seemed well suited for each other. We made a salad for lunch with greens from the garden. We hung out and talked in the living room for hours, waiting for Judd to get home from his daily chores at a neighbor's farm. It was a typical summer day at Deer Creek.

On an ordinary morning I came down to the kitchen to make coffee. Even though I was still half asleep, I felt something was amiss. I sat at the kitchen table listening to the coffee percolate. I glanced out the window. Staring back at me was a big cow's head. *What the hell?* I looked outside, and there were cows all over the yard. I yelled up the stairs for everyone to come down.

Judd said, "I'll call the farmer and let him know that his cows got loose and are all over the place. Don't go outside because there's a bull out there watching us."

Not too long after the phone call, the farmer and his son drove up and rounded up the cows. The farmer said, "These cows are very young, about a year and a half. I found a few of them hiding in the old barn across the road. They seemed frightened and couldn't figure out how to get out. I don't understand what happened to the old barn door; it's gone." I didn't say anything, but everyone turned to stare at me.

In the dining room off the kitchen was a large wooden picnic table, which we named the Beggar's Banquet table. Kelly and I sanded and varnished it, and we were building two benches to go on either side. We were learning some carpentry from Daisy and Jeremiah who built their own cabin. It was the first time I'd used an electric hand saw. It was a powerful feeling. The aura around what is men's work seemed to dissolve in the buzz of the electric saw.

Every Thursday night, there was an auction in a barn not far from us.

It was the social event of the week, where you got to meet your neighbors. Whitney made friends with a woman at the auction named Meredith, who invited us to come see her stables and horses— these stables were more like suburban houses. There were a few horses neatly housed in their personal stalls. They all looked well cared for, and were waiting for pets and treats. Her horse was named Glory. We watched Meredith groom her and tend her hooves. She spoke to Glory softly, making a fuss over her. Glory was going to the blacksmith's in a few days, and Meredith asked us to tag along. I couldn't pass that up.

The blacksmith knew everything there was to know about horses. He seemed to be someone from another time and space. His eyes sparkled from the fire as he put Glory's horseshoe into the coals. I watched him doctor Glory's hoof and re-shoe her. He handled Glory like a dream. The setting was totally foreign to me, yet it felt familiar, as if I had been around it at some point in my past. Another life perhaps?

Whitney and I decided to hitchhike to Cape Cod to spend a week over the Fourth of July in that quaint resort of Provincetown, Massachusetts. Hitchhiking was strange at the beginning. We weren't sure which rides to take and which ones to turn down, but we made it to the Cape in three rides. The first ride was with a guy in a pickup, who told us he was working the Fourth of July weekend for big bucks. He took us pretty far. The second ride was with a sheriff, who took us all the way to Worcester. I had the impression he didn't like the idea of two young women hitchhiking alone, and he warned us about the crazies out there on the highway. It wasn't long after he dropped us off that we got our final ride with a woman in a VW bus.

Whitney Kennedy had friends at the Cape who offered to put us up for the week. As soon as we got there, we threw our packs down and hit Provincetown, drinking in all the bars. We were having a blast, as Peggy Lee sang "Old Cape Cod" on the jukebox. One of the guys who lived at the house we were staying in, George, was a great guitar player. He had a twelve-string that he let me fool around with. I'd listen to George play his guitar while I recorded thoughts in my journal.

George said, "I have a friend who constructed a tower of old barn wood and glass. I'll take you girls to see it." He fetched a pencil and drew a picture of it in my journal.

TOWER OF BARN WOOD AND GLASS

We went to see the tower, and I loved the concept. It was constructed around a large tree, and was surprisingly spacious inside. I imagined myself living in the tower, and creating an art studio at the very top under the glass dome. It would be perfect for painting and drawing.

George's friend claimed he was half Native American and half Italian. He took a liking to Whitney, with her tall, thin frame and red hair. After a day at the beach playing on the sand dunes, the four of us went to a famous gay bar in Provincetown, the Back Room Bar. Mr. Gay himself, Queen of the Playhouse, sported whips and chains on the dance floor, fluttering his oversized fake eyelashes. We danced and drank well into the night.

Despite George's youth—he was only eighteen—he seemed really hip and cool. That night the four of us got stupid drunk and went to see the fireworks at midnight to usher in Independence Day. We staggered back to the house and collapsed in the living room. George played his twelve-string for a bit. At some point, he leaned over and whispered in my ear, "Let's go to my room."

I followed him, and it wasn't long before the alcohol I'd consumed washed any judgment right out of my head. I am sure he had no idea that I was twenty-seven, but I knew he was eighteen when he blew out the candle. I fell asleep to the sound of the bells chiming in the church tower at the end of the road.

When our week at the Cape was over, Whitney and I splurged and took the train back to Deer Creek. George and the Italian Indian drove us to the railroad station. The train went along the ocean for a while, past swampy deltas and tall grass, and then it flew through the Hudson River Valley. The porters on the train took a liking to us. They snuck us hot cornbread from the dining car, which we ate with lots of butter. The train went over bridges with rivers below. It was quite a scenic ride. We'd called the house at Deer Creek before we boarded the train, and Kelly was there to pick us up at the Hudson Train Station.

I was reading *The Good Medicine Book* by Adolf Hungry Wolf, all about life in harmony with nature. I jotted the following passage down in my journal:

> Go where you can see the crops that provide the food for your table. Go where you can wander for hours and think freely. Go where you can enjoy directly the fruits of your labor. Go and become what you think you are.

At the very end of July we went to a music festival, the Summer Jam at Watkins Glenn, New York. We parked the car in the town and planned to hitchhike to the Watkins Glen Grand Prix Raceway, where the music was happening. We walked along the streets in town and stopped in an ice-cream shop. We met a cool guy, Reed, who was also on his way to the festival. He was a little wild-looking with a bright-green bandana around his forehead, which held back his long hair. We sat down at a table, and Reed sat with us. I ordered a black-and-white ice-cream soda.

Reed said, "I've never heard of that before."

"Share mine!" I pointed one of the straws his way.

"Wow, I really like it," he said.

"Well, how can you go wrong with vanilla ice cream, chocolate syrup, and whipped cream?"

We all walked out of the ice-cream shop together. The traffic was backed up for miles, so we ended up walking to the Raceway Park. There were so many bands—the Grateful Dead, the Band, and many others. It was a totally crazy and chaotic scene. We heard on the radio that there were approximately six hundred thousand people in attendance, two hundred thousand more than attended Woodstock. There were two guys who parachuted into the festival, but one of them got tangled up in the trees and died. The idiot made it into the newspaper all right, in the obituary column!

It rained hard while one of the bands was on stage. There was no place to move, so we just stood there getting drenched. We walked down a hill with plastic garbage bags over our heads while the Allman Brothers were playing. There was an ocean of people, and at that moment, I was okay with having missed Woodstock.

Reed said, "Let's exchange phone numbers in case we lose each other." Luckily we did, because at some point I lost Reed in that sea of people, and never found that damn green bandana he told me he'd be waving.

Reed called during the week. He was sorry we lost each other in the crowd at Watkins Glen. He said he was coming to see me on the weekend. I gave him directions to Deer Creek and told him I looked forward to seeing him.

I was into stained glass, my newest artistic endeavor. I had a worktable set up in the tool shed off the side of the house. The room was perfect for crafts. I looked around for glass chips in secondhand shops, and any scraps or fragments I found on the streets in surrounding towns. Working on stained glass projects was very therapeutic. I was using the soldering iron on a stained glass sailboat, when I heard a car horn outside. It was Reed.

I ran outside to greet him and took his things inside. I gave him a tour of the house, then took him outside to show him the property. We went through the kitchen and out the back door. We walked to the bridge over the stream, and through the apple orchard. Reed whipped a joint out of his pocket. We sat on top of the hill smoking the joint and watched the sunset.

He seemed really affected by the place. He commented "Ya know, Deer Creek is like a little piece of all the places I've been to and dug, all wrapped into one plot of land."

We thought we saw some deer up on the hill—the deer loved our place—but on closer inspection, they were just shadows made by the shrubs in the mist.

Reed laughed and said, "That was some powerful weed!" Reed had long, kinky, brown hair and blue eyes. He told me his father was black, and his mother was white. His parents had met in Germany when his father was in the service. They moved back to the States when Reed was eleven.

After the sun set we walked back down to the house and hung out in the living room. Everyone liked him. I took him to the worktable in the tool shed, and showed him the stained glass sailboat I was working on.

"Now that's really cool," he said.

"I don't have much glass left, but I'm planning a trip into New York City soon to visit my family. I'm sure I can find glass there."

I told him to bring his things up to my room, and he smiled in anticipation. As we entered my room, he took one look at the barn door behind my bed and started laughing. I asked, "Don't you like it?"

"Yeah, it's really cool, but how did you get it up here?"

"It's a long story."

After we had sex, we stayed up all night talking about all the things we wanted to do with our lives. We never went to sleep, so we decided to watch the sunrise. We walked to the apple orchard out back, and the colors were golden as the sun rose over the barn. When we got back to the house, everyone was already seated at the Beggar's Banquet table eating breakfast. Kelly and Whitney smiled, but Judd rolled his eyes at me.

Judd asked Reed, "Are you hungry?"

"Yeah man."

"There's batter for pancakes in the kitchen, and a bowl of fresh black raspberries that were just picked out back."

"God, I love this place," Reed said.

"There's a bunch of people going swimming at the quarry today," Judd said. "Do you want to come along?"

"Hell to the yeah!" Reed answered.

Reed and I walked to the kitchen and made ourselves pancakes.

I said, "I'm trying to enjoy every moment of summer, because I know when winter comes, it's going to get really rough up here."

"Well, this is the country, so you can expect it to be really cold with lots of snow," he said.

"I was trying to put that thought out of my head."

We both laughed.

The water in the quarry was cold and crystal clear, and the bottom seemed fathomless. Our friends were already sunning themselves on large flat rocks when we got there. Reed was something to behold. He had the body of a mythical god, and the hair of a merman. I could tell he was a Leo by his crazy mane of hair. He seemed to be in heaven, and must have dived off those rocks fifty times. I sat on a rock watching him, admiring what I saw. Kelly and Whitney nick-named him Tarzan. Reed ate that up.

When we were back at Deer Creek, I went out to the garden to pick lettuce and tomatoes for a salad. After dinner, Reed and I walked up through the apple orchard to watch the sunset from the top of the hill. The sunset turned everything golden, as if in a dream. The farmer's cows were at the top of the hill. I was a little afraid, but Reed didn't flinch. We sat there for a while.

REED WITH COWS

He put his arm around me and said, "This place is awesome, and I really enjoyed being here with you."

He leaned in and kissed me, and I lay my head on his shoulder. He told me he was going to school in Germany in the fall. I wasn't planning on a big love affair, so I wasn't disappointed. I was happy for the time we'd spent together. We walked back to the house, Tarzan with his arm around me.

When Reed left after the weekend, Whitney asked, "Are you gonna miss Tarzan?"

"No. It was really nice, but it wasn't anything heavy."

It was August, and the summer was more than half gone. I was working in the garden when Kelly called out, "Adriana, you have mail." I saw a large box on the kitchen table. I looked at the return address; it was from Reed. I couldn't wait to open it.

The box was filled with pieces of colored glass of all sizes and shapes. There was a card inside that read: "I hate to see an artist without materials. Enjoy. Love, Tarzan."

Adriana Bardolino

SEVENTEN

WHEN WORLDS COLLIDE AT DEER CREEK

The *Farmers' Almanac* is an annual North American periodical that has been in continuous publication since 1818. It is time-tested and generation-approved and is a compendium of knowledge.

—*The Farmers' Almanac*

I was sitting in the kitchen at Deer Creek waiting for the soda bread to rise. Kelly was at the stove making preserves from the black raspberries we'd picked earlier that day. Whitney had gone up the hill to watch the sunset. I could hear the Rolling Stones singing "Angie" on the stereo in the living room, and the vodka I was sipping was unleashing my creative energy as I wrote in my journal. It had been a productive day. I'd made a batch of granola, fixed the ladder, watered all the indoor plants, worked in the garden, and did some yoga.

Judd Thatcher wasn't around. There was discord going on between Kelly and Judd. Hell, they got the upstairs bedroom with the working fireplace; wasn't that enough to save the romance in their relationship?

The summer had flown by, and it was the end of August. We found out something about corn. You have to plant a lot of it, row upon row, for it to pollinate and produce. I guess we didn't plant enough because all we got out of the corn crop was a measly four ears, one for each of us. But when I buttered it and took a bite, I said, "Now that's what corn should taste like." Everyone around the table laughed.

That week Nola and I walked through the woods behind the house totally nude. It was a strange sensation walking in our bare feet over leaves and past shrubs that brushed against our bodies. It was like a race memory of being tribeswomen who wandered away from their camp to scavenge for berries and ferns but got lost in the process. We stopped at the stream and went swimming. Nola was Jeremiah Murphy's ex-wife. They had a son together, Jules. Nola had a new, very young boyfriend, Tristan. It was crazy how Jeremiah and Nola divorced, and they both ended up choosing much younger partners. Tristin wanted to live with us at Deer Creek when Whitney Kennedy moved back to the city. I liked the idea; I thought it would change the dynamic of the household for the better. Besides, we'd see a lot more of Nola.

That night I wrote in my journal:

> Free and beautiful, my naked body wanders through the woods. My feet shuffle bare through the grass and leaves. The wind caresses every inch of me, and blows my tiny hairs and my mane. I feel like a wild animal. The sun touches my body softly, making it bronze, feeding me energy from above. My eyes look golden with my hair sun-bleached lighter. I am in harmony with Mother Earth.

My mother had called to let me know that my father was in the hospital. I needed to get to the Bronx as soon as possible. Kelly dropped me off at the train station in Hudson, which sometimes felt like the last stop on earth. The station was usually deserted, but there was an old woman standing on the platform. She looked like she'd probably taken that same trip thousands of times. We exchanged glances. The air was brisk, and the scene was bleak. So different from the warm bed I roused myself from earlier that morning.

The train into New York City flew through the Catskill Mountains and over the tracks along the Hudson River. I read, drew, or wrote in my journal, maybe even dozed off. My mind often wandered as I listened to the sound of the train wheels gliding over the tracks. I was thinking that no one in the valley interested me, and I felt lonely a lot of the time. I fell into a half state of sleep and dreamed about waking up next to Bobby Becker. He'd stir during the night and put his arm over my chest. He made me feel cared for and secure. I was missing him and wanting to feel him all around me. But catching Bobby was like Donovan's song "Catch the Wind."

When the train pulled into Penn Station, I hopped another train to the Bronx.

My father had minor surgery and was already home recovering. Things seemed weird between my parents; in fact, they were outwardly hostile to each other. They had always bickered, but this was downright brutal and painful to witness. It wasn't so much what they argued about; it was the cruel words they used.

Andre said, "I'll leave; you don't need me anymore!"

Vita answered, "Why don't you get sick and die?"

I'd heard that sort of thing all my life while growing up, and I knew it was a source of my unhappiness and insecurity. My mother wore the pants in our family; she supported us and often said, "If it was for your father, you wouldn't even have a pair of shoes." On occasion, my mother would call my father's barbershop, only to find out that he'd closed it and gone to the beach. I am sure my mother felt frustration and disappointment in his lack of ambition. It oozed out every so often in their arguments. I think she resented being the breadwinner of the family. She always said, "Adriana, make sure you have your own money in a separate bank account. Never depend on a man for anything. If you are not happy, you can walk out the door." I suppose it made me independent, but it also made me afraid to share and trust.

I arrived from upstate with a bad cold, and my father wanted me to put Vicks VapoRub on my chest. I said, "Dad, I don't use Vicks anymore; I use Tiger Balm."

To which he answered, "I'll put Vicks on your chest if I have to slap you around." He'd never spoken to me that way before. Maybe he was imagining me as a child, and putting Vicks on my chest was something he would do when I was sick. Maybe he felt I was out of his control, wishing that I was that little girl again.

My father only hit me once when I was a child, and the event is burned in my memory. My parents were going to an affair at a nightclub, and my father was at the bathroom sink shaving with a barber's straight razor. He swished the razor back and forth on a long leather strap to make it sharp. I was hanging around his feet wanting attention, pulling on his trouser legs, and making a pest of myself. He kept telling me to stop, but I wouldn't listen. My father lost his concentration, the razor slipped and cut his face. He was so angry he took that leather strap and wacked me hard with it a few times. I was shocked and sat there crying on the cold tile floor.

Then my father picked me up, hugged and kissed me, and said, "I'm sorry, my darling. Don't cry. Daddy's sorry. I didn't mean it. I love you so much."

At my parents' apartment I was feeling like I was that helpless child again. I wanted to run away, but all I could do was sit there listening to them yell at each other. I felt sorry for them and for myself. I was relieved that my father was recovering, and I wasn't staying long.

I was happy to return to Deer Creek in the country after spending a few days in the Bronx. The last days of August brought tribal splendor. The whole clan, all of our friends, spent the day at Gooseberry Farm. A waterfall fed into a stream forming a large body of water that became a small lake. It was the perfect swimming hole. It was a secluded place, so we all took our clothes off and went skinny-dipping. We lay out on the rocks worshipping the last days of summer. We made paint with spit and rocks and painted each other's bodies; we loved doing that.

Somehow I managed to lose the friendship ring that Romeo had given me during our summer of love. It drifted to the bottom. I dived down and searched for it, with no luck. I came out of the water upset, and looked for a blanket to lie down on. Two of the guys painted my body in a kind of ritual, as if to the goddess Isis. Maybe I imagined I was her. Lucas, one of the guys painting me was doing it in a way that was very sensual. I got up and waded into the water to wash the paint off, and he followed me in. The paint wouldn't come off so I dove underwater, and Lucas dove in after me. He met me head-on, under the surface, and planted a kiss right on my lips. It was like a scene from an old Esther Williams movie. I had a feeling he planned that. Something shimmery at the bottom caught my eye. I dived down to check it out, and it was my ring.

I burst through the surface of the water holding the ring, with my arm straight up in the air saying, "I guess the Isis ritual worked."

Lucas smiled at me, and we both laughed. His green eyes sparkled from the reflection of the water, and the droplets on his dark hair and beard danced in the sun. I put the ring back on my finger, and we walked out of the water together.

> Your clothes conceal much of your beauty, yet they hide
> not the unbeautiful. And though you seek in garments
> the freedom of privacy, you may find in them a harness

and a chain. Would that you could meet the sun and wind with more of your skin and less of your raiment. For the breath of life is in the sunlight and the hand of life is in the wind. Modesty is for a shield against the eye of the unclean. And when the unclean shall be no more, what were modesty but a fetter and fouling of the mind. And forget not that the earth delights to feel your bare feet, and the wind longs to play with your hair.
—Kahlil Gibran, *The Prophet*

In late afternoon the sky began to darken so we knew rain was coming. We quickly got dressed, gathered our belongings, and left Gooseberry Farm. I rode in the back of Lucas's pickup truck with Nola and a few others. We glided past farms, with cows chewing and horses playing, and—unlike the corn we planted—the corn we passed stood tall in a field and in multitude. The stormy gray sky with streaks of lightning in the distance gave everything an El Greco quality. The wind was a tempest in the back of the truck tossing our hair. By the time we reached Stillwell's Farm, where Judd worked, it began pouring rain. We jumped out of the back of the truck and ran to the barn, wet and shivering. We could feel the electricity of the storm as we watched the rain come down in waves. I peered out through the barn door at the horses standing motionless in the field, with the driving rain coming down on their backs. We helped Judd do his chores with the horses, feeding them oats and hay.

The sky must have been falling because Bobby Becker came to Deer Creek for the Labor Day weekend. We had a lot of people visit on that last official weekend of summer—Ross Grant, Suki Rosmond, and a few other friends from Staten Island. Ross was on his way to California with Suki, and was trying to convince me to come stay with them when they were settled. They were family to me, and I loved having them at the house, even if it was only for the weekend. I gave Suki, my Virgo sister, a shell necklace I'd made for her, and she loved it. I told them I'd seriously think about California.

Bobby Becker loved the barn door behind my bed and roared with laughter as soon as he saw it. He said, "That is really something. We'll rattle that thing as often as we can over the weekend. But how the hell did you get it up here?"

"It's a long story."

It had been nearly two months since I'd seen him, and it was all so delicious. We lay there holding each other in the dark, and I felt warm and plush like crushed velvet sleeping with Bobby's arm over my chest. I was totally okay with Bobby wrecking my room.

Before I knew it the weekend was over. Bobby went back to the city with no specific plan to return. He did mention that he looked forward to seeing me on Staten Island the next time I was in town. How strange it is when worlds collide. We are all, each one of us, like a miniature universe. These intricate networks get attracted, spin, and revolve around each other. We latch on like random molecules. Then, at some point we separate, and go hurtling through space again, alone—at least that was how I experienced it.

The Scarlet Letter by Nathaniel Hawthorne was required reading in the lower grades. Even though the book was written in 1850, women in the present day were still blamed as the source of infidelities—and with events that followed, I soon became much like the protagonist, Hester Prynne.

It was September 1973, and fall was in full swing. Out of all the men I met in that tight-knit rural community, Lucas Garzetti was the one who caught my attention. He was a big, strong guy, a carpenter, and a good friend of Judd's. He had been to our house many times; in fact, his truck was parked in our driveway on a regular basis. I never thought much about him until the day we all spent at Gooseberry Farm.

Lucas walked into the kitchen at Deer Creek. "I don't see Judd around. Can you give him a message?"

"I will," I said, "Hey do you want coffee?"

"Sure. I've been running errands all day long in my truck. I'm cold, and a cup of hot coffee sounds really good to me." He sat down at the kitchen table, and we had a nice chat.

I didn't know much about him, except that he built houses and was an all-around nice guy. I heard that he and his wife, Connie, were estranged, but I wasn't judging.

I said, "Lucas, I want to partition off an area of the tool shed to make a dark room."

"I can definitely help you with that."

A few days later, Lucas Garzetti showed up at Deer Creek with two-by-fours and sheets of plywood. When he saw the wood-burning stove in the tool shed he remarked, "You're definitely going to need that stove in the winter if you want to work in here."

I felt an instant connection to him, and we became friends. But it didn't stop there, because somewhere along the way our relationship escalated into something more.

Kelly took note of the way we were paying attention to each other and said, "Be careful, Lucas is still married to Connie. They just finished building a house, but they never moved in. I heard they're going through a rough patch. I think he's living at the new house, and Connie is still at the old house."

I paid no heed to Kelly's warning and looked forward to Lucas's visits. One day, when we were working on the partition for the darkroom, he reached for me and planted a kiss on my lips. I was a little stunned, but I liked it. As big and strong as Lucas was, he had a sensitive side. I didn't want my joy to become his wife's pain, but it just happened that way. We began showing up together at neighborhood gatherings, and shopping together in town. I rode around with him in his pickup, and people took note of me—not of Lucas, but of me. Everywhere I went in town, people stared at me as if I had a big scarlet letter A embroidered on my sweater. Well, I was the other woman.

Lucas and Connie had a two-year-old son, who regarded me with a wary eye, and I understood that. I wasn't his mother. I loved spending nights by the fireplace in the new house Lucas built. I had just finished a charcoal drawing of a Native American woman, which I framed and gave to Lucas as a housewarming gift. The new house was our hideaway. Although Lucas and I seemed good together, I had the image of an ending in the back of my mind.

CHARCOAL OF NATIVE AMERICAN WOMAN

Confessions of a Hippie   **241**

I discussed Lucas Garzetti with my father, of all people. "Adriana, married men always go back to their wives."

I figured my father was right, and that the affair would probably end that way, but I couldn't stop myself. There weren't any other men in the valley to whom I related on a deeper, meaningful level.

My parents came to Deer Creek for a weekend, the same weekend that Lucas fixed our chimney. Some of the bricks had caved and fallen down, and the fireplaces would not draw properly. It was the end of September, and before we knew it, winter would be upon us. The fireplaces had to work well because the house was not insulated. I was not aware that, by law, the top of a chimney had to be a certain distance from the peak of the roof for fire safety. Fortunately Lucas knew all about that stuff.

My mother got a big kick out of watching Lucas straddle the roof with bricks and cement to build up the chimney. The end result was that the fireplaces worked well that winter. My mother enjoyed taking Kelly's family dog for walks along the country road with me. She and I were making an effort to get closer, and mend fences from our past relationship.

The affair with Lucas went on for a while, until one morning, Lucas showed up at Deer Creek with his son in his arms and announced, "I left Connie."

A cold chill ran up my spine, and in that moment I realized it wasn't the end result I had expected or wanted. Lucas and Connie were high school sweethearts, and I figured that he'd never lived on his own. I thought he might be looking for me to fill her place so he wouldn't be alone.

I begged him, "Lucas, think about what you're doing. You need to live alone for a while before deciding to become a couple with me, or with anyone for that matter."

Lucas seemed surprised at my reaction. He stood there and stared at me blankly.

"Think things through. Figure out what you really want," I said. I felt that he was looking for security, and I was not the type to be someone's security blanket. Hell, I wasn't even secure within myself.

He continued to look disappointed at my reaction to his announcement and remained silent.

"Lucas, remember the first time we made a fire in the fireplace in your new house? You broke down crying, saying that it wasn't right, that you and Connie should be making the fire."

He looked at me, and for a moment I thought I was getting through to him. Their son was being shifted between the two of them, and I felt as if I was in the middle of a big mess. It was like lying on a bed of rusty nails, afraid to move one way or the other.

Without saying a word, Lucas turned and left me standing in the kitchen. He slammed the door and walked out to his truck carrying his son, and drove off.

It was Halloween, and there was a big party at Logan's Bar and Grill. I was nervous because Lucas's wife, Connie, was going to be there. I'd run into her a few times before, and it was always uncomfortable for both of us. How could it be any different, two women wanting the same man? But the night turned into a bit of magic.

As the night progressed, and we all got thoroughly liquored-up, our grievances seemed to dissolve away like a patch of snow in the afternoon sun. Connie and I began dancing together, and our friends surrounded us. Lucas stayed away, and let us do our thing. I looked over at Lucas—my friend, my lover—and he looked relieved. I hugged Connie, and she hugged me back. I hoped she realized that it wasn't me, but Lucas who was disloyal to her. There was a problem between them that had absolutely nothing to do with me. Perhaps I was a safe harbor for him while they were going through a change in their relationship.

Eventually, Lucas did get his own apartment in town, and the new house he built sat empty. On one of my visits to his apartment, I noticed partially burned candles on the dining room table. He confessed that he'd begun seeing Connie again, and they were trying to work things out.

Wow, I thought, *my father was right*. I was tired of the love triangle, and distanced myself from Lucas. Somehow through it all, he and I managed to remain friends.

This seemed like the perfect time to take a break and escape to the city. I needed money badly. The only work I'd been able to find in the valley was a wallpapering job with Daisy Holmes. With Daisy's carpentry skills and my fabric design experience, we successfully pulled it off. Doris, the woman whose house we wallpapered, was so pleased she paid us a little extra. We drove away in Jeremiah's truck counting the cash and laughing. But jobs like that were few and far between. I worked at the market research company in Manhattan, and stayed with my parents in the Bronx. While in the city I called Troy Bloom on Staten Island to see how he was doing.

We had a very civil, even friendly, conversation. He told me he was having some friends over for dinner on Friday night, and invited me. Against my better judgment I accepted. On the ferry ride to Staten Island I ran into a friend who took me to a neighborhood bar for a few drinks. I was feeling tipsy and called Bobby Becker and asked him to come to dinner with me. Troy was surprised to see me show up with Bobby. I looked around Troy's attic apartment, which had all of our old furniture, arranged very differently than I would have configured it. A mirror we had picked up on the street, which had been on the dresser in our old bedroom at the Waverly Street house, was standing on the same dresser in this bedroom.

Bobby leaned over and whispered in my ear during dinner, "You're staying at my place tonight, aren't you?"

I whispered back, "What do you think?"

After I made some money in the city I returned to Deer Creek and was happy to be back in the country.

Kelly got into the habit of consulting the *Farmers' Almanac* on a regular basis for everything—whether it was how to can tomatoes, how to keep the cats away from the birdhouses, or how to build a fence around the garden. She claimed it was all right there in the *Farmer's Almanac*. To our delight, there were apples in the orchard, and we did a little picking every day. Kelly and Whitney started canning and drying apple slices, according to the directions in the *Farmer's Almanac*.

DAISY HOLMES, TAPPING A MAPLE TREE.

Daisy Holmes came by with a few buckets to show us how to tap maple trees for their sap, so we could make our own maple syrup. While out in the woods tapping maple trees, we heard gun shots. I knew it was deer hunting season, but hunters were not allowed on private land, and they sounded way too close. I called the farmer who kept his cows there in the field. I was sure he didn't want them spooked. He thanked me for letting him know, and told us not to worry; he'd deal with the hunters himself.

Later that afternoon, we began digging up potatoes and storing them on a shelf in the basement. We were getting prepared for the coming winter.

I picked up a large desk and a chair at the Thursday night auction, and it was the perfect addition to my bedroom. It was a rather large room, but I liked the sparseness of it. The fireplaces on my side of the house were not in working order, but it was still nice to have one in my room. On the mantel I displayed the colored-glass bottles I had collected, and photos of my family and friends. I also exhibited a vase I'd made in pottery class with Adam Hirschfeld, and I filled it with dried wildflowers I had gathered during the summer.

My cat, Sabrina, loved it in my room, and I would often find her sleeping on my bed during the day in the tiniest ray of sunshine that streamed through the window. Sabrina liked to wander outdoors at night, even on the coldest nights. One night I woke up to the screams of a creature, and Sabrina making strange, high-pitched noises. I sat up and reached for the flashlight I kept on the night table beside my bed. I was completely stupefied to see a large mouse on its hind legs, fighting with Sabrina. It was quite a scene. I yelled, "Get that thing out of here!" Sabrina loved to bring her trophies to my room, and I'd often find the head and spine of a mouse or a bird, but this was the first time she wanted me to witness the actual fight. After that, I had a difficult time falling back to sleep.

Now that the chimney was fixed, we began using the fireplace in the living room just about every night. It was the beginning of November and getting cold. There is something so basic about making a fire. It's probably ingrained in our DNA. Since prehistoric times, fire has been used for so many things— keeping warm, warding off animals, making tools, cooking food, even in worship rituals. As the season progressed I became an expert at making a fire, and everyone at the house called me "Fire Girl." Jeremiah Murphy told us to chop as much wood as we could and stack it in our basement every chance we got, and we'd be happy we did when the snow started flying.

Whitney Kennedy moved back to Staten Island in the city, and Tristan,

Nola's young boyfriend, moved in with us at Deer Creek. He was in a band, and his bandmates often came by to practice. I so looked forward to those nights. Tristan's addition to the house was positive, which eased the discord going on between Kelly and Judd.

SKETCH FOR WOODCUT.

Everyone around me was into wood and carpentry, so I began experimenting with wood cuts and ink on paper. Tristan and I were in town picking up supplies at the hardware store, when we ran into a man who said that he'd never been to New York City. In fact, he'd never been more than twenty miles from that town. I was a little shocked but made an effort not to show it. To think that people lived in such a narrow universe amazed me. Although the man seemed content with it, I had a difficult time relating.

Tristan said, "There are a lots of people like that here."

"I find it difficult to comprehend," I said. "Then again, who thought I'd own a drill and a toolbox."

Tristan laughed heartily, "That's not your drill!"

"It is," I protested.

'No it's not," he insisted.

"Tristin, it is."

Tristan shook his head in disbelief.

When we got back to Deer Creek, Tristan took me straight into the woods behind the house. He was helping me overcome my fear of the chain saw. I was timid and afraid at first, but, eventually I gained confidence. In no time, I heard the sound of three dead trees falling. The thud as they hit the ground was unfamiliar but awesome. Then we sectioned off the trunks for firewood and created a chain of people. We passed along each section of wood to the next person, and the next, and the next, until another threw the wood into the basement. The last person in the chain, standing in the basement, stacked the wood neatly against the wall. That night I sat up in bed and wrote some thoughts in my journal:

Flashed on an old boyfriend today while I was walking with you through the hardware store. I haven't thought about Zackery Darcy in a long time. Maybe it was the way you smiled, or the way you laughed, and there he was in front of my face. I felt so unsure of myself because you assumed the drill I was holding wasn't mine, even though I told you it was. You assumed it couldn't possibly belong to me, and suddenly I was unsure of myself. Zack used to do that to me. Isn't it crazy how I lost my own knowledge for a moment and had to question if the drill was actually mine?

It was the beginning of December, and I was alone in the living room at Deer Creek. I loved staying up after everyone had gone to bed. I'd lie on the couch watching the fire in the fireplace—a fire that I'd made myself. Looking out the window, I could see snow flying while I was warm and cozy inside. I watched it for a while, and a pleasant memory popped into my head—the day that Adam, Max, and I took LSD, walked through a blizzard to Riverside Park and went sledding. Those were such beautiful memories, and I wondered where they both were at that very moment. It all seemed like a lifetime ago.

I was still happy with group living, but it seemed different somehow. It was not like living on the commune, which was more like a family. We were older now, and none of us was experiencing life with that total abandon of youth. In the early days of the peace-and-love movement, life flowed easily, and we flowed right along with it, perhaps aimlessly at times. We were tossed by our whims and desires, and didn't dwell on the consequences of our actions. I think we became somewhat jaded as we got older. In our youth, we are idealistic and forever hopeful. As we get older, we guard our feelings, and become reluctant to give it all away.

EIGHTEEN

STORMY'S PUB

"Love is the only freedom in the world because it so elevates the spirit, that the laws of humanity and the phenomena of nature, do not alter its course."

—*Kahlil Gibran, "The Broken Wings"*

The Christmas season is a magical time, and it was no different in the Catskill Mountains. That year there was a lot of snow in big drifts, howling wind, and freezing temperatures, which led to nights in front of the fireplace. Pine boughs were woven along the bannister of the staircase in the house at Deer Creek, and the fragrance permeated throughout. The scent of fresh pine mingled with fresh-baked apple pies— made with the apples from our own orchard. I displayed a bunch of pine on the mantel over the fireplace in my bedroom, and dangled little crystals from the branches. It was all so festive. A bunch of us trod through the snow in a forest not far from Deer Creek, looking for a Christmas tree. We brought along a flask of bourbon to keep us from freezing to death. (It works as well as antifreeze on a car engine.) That night, we decorated the tree with homemade ornaments, and strung popcorn and cranberries. Even without lights the tree was an awesome sight.

Adriana Bardolino

SNOWY BARN ACROSS THE ROAD.

We had some wild weekends in the neighboring town of Forestville at a place called Stormy's Pub. On Saturday nights we'd head over to the pub for drinks and a dose of country and western music. It was a good respite from the brutal winter raging outside. It was mostly a beer joint, although there was a full bar. Some nights, shots of tequila were in order while pitchers of beer were flowing.

I was sitting at a table with Lucas Garzetti, who was telling me all about how his wife Connie dumped him, and had a new boyfriend. I was half listening to his sob story when I happened to glance over at a table of guys sitting near us. One of them was wearing a brocade jacket. His long wavy brown hair shook when he laughed. It was a crazy laugh. I thought he resembled an eighteenth-century king—maybe it was the brocade jacket. Our eyes connected. A special vibe flows between people in a magnetic field.

Lucas said, "Are you hearing what I'm saying? Connie left me."

"I'm sorry Lucas, truly I am." I was happy that Lucas and I were still friends, but I had no intention of getting intimate with him again.

That winter I received a forlorn letter from Maxwell Robinov. I hadn't heard from him in a very long time. He sounded sad, lonely, and nostalgic for our early days on the commune in the Yellow House. He spoke of the comfortable eons of Route 28, and reminisced about strawberry tea and maple nectar. He wrote, "**It was my home.**"

How could any of us forget that epic summer we all shared in the old yellow farm house, or Max's survival bread? His letter was so poetic and beautiful that it made me cry. He signed the letter simply, "**Max**." I tucked it into my journal for safekeeping.

The next Saturday night we piled into the car and drove to Stormy's Pub. Bud Henderson and the Buckeyes were playing. We got a table, and Judd went up to the bar and brought back a pitcher of beer and glass mugs. It was a particularly busy night, and people were there from all over the county.

That guy I'd seen the previous week was standing at the bar holding a mug of beer. He was all lit up, wearing a crazy tie-dyed bandana. He was tall, solid, and as good looking as an actor. Sargent Preston of the Yukon had nothing on this guy. I pictured him in a red Canadian Mountie uniform. His eyes connected with mine, and the next thing I knew, he was walking over to our table with a pitcher of beer. He smiled at me, sat down and filled my empty glass without asking. He was downright charming, and he already had me with that smile and crazy laugh.

"I'm Peyton Parker. We have friends in common," he said, as he raised his beer mug and took a gulp.

"I'm Adriana Bardolino from Deer Creek, originally from the Bronx."

A big grin broke out on his face. "I'm staying at Finnegan's house in Forestville. I think Judd knows Finnegan."

Judd nodded in affirmation.

"Are you from around here?" I asked.

"No. I'm from California, but I'm staying here for the winter—that is, if I can survive the cold."

We both laughed. We were involved in our bar banter when his friends at the bar yelled out, "Hey Tubs!"

"I've got to get back to the bar," Peyton said. "We have a bet going on a game." As he got up, he grabbed his beer and said, "But you and me—I know we'll be seeing each other again."

I watched him walk back to the bar. Cupid shot his arrow straight to my heart, because it was love at first sight.

Kelly asked, "What was that all about?"

I shrugged. "I'm not sure, but I think I like him."

"Well, he sure seemed interested in you!"

Little did I know that it was the beginning of a winter romance we both sorely needed. I went home, but couldn't forget his face.

I was excited about going to Stormy's Pub that next Saturday night. I was afraid I'd see him again, but even more afraid I wouldn't. Sure enough, he was there standing at the bar wearing that damn tie-dyed bandana. He grabbed my arm as soon as he saw me walk through the door. I hung out at the bar with him, and we talked and drank. We did a few shots of tequila. I guess we both needed some courage. The band was playing that Eagles' song "Tequila Sunrise." (Funny, I still think of Peyton Parker and Stormy's Pub whenever I hear that song).

I was lost in a cloud of infatuation as he talked about himself, and I got drawn into his world. Judd came to the bar to say that it was time to leave, but before I could respond, Peyton said, "I'll make sure she gets home."

Judd asked me, "Are you sure?"

I looked at Peyton, who hadn't taken his eyes off me, and answered, "Yeah, I'll be fine."

Peyton said, "Judd, she'll be safe with me."

When it was closing time we left the pub and drove to Finnegan's house along the snowy roads. I sat in the back seat with Peyton and his friend Wally. Everyone called him Uncle Wally, but he didn't seem much older than the rest of us. As we entered the living room of their house, I saw that the focal point was a large gas heater in the middle of the room. It was really cold in there, so Uncle Wally turned up the heat. It did a great job of heating the living room, but the rest of the house was frigid. None of these old houses upstate were winterized. It was possible that people used them for summer homes at one time, but as the population grew, the houses were needed as permanent residences.

A woman walked into the living room. Peyton introduced us. "Adriana, this is Wanda, Finnegan's wife."

We smiled acknowledging each other.

Peyton and I sat at the kitchen table, but I didn't take my jacket off. Finnegan made us hot tea, which I held with both hands, hoping my fingers would thaw out. I walked back into the living room when I heard a piano. I couldn't imagine how Wanda's fingers worked when mine were still frozen from the car ride to the house. I sat down and listened for a while. I flashed on a pleasant memory from Berkeley. I closed my eyes and saw my friend Dharma, sitting at that old honky-tonk piano, with her long red hair below her waist. She would sit barefoot in a long dress, with a cigarette dangling from her lips, her blue crystal earrings bobbing to the music. My memory was interrupted when Peyton sat down next to me on the couch.

He squeezed my hand and whispered, "Let's go upstairs." He didn't seem like the whispering type. I followed him up the stairs nervous, but excited.

There was a cat sitting on his bed, which began meowing as soon as he walked through the door.

He sat on the bed petting her. "Sapphire likes to sleep in here."

"It's all right, I love cats. I have a cat named Sabrina."

It was strange, the way we connected right off the bat, as if it was meant to be. He reached for my hand and said, "You know, I liked you the first time I noticed you at the pub. You were sitting at a table with a guy."

"Oh, that was a friend of mine, Lucas Garzetti."

He stood up and put his arms around me. At first he just hugged me. I could feel him shaking a bit. I figured he was just cold. He said, "I haven't done this in a long time."

I looked at his face, surprised. "That's okay."

"I was in Germany for a year and a half, and I landed in New York and thought I'd mellow out here with my friends before heading home to California."

I waited to hear more of his story, but he grabbed me and kissed me. It was so cold in that room that we lay on the bed fully clothed, slowly peeling our layers off, piece by piece. We began to laugh, which put us both at ease. He kissed my body all over, like he hadn't been with a woman in a while. I swept his hair aside and kissed the back of his neck. Instead of a chain, he wore a thin leather chord around his neck with a large glass African bead.

The candle on the window was flickering, and when I glanced at it, I noticed ice on the inside of the window. I said loudly, "There's ice on the inside of the window!"

Peyton laughed, sighed, and said in a low, sexy voice, "We'll burn that off pretty quick."

On Sunday morning, Sapphire the cat woke me by scratching at the window, wanting to go out onto the roof.

Peyton opened his eyes and took my hand. "Why don't you stick around here with me today?"

I thought, *I guess the two times we made love during the night wasn't enough.* I smiled and nodded. He jumped on top of me, and we did it again. I loved the way he approached the sexual act like a child in wondrous joy. He'd mentioned being a Taurus, and I could tell he loved earthly pleasures.

When we were finished, he laughed and said, "See Stormy? No more ice on the inside of the windows."

We affectionately called each other Stormy, after the name of the pub where we met. I was still cold, so I pulled the blankets over my face, just enough so I could still watch him get dressed. I was very much physically attracted to him, and I felt strong chemistry between us.

He said, "I'll go downstairs and see what's for breakfast. Come down whenever you want." He closed the door behind him, and I lay there looking at everything in his room. I noticed a box on the dresser. I got out of bed to investigate. The box was filled with various little trinkets, and a small vial labeled "Musk Ox." I sniffed the vial, and it smelled of him. I would remember that smell for a long time to come.

When I finally got dressed and went downstairs, I found Peyton in the kitchen doing something with a small contraption on the table. "What is that?" I asked.

"It makes yogurt."

"I never got into yogurt."

"Well, Adriana, you're going to love this." As he mixed all the ingredients together and turned the timer on, he mentioned that he was a vegetarian and hadn't eaten meat in years.

I stared at him because I'd imagined all vegetarians were slim, but Peyton had a pretty solid form. Later on, when the household was up, Wanda made pancakes. I tried some of Peyton's yogurt and loved it.

The guys asked me if I played poker, and that was music to my ears. An all-day poker game ensued. Everyone kept calling him Tubs, which made no sense to me. I got up to get a drink of water, and Peyton yelled after me, "Hey Stormy, get me a glass too."

I brought the two glasses of water and set them down on the table. He lifted me on his lap and ran his tongue along my lips darting it in my mouth. I looked at him and said, "Tubs," in a slow, drawn-out sexy voice. We began passionately kissing, and the guys began whistling and pounding on the table. I ended up losing five dollars that Sunday, but it was well worth it.

On Monday, I didn't want to leave, but I had to get back to Deer Creek. Finnegan drove us to my house. I kissed Peyton goodbye, and they both smiled and waved as I walked up the driveway. We had plans to see each other in the next few days.

I found Nola was sitting at the kitchen table with Tristan, and Kelly was cooking something on the stove.

Tristan asked, "So how was your weekend?"

"It was great," I said, and he smiled at me. Sabrina heard my voice and came thumping down the stairs.

Kelly said, "We didn't see her the whole time you were gone."

I picked her up and she began purring. I kissed her, and she squinted her eyes and looked at me with love.

Tristan said, "The stream out back is frozen over. We should go ice skating before it thaws out."

"I don't have ice skates," I said.

Tristan smiled. "Who needs skates?"

Peyton Parker called the very next day to tell me it was crazy how he missed me already. I told him we were going ice skating on the frozen stream at the back of the property. He said he'd be over with the guys a little later. Peyton showed up wearing a bulky, full-length, fur coat, Wally and Finnegan tagging along behind him. We all headed to the stream out back. One by one, we glided along the frozen surface. It was a riot watching Peyton in that big fur coat; he had a funny technique that had us laughing hysterically. He'd jump on the ice with such a force that it propelled him well down the stream, farther than anyone else.

I took Peyton's hand and said, "Hey Tubs, let's walk up to the top of the hill. I want to show you the property." We walked away from the others, who were still careening along the frozen water.

We trudged through the apple orchard, and up the side of the hill through the packed snow. The sun was out, but it was still chilly. We sat at the top of the hill for a while. Peyton said, "How old are you Stormy?"

"Twenty-seven."

He smiled. "Really? I'm twenty-seven too. You know, this is a nice piece of property. I really love it here."

"Stay for a couple of days," I said.

He smiled and hugged me. "I think I will."

When we walked back down to the stream, everyone had gone. We found them back at the house in the kitchen talking and laughing, and there was whiskey involved.

Peyton said, "Oh, I'll have some of that."

We all hung around in the kitchen drinking and telling stories, thawing out from the cold. I took Peyton upstairs to show him my bedroom.

As soon as he walked through the doorway and saw the barn door behind my bed, he said, "Whoa, what the hell? Oh, we're gonna have some fun up here tonight Stormy!"

That night, after everyone had gone to bed, the two of us hung out on the couch in the living room. I was wearing a long skirt and a sweater, feeling toasty. I walked to the fireplace to stoke the fire. I heard Peyton say, "Come over here Stormy." I turned around, and he was seated on the edge of the couch. I noticed he had pushed his pants down. I walked over and stood in front of him. He pulled my skirt up and slipped my panties down, and I put my legs over his lap.

"Making up for lost time, are you?" I asked.

He seemed oblivious to my words, as if in a trance. He said, "Stormy, you're not wearing a bra."

I began moving up and down while he was fondling my breasts and making the nipples hard. My long hair was laying on his shoulders.

"Oh God, Stormy I can't stop," he said, and in a moment it was over.

I put my arms around his neck and said, "Its okay."

He gave me a soft kiss on the lips. I lay down on the couch and put my head in his lap. He played with my hair, and we watched the fire for a long time. I was feeling intense about Peyton Parker, and wondered if he was feeling the same.

When the fire was down to embers we walked up to my bedroom. He began laughing as soon as we passed through the doorway. I said, "What's so funny?"

"That barn door—I just can't get over it. How the hell did you get it up here anyway?"

"It's a long story."

I searched around the room for candles and matches. I lit the candles and set them in a dish on the nightstand.

He sat on the bed looking up at me. "It's your turn now, Stormy."

The room was cold, but we were still warm from the fire. We got into bed, and he began making love to me.

Peyton hung around with me at Deer Creek for a few days, and it was sugary and mellow. I was so comfortable with him, and we were good together. As soon as he went back to Forestville I missed him. We planned to meet at Stormy's Pub on Saturday night.

There were so many people at our house on Christmas Eve, including our neighbor Geordie, and Lucas Garzetti who'd crafted a god's eye for me as a gift. I made my mother's famous eggnog, and followed her recipe to the letter. I added lots of rum and bourbon, spooned vanilla ice cream over the top, and sprinkled it with nutmeg. I let it sit in the refrigerator for an hour, as the ice cream melted and created a heavenly foam on the top. It was killer, and everyone loved it. It turned out to be a beautiful night. In the spirit of Christmas, gifts and all, I prayed for love and peace for us all. Peyton stayed over that night, and all was merry and bright.

By January 1974, the winter was in full swing in the Catskill Mountains. We got really drunk on tequila at Stormy's Pub one Saturday night, and Peyton and I were thrown out for being lewd on the dance floor. We stumbled out the door and fell laughing in the snow, too drunk to be embarrassed. Our friends drove us back to their house in Forestville. A bottle of beer was passed around the back seat. Peyton sang along to the new song by the Steve Miller Band, "The Joker," playing on the car radio.

I laughed and said, "He thinks he's a space cowboy." Peyton sang, "Yeah, I'm the gangster of love."

Uncle Wally just shook his head.

When we arrived at their house we continued drinking. That night we stayed up talking most of the night. Peyton mentioned that Wanda and I were the only two women he'd met in the Hudson River Valley that he related to on a deep level. That was when he admitted that he'd been in prison in Germany, and why he was there. I sensed anger and frustration as he was talking, and wondered if I was just a bridge from that experience back to his life in California.

In the morning I opened the window to let Sapphire out on the roof. I could hear the water in the brook that passed by the house, but I couldn't see it.

Peyton said, "Stay in bed. I'll go downstairs and see if Uncle Wally made coffee."

When he didn't return, I got dressed and went downstairs. I could smell the coffee, and I heard voices as I approached the kitchen. I heard Uncle Wally say, "Did you tell her yet?" I didn't hear an answer. They both acted like nothing was going on when I walked in, so I played dumb. Uncle Wally handed me a cup of steaming hot coffee, and Peyton looked at me with a serious expression on his face.

There was a football game on, and the guys were all whooping and hollering in the living room. I put my Airforce parka on and went outside for a walk in the woods behind their house. Amid all the snow around me, I had flashbacks of Colombia, South America—the heat, the red-hot sunsets, the dampness of the jungle, and the heavy rains. It seemed to be a memory I just couldn't shake. I thought about all the nights I'd spent alone there before I met Luka. I'd lay awake alone on a grass mat listening to the sounds of the night, the moonlight putting a spell on me. Luka flashed before my eyes, and I saw us in the shower at the house of El Capitan Morales. I'd sing a song as the water rushed over us. Luka would smile and say, "Is beautiful."

I was so lost in my daydream that I didn't hear the snow crunch behind me. I was suddenly brought back to reality when Peyton wrapped his arms around me from behind. He was wearing that fur coat he dragged around everywhere. He kissed me, "I have to talk to you about something."

I felt my stomach turn over.

He said, "We'll talk later, okay?"

I nodded, smiling, although my insides had a different reaction. He put his arm around me and walked me back to the house.

I had been spending all my weekends in Forestville, and up until now it was a joyful experience. I felt at home among these folks. That night after we made love, Peyton sat up and said, "I've been meaning to tell you something, but I didn't know how. There's a girl back in California. I haven't seen her in a long time. I have no idea how I feel about her after all this time, or how she feels about me. But we've been together since high school, and she's always been my girlfriend."

I didn't say anything; I just let him talk.

He took my hand and said, "This has happened for us Stormy. It was like fate stepped in and brought us together. Whatever the future brings, whatever goes down, this is ours forever!"

I looked at him, disappointed, but I stroked his hand. My reaction was very Zen, although inside I was torn up. I thought of that phrase my mother liked to use, Que sera, sera, and said, "Whatever is meant to be will be?"

"I don't know exactly when Stormy, but she's coming here soon."

I understood about past loves—some of my own who I still thought about, one of them just earlier that day.

Then he said, "You and me—we seem to overlap in places."

Overlap, I thought, *that's common ground between phenomena; coincide partially or wholly.* I wasn't sure what he meant, but it sounded just the way I felt about us.

I went back to Deer Creek the next morning and tried to forget his words, but I couldn't. I wondered if what I was feeling was an illusion, and that I had let my emotions run away with me. I busied myself with chores, and there was always plenty of those.

Judd was driving to Albany to take care of some business, and since Kelly was substitute teaching that day, I told him I'd go on that long drive with him. Besides, I wanted to see the state capital. My mother's brother Victor was one of the designers of the marble at the state capital in Albany, New York.

Funny, I'd just written in my journal that week, that it was one of the best years of my life. My mother used to say, "If you start the day laughing, you could end the day crying." I wondered if my joy would somehow turn to sorrow.

Peyton called a few days later to tell me that the guys were driving to Woodstock for a happening called Joyous Lake, and was taking me along. Of course, I went. They came to pick me up in a Triumph.

I asked, "Are we all going to fit in this thing?"

"You're sitting on my lap Stormy," Peyton answered.

I squeezed in on his lap, and he gave me a sloppy kiss on the mouth as the car lurched forward. I think I was in love, because everything around us was beautiful and had a glow. (I'm convinced that love is better than any drug.) A joint was passed around, and we all got into a crazy mood.

The James Cotton Blues Band was playing when we arrived. They were fantastic and really rocked the place. When James Cotton took a break he sat at our table. He bought Peyton and me a drink, and that was really cool.

Driving back to Forestville after the concert, a flask of whiskey was passed around the Triumph. Peyton got totally drunk and rambled on about Geordie, my neighbor at Deer Creek. "Geordie's always at Deer Creek trying to get into your panties. He probably comes around when I'm not there to fuck you." Peyton could be really stubborn when he was twisted, a typical Taurus.

The guys in the car were all snickering, but I got angry. He wouldn't give it up or get off the subject. True, Geordie liked me, and Peyton probably picked up on it, but I never had sex with Geordie. We were just friends. He was jealous, plain and simple.

Peyton was out of it when we got back to their house in Forestville. Uncle Wally helped me get him upstairs and into bed, and I had him to give me a ride back to Deer Creek.

I received a letter from Suki Rosmond, describing how beautiful the house was that she and Ross were renting on the Russian River in northern California. She wanted me to seriously consider living there with them for a while. I found myself in a tenuous situation again. My relationship with Peyton Parker lacked clarity, yet I couldn't pull myself away. I thought of her offer, but all my trips to California seemed to end in disaster.

The next Saturday at Stormy's Pub, Peyton and I were dancing and making a conscious effort not to be lewd. He held me tightly and gave me a tender kiss on the lips. He kept looking right into my eyes. I was so high on love, and I thought he was too. While on the dance floor, the band played our song "Tequila Sunrise." He smiled and spun me around while singing the lyrics. I knew I wasn't just another woman, but were they his words or just the song lyrics?

I realized that it's not so much a place that becomes home, but a person who becomes home. Wherever they are, you want to be, and that's home.

Peyton's expression changed, and he became serious. He squeezed me tighter and said, "You and me—we mesh."

I thought, *Mesh—fitting together, work together in harmony, interlocking.* Yeah, that's how it felt. But why did I feel the need to analyze his words? My happiness was clouded with uncertainty.

It was the end of January and Peyton's California girl hadn't shown up. Why was I willing to play second fiddle to another woman? The answer eludes me. Perhaps I was hoping in the end he'd choose me.

Peyton spent a few days with me at Deer Creek. We cooked, baked bread, took walks around the property, and hung out by the fireplace each night. For me they were days filled with joy and love. I felt content, devoid of anxiety, or want, except for him.

In Forestville, the guys got hold of a deer hide. I sat on the ground like an Indian squaw outside their house watching Peyton stretch the hide on a frame. I imagined he was an Indian brave, with his wild hair blowing in the wind. To me, he seemed happy and content.

Moss appeared in the areas where the snow had melted. The air was electrically charged, and we felt it. There were buds on some of the trees, and I hoped they wouldn't get killed in a Pre-spring frost.

In February, Ross Grant came to Deer Creek for a visit from California. He had Marty Feinstein with him, who was already living with them out west. It was good to see Ross again. He was family. They were telling me how great their house was on the Russian River, and that I should come and live with them.

We were listening to the radio when they announced that Patty Hearst had been kidnapped by the Symbionese Liberation Army in San Francisco. Crazy shit seemed to happen in that state, and I was having second thoughts about going back there again.

Strangely enough, Matthew Romeola, a.k.a. Romeo, called while Ross was visiting, and I figured Ross had something to do with the call. Romeo began working on me over the phone. "Honey, you're out to lunch for not coming back to live in California. What the hell are you waiting for?" He mentioned that he might have to come to New York to see me if I didn't get there soon. I'd heard he had a new girlfriend, so I wondered why the urgency?

While Romeo and I were talking I pictured his green eyes and soft face. I felt a warm sensation in the pit of my stomach. But after I hung up the receiver, I recollected how I'd left him, and California, a destroyed and broken woman.

Peyton Parker and Uncle Wally had friends who had a loft in New York City. They were planning a visit, and Peyton was taking me along. Their friend's loft in Manhattan was way more modern than the place my friend Ruby Hoffman had. It was occupied by a bunch of guys, and there were girly posters and trashy sex magazines everywhere. There was plenty of cocaine being passed around.

Peyton put his tie-dyed bandana around his wild hair and slipped into his fur coat. He took my hand, and we left the loft to roam around the city. He'd never ridden on a subway, so I took him to my parents' apartment in the Bronx.

He freaked out on the train. He hung on to me saying, "Don't let go of me Stormy. I'd be lost in this metropolis without you."

The next day I took Peyton to Greenwich Village. He walked around curiously looking at everything, as if we were walking on the surface of a different planet. We were having a rip-roaring time in New York City. Any thoughts of Peyton's California girl completely vanished into the smoggy air—well, at least for me.

After a few fun filled days in New York City, we drove back upstate.

Winter was still raging in the Catskill Mountains, with snow everywhere—a very different climate than in the city.

Peyton's California girl never showed up. Woman's intuition told me that she'd heard he was hanging out with another woman, so she stayed away. I didn't want to go back to Deer Creek just yet. Judd and Kelly weren't getting along, and there were weird vibes at the house. Kelly Cooke wasn't the type to share her feelings, and Whitney Kennedy had already moved back to Staten Island. I felt estranged there. The aftermath of life on the commune, beginning with the Waverly Street house, and then Deer Creek, was friendly but different. I loved everyone, but it just wasn't the same as life on the old commune.

Peyton and I were heading upstairs to his bedroom when he turned around and went back downstairs.

"Where are you going?" I yelled after him.

"You'll see!" he said, his wild hair shaking as hopped down the stairs laughing.

I went into his room, got undressed, and slipped under the covers because I was cold. He returned with a big grin on his face, holding two jars.

"What's that?" I asked.

"Yogurt and honey, cause you're so snarky and sweet!"

He pulled the covers off me and began spreading the honey and yogurt on various erogenous places on my body. Oh God, the room was so damn cold, but all I felt was the heat of his breath and his mouth on me as he ate it off. I suppose he had all that time in a prison cell to think of things he wanted to do to a woman, and I was the beneficiary. When we kissed though, and when we made love, it was more than just sex— at least for me.

Soon it was spring, and Peyton Parker was going back to California. We were in his bedroom in Forestville; I hadn't been home to Deer Creek in days. He said, "Stormy, it's time for me to face the music! Jesus, I haven't been home in two years." He added, "I'll call you at Deer Creek in a few days, or if you're not there, at your mom's. And you'll be coming to California soon anyway."

I smiled but didn't say anything. I wondered if we even had a future together. I was planning to stay with Suki and Ross, so I gave Peyton the phone number of the house on the Russian River.

It was an emotional goodbye for me the day he left. I felt as if I was hurtling through space and the unknown again. I drove with Uncle Wally, and we dropped Peyton off on the side of the turnpike. He was hitchhiking to the airport. We kissed goodbye at the entrance.

Peyton looked back and shouted, "I'll be calling you soon," and mouthed a kiss.

As Wally and I drove away, I watched Peyton disappearing through the rear window until he was a tiny dot in the distance.

Uncle Wally rested his hand on mine. "Don't worry, you'll see him again."

I half smiled because I wasn't so sure.

Emptiness followed. Days went by with no word from Peyton. Days turned into weeks, and weeks turned into months. He was gone completely, as if it all never even happened. It was as if someone had shaken me awake from a beautiful dream, and I wanted to fall back to sleep again but couldn't.

I had packed all my personal belongings in the house at Deer Creek. I planned to stay with my parents in the Bronx before leaving for California. My room at Deer Creek was bare, an empty shell. I left all my plants with Kelly. I gave my cat, Sabrina, to Troy Bloom—she was familiar with him.

Stormy was gone, and I was alone again. I threw the three Chinese coins, and the I Ching gave me its ancient wisdom, "It furthers one to cross the great water." I wasn't sure what that meant. All I could think of was how much I missed Peyton, and wondered if he thought of me at all, or if he just went home and resumed his former life. I felt dead inside, as if a flame had been snuffed out.

At my parents' house in the Bronx, I went through the boxes I had mailed to myself from upstate. I saved only the bare minimum of things. As soon as I opened the box of trinkets Peyton had given me, I smelled the Musk Ox. I pictured his bedroom, and all the nights we'd spent together flashed before my eyes. Then I faced the possibility that I would probably never see him again. After I cried it all out, I fetched my journal and jotted down Confucius's words:

> Do whatever brings you to life, then, follow your own fascinations, obsessions, and compulsions. Trust them. Create whatever causes a revolution in your heart.

I did see Peyton Parker after that, spent time with him after that, and made love with him after that. But in a strange way, I never saw Stormy again.

NINETEEN
A COSMIC JOKE

Water gives life to the ten thousand things, and does not strive. It flows in places men reject, and so is life. No fight, no blame. Yield and overcome, bend and be straight, empty and be full, wear out and be new. In the spring some go to the park and climb the terrace. But I alone am drifting, not knowing where I am. Like a newborn babe before it learns to smile. I am alone without a place to go. I drift like the waves of the sea, without direction like the restless wind. Everyone else is busy, but I alone am aimless. I am different. I am nourished by the great mother. Empty yourself of everything. Let the mind rest at peace. The ten thousand things rise and fall, while the self watches for their return.

—*Lao Tzu, Tao Te Ching*

I had given my deposit on a van ride to California for the first of April. I was leaving all my precious belongings with my parents in the Bronx and just winging it. Kelly Cooke was still living at Deer Creek. She invited me to stay with her for a few days before I left for the West Coast. Judd Thatcher was out of the picture now, and a new guy, Johnny Doyle, had Kelly's attention. I took the train from Penn Station to the Hudson Station, where Kelly picked me up.

On the drive to Deer Creek she filled me in on all the changes at the house. She told me all about Johnny Doyle and how wonderful he was. "You know, Johnny and I are the same size, and we wear each other's clothes."

I stifled the laughter I felt bubbling up in my throat.

"I dated a guy named Jake, briefly," she continued, "but he really freaked me out."

"In what way?" I asked.

"He shot and killed his dog because the dog wouldn't stay out of the garbage."

That Saturday night we went to Finnegan's house in Forestville, and I was happy that Uncle Wally was still there. We all got into Finnegan's truck and drove to Stormy's Pub. The atmosphere was festive, as always. I danced, drank, and had a good time, but for me, the magic was gone. Wanda, Finnegan's wife, stayed untill 3:00 a.m., closing time, which was strange because she had never come to the pub with us before. Our neighbor Geordie was there. He bought me a few shots of tequila, and we had a profound conversation. One of Peyton Parker's close friends wanted me to go home with him, as if he and Peyton were somehow interchangeable. Jake, Kelly's friend, was sitting at our table. He seemed like a nice guy, but I kept picturing a dog lying on the ground, crying, and full of blood from a gunshot wound. (Who the hell shoots their own dog for getting into the garbage? Sick bastard!) Without Tubs, Stormy's Pub had lost its luster.

Daisy and Jeremiah came to Deer Creek and took me to their cabin on the mountain. Our neighbor Geordie came along for the ride. It was good to be back at Thoreau's Cabin, which is what I affectionately called it. I felt more at peace at their place, where there were no memories to haunt me. There was no electricity or running water, but they had a system worked out. We sat around by the light of a kerosene lamp that night and played music. I shut my eyes and was aware of nothing but the sound of Geordie's mouth harp, with its bluesy vibrations.

Jeremiah Murphy and Daisy Holmes lived close to the land. They bartered and shared with their neighbors. Jeremiah sanded the floors in his neighbor's house in return for potatoes and fresh eggs. I saw ducks, hogs, and sheep on the mountain, and wondered if any of them were for food.

One of their neighbors was an extraordinary character. She was an artist and a world traveler. She took us to her antique shop in town. She worked with leather, beads, shells, and feathers. Daisy told me she had dived for barracuda in the Florida Keys, hauled lumber through the swamps of the Everglades, and fixed houseboats. She was missing the entire top row of her front teeth from a motorcycle accident, and her jaw was wired shut. She showed us her life's collection of old beads, clothes, bones, and trinkets. The store was filled with antique furniture, plants, furs, and unfamiliar spices and herbs. I felt as if I was in a holy place, as if she were a shaman. I was like an opium-eater in a field of poppy flowers. The place was filled with dreams and precious things, and it felt sacred. My soul was set free up on the mountain.

I spent the last few days before I embarked on my trip out west with my mom and dad in the Bronx. I watched my mother bake a pumpkin cake, which was my father's favorite. It was comforting to see a spark of love between them.

I made a last trip into Manhattan and searched my soul for feelings about the city. I loved it, and I hated it. All the things that made New York City such an intense place—car horns blowing impatiently, newsstands on just about every street corner, whistling steel workers, pimps and hookers, flashing neon lights, and music trios on street corners, and in the subways. People of all colors marching to and fro, a true melting pot. Immigrants flooding in from all over the globe, making money to send back to where they came from. The gray masses riding the subterranean trains. Where else can you get a chocolate egg cream or a real bagel? Wherever I went, this place was in my heart. You cannot hate something you've never loved. I saw Lightnin' Hopkins and the Dixie Hummingbirds that night. It was an awesome concert.

When I got back to my parents' apartment in the Bronx, I had an honest conversation with my mother. I told her how lost I felt, and that I was unsure about my next move in life. I told her I was brokenhearted again, and had misjudged someone's attention.

My mother looked at me complacently for a moment.

She sighed and commented, "Que sera, sera!"

I was glad I'd chosen to go the van route to California as opposed to flying. It gave me time to think about where I'd been, and where I was going. I thought about the first time I'd taken the love bus, how my excitement overcame my fear. But I wasn't twenty anymore; I was twenty-seven. On the van there was an eighteen-year-old girl who was running away from home. I tried to think back to when I was her age.

I had very restless sleep in the van, and had some crazy dreams. My brain seemed to be processing recent events, as well as older ones from my past.

I recorded two of the dreams in my journal:

I dreamed that I was settled into life in California at Ross and Suki's house, and both Romeo and Peyton came to visit me. For some reason, I found them both very unattractive. I took this to mean that in reality, they may have changed, and I might not like who they'd become.

The other dream was that I had a baby girl, and she was sitting on my lap in the New York subway. It was winter and very cold, but I had no blanket for her. An old woman walked over with a blanket and covered her. I kept staring at the baby, and couldn't believe she was mine. I loved her, and she made me happy. I couldn't figure out who the old woman was. I took this to mean that I had regret over lost life. That things would have been okay if I had a baby when I was much younger. That both the baby and I would have been safe. Then I thought maybe that baby was me.

The house where Suki Rosmond and Ross Grant lived, along the Russian River in northern California, was really beautiful. Bay trees and Fleetwood Mac permeated the atmosphere around that very modern house. There was a fireplace in the living room which was painted with an Egyptian motif. Ross gave me his room, which was a separate structure off the main house. A cacophony of chickens, turkeys, peacocks, goats, and geese moved freely about the property. Occasionally, the peacocks would wander inside the house. We had to be very still, so as not to scare them. Suki told me that they were very delicate and could easily break a leg.

When heavy rains came, the main road flooded, and we needed a canoe to get to and from the house. My days were filled with sun, music, granola, and healthful smoothies. My nights in bed were filled with confusion and inner turmoil.

Star Green came to visit and took me back to San Francisco with her. She had an apartment in North Beach, right across the street from the San Francisco Art Institute. On my first day there, we visited the art school I had attended. As we roamed through the halls, artists were working in studios and lingering in doorways talking. Memories flooded my brain prompted by the smell of the paint. I flashed on how I'd left that place midsemester. My stomach nearly dropped out. I was relieved when we finally left.

It was a perfectly sunny day, so we walked up and down the hills of the city. We hung out with so many new people that I couldn't keep track of their names. One of Star's friends played the flute so beautifully. We lay on the grass in front of Saint Peter and Paul's Church in North Beach, listening to him. It was spring, but the sound of the flute transported me back to the past winter, to one of the nights in front of the fireplace at Deer Creek—a friend of ours, who claimed to be an Italian Gypsy, taught me a Sicilian shepherd's song on the guitar. It all seemed so long ago. My world was all mixed up, and my head was filled with memories which clouded the present.

The next day we went on a road trip to the ocean with Star's friend Bailey. He was quite funny, and we laughed a lot that whole day. We drove north along the coast to Mendocino, and then to Russian Gulch where we sat on the beach among the driftwood. We ate provolone cheese with sourdough bread, and we finished off two bottles of champagne. I stayed in the city with Star for a few days, and it was good to be close to her again. Looking back, I think I was hanging on to the individual members of the commune for some stability in my life.

RUSSIAN GULCH

When I returned to the Russian River I received an unexpected phone call from Peyton Parker. He announced that he was coming to visit me. I hadn't seen or heard from him in two months, not since we kissed goodbye on that turnpike in Upstate New York. I had so many questions, and had felt let down. I was nervous about our reunion.

I thought my heart would stop when he walked through the front door. "Hi Stormy," he said with a smile, and kissed me on the lips. I wanted to grab on to him and never let go, but held back. When we embraced, all the sadness and resentment seemed to disappear. He looked so good, and I took note that he'd come alone. I supposed he wanted to see how he felt with me, if we still had a connection. We spent the day together, and being with him again was a bit overwhelming. I felt as if a light was turned on inside of me. We reminisced about the winter we'd spent together in the Catskill Mountains. There was no mention of his California girl, and I didn't pry. Perhaps I didn't want to know. We made love, and afterward, he said, "Stormy, it was the best ever." He took something out of his pocket. It was the glass African bead he'd worn around his neck on a leather chord. He handed it to me, "I want you to have this."

I took it and said, "Tubs, I'll treasure it forever. Being together with you feels holy."

He took my hand, stroked it and said, "It's spiritual, the energy flowing between us."

Yet I heard no plans from him about the future, and when he left, I felt deserted and empty again. I almost wished I hadn't seen him, that we hadn't made love. My heart felt as if it was in an old-fashioned washing machine wringer. A few days later I heard through the grapevine that Peyton Parker went on a camping trip to Hawaii. It all seemed like a cosmic joke, and the joke was on me.

My cousin Gia and her husband, Stu, came to the house on the Russian River. I gave them the room I was staying in, Ross's room, for privacy. We had a joyous visit, but I think they noticed my state of mind, although they didn't comment. They were on their way to Lake Tahoe and asked if I wanted to come along. I'd been to Reno but had never been to Tahoe, so I went with them. We embarked on the journey and got as far as the foot of the mountain. There had been a lot of snow the night before, and there was a line of cars at a checkpoint, waiting to drive up the mountain. We were turned away because there were no snow chains on the tires of their rental car. It was good to be with family, although it was a short visit.

I was being tossed around like a football from one friend's house to another. Matthew Romeola a.k.a. Romeo, my boyfriend from the summer of love in the Yellow House, told me that his new girlfriend, Bella McTavish, had an apartment in the Mission District of San Francisco. He said, "I'm going on a trip to South America. There's plenty of room at Bella's apartment. Why don't you stay with her?"

I knew this was a bad idea from the get-go. How the hell would it ever be a good idea, living with your old boyfriend's new girlfriend? How would I feel when they were together? He was such an important love in my life, at an important time in my life. I don't know what I was thinking. Perhaps I was just holding on to that communal string through Romeo. I still felt love for him, even though it seemed like a lifetime ago that we were a couple. I guess once you love someone deeply, you always love them in a way, and a strong connection remains. I was looking for a job in the city, so against my better judgment, I moved in with Bella.

Bella was a tall, skinny blonde, a bit dizzy at times, but sensitive and sweet. She seemed to be everything I was not. Romeo's best friend, Casey Cutler, was living there as well. Everyone else came by to visit all the time, and at the beginning, it was like being back on the commune. I never saw Brent Beachwood (Beach) though, and figured something had broken their friendship. Star never talked about him either, not since they'd broken up. I remembered when the guys first showed up at the Yellow House that magical summer, the three stooges were always together.

Lots of drugs were passed around every night, and I think they masked my inner feelings. It was difficult watching Romeo and Bella together, and I wondered if I was punishing myself for something.

I took a day to walk around the city by myself. I hopped a cable car to Van Ness, where the love bus had dropped me off seven years ago. I had been bouncing back and forth between New York and California for a long time. They were places with such different mindsets; I think, inwardly I was searching for someplace new and different. I passed an old-fashioned diner, walked in, and sat at the counter. I ordered a cup of coffee. When the guy behind the counter set it in front of me, I suddenly began crying uncontrollably.

"What's wrong, miss?" he asked.

I threw some money on the counter and ran outside into the street. I felt lost. It was gone; it was all gone—the summer of love, the commune, all the beauty and togetherness we shared, my youth, my innocence, everything!

I was an empty shell with memories. I felt aimless with no direction or vision for the future. I began walking. I don't know how far or how long I walked, but I just kept going until I reached Bella's apartment. I knocked on the door, and Bella opened it. When she saw the expression on my face she hugged me, put her arm around me, and walked me inside.

Someone told me about an old Chinese man named Lin Wong Foo in San Francisco, who gave personal readings from the I Ching. I sought him out and went to his apartment. I knocked on the door and waited. A rather small Asian man came to the door and let me in. I showed him my three coins, which I carried everywhere. He told me that my coins were over two hundred years old, and from China. He asked me if I'd like an I Ching reading from his old book, and I told him that I did.

He led me down a long hallway to a dark room lit only by candles. We sat down on the floor facing each other with our legs folded, and were silent. Then he told me to think of my question and to concentrate only on that. I thought of my question as I threw the three ancient coins. He burned incense and called my name to Fu Hsi—Fu Hsi was a mythical Chinese emperor, who supposedly lived about 4,500 years ago, and was credited with the invention of the I Ching. I loved the way the I Ching explained the human condition according to the laws of nature. Lin Wong Foo read me my response, which was very profound. The passage that remained in my mind's eye was, "It furthers one to cross the great water." I had received that response so many times in the past that I began to wonder if there may literally be an ocean I needed to cross. I left there feeling calm and content, as if I was somehow in communion with the ancient spirits.

Bella and I seemed to get along while Romeo was in South America. When he returned, a lot of guys—friends of his—hung out at Bella's apartment. One of them, Justin Jordan, was a trumpet player in a famous band. There were about eight members, all wind and brass instruments. He was average height, and on the thin side. He had a mass of kinky blond hair which he kept in a long, thick braid, tied with a leather strap and some beads. He was very quiet, sweet, and had a chipped front tooth. He was an attractive and talented guy. There was always an empty room for friends at Bella's apartment, and Justin stayed there a lot. As I sat in my room writing or drawing, I loved listening to him practice on his horn in the next room. I was always drawn to musicians, and Justin was no different.

Justin would often invite me into his room, and I would lean against the wall with my eyes closed listening to him practice. During one of his practice sessions, he gazed down at me and held his hand out, and I took it. He put the horn down, knelt in front of me, and took my other hand. He said, "I've wanted you for a while now." We smiled and began to undress. We lay down on his bed and had sex. The faint smell of jasmine surrounded him, and his thick blond hair got loose and streamed across the pillow. When we were finished, he sat up, picked up his horn and began to play again. I continued listening, with a little more interest and connection. After that night, we usually stayed together when Justin was at Bella's apartment.

When Justin Jordan's band played in San Francisco, we all went to the concert. I listened to the notes streaming out of his horn, and felt as if I was seeing him for the first time. That night he was on stage blowing his guts out on the trumpet. Even though we'd been intimate before, I felt renewed excitement.

After the concert, and a night on the town, we streamed into the living room of Bella's apartment. It was really late, but none of us was in the mood to go to sleep. Justin had some cocaine and passed it around on a mirror. After the coke, lines of heroin were passed around. I was reluctant seeing heroin as a death drug, but Romeo said, "Try it. It'll take the edge off the coke." I snorted a little. All it did was make my nose itchy, and Romeo laughed.

Justin saved some coke for just the two of us. He stood up and took my hand, and as we walked out of the living room together, Romeo followed us with his eyes. I wondered what was going through his mind. Justin and I did some more coke in my room. He lit a candle, and we lay there buzzing. For a moment I felt suspended in time. I thought, *Musicians are a strange breed. They are married to their instruments.* Justin played a beautiful horn, and they became one—the brass and the man. The music would burst from his soul, through his trumpet, and out over the hills. It was a spiritual thing, a beauty that stirs from within. Justin always said, "Things that accord in time vibrate together."

I'd been in California for a few months when I finally found a job coding at a market research company in the Embarcadero. A trolley ride was my daily commute. Ross and Suki came to Bella's apartment for a visit and handed me a letter. It was from my friend Geordie, back East in the

Hudson River Valley. Geordie said some heartfelt things—that there were only a few people in our lives that we will always remember, people with whom we had common life goals and a connection. It was a beautiful letter. I certainly missed his bluesy harmonica, and his true friendship. I felt as if the people around me on the West Coast spoke in riddles. I was forever attempting to decipher the meaning of their words.

It was my twenty-eighth birthday, and it was one of Bella's friend's birthday as well; we were two Cancers. They threw us a party. Everyone was there—Romeo, Casey, Justin, Star—and Peyton Parker called me from Hawaii. Among my presents were a pre-Colombian bead earring, a freshly cut red rose, the promise of a tattoo, a bunch of exotic sea shells, Maxfield Parrish prints, and a woven belt from Peru. Also in front of me was a large mound of cocaine on a mirror, all for me. I did so much of it that night that I thought my heart would jump out of my chest.

Nights like that were common at Bella's apartment, and still, I managed to get up for work the next day. But I was getting jaded on the nightly routine, and I wanted out. Thank God I did not have an addictive personality. When the drug was there I enjoyed it, but when it wasn't around I didn't miss it.

Romeo and Bella went on a buying trip to South America together. They had plans to open a small gift shop, and in South America, they found a source for cheap goods. I was left to deal with Casey Cutler, who could be a handful. I was at work when there was an emergency telephone call for me. It was Casey, calling me from the hospital. Somehow, he managed to smash his leg.

I rushed to the hospital and found him in a ward with twenty other men of varying ages. It was the most depressing place. I witnessed, firsthand, how people without money were treated. I brought him some fresh fruit, but all he wanted was booze. I washed his long, strawberry-blond hair, which was not an easy task. The way he looked at me, with such love and appreciation, warmed my heart. He wasn't the easiest person to deal with, but in that situation, he actually seemed grateful. Doing this for him made me feel good. Maybe it resulted from the mere act of selflessness, which was something I was not familiar with. In the end, I realized that I am my brother's keeper.

Casey watched me with a serious expression as I poured the dirty water in the sink. He said, "I never told you this, but remember the day Romeo and I took you to the airport? When you left us in California and moved back to the commune in New York....after you got on the plane, Romeo sat in a chair at the gate, broke down and cried. So don't ever think he didn't love you very much, because he did."

"I wish he would have shown me how he felt back then, but he just let me walk away," I said.

Casey frowned and laid back down in the hospital bed. I stayed for a bit, then kissed him on the forehead and left.

When I got back to Bella's apartment, someone told me that Peyton Parker had called again from Hawaii. *Damn it! I missed his call again*, I thought. But at least I was still somewhere on his radar.

I met Star at a coffee shop in the city after work, and we had a nice chat. She said, "Did you hear Nixon resigned the presidency!"

"Yeah, over the Watergate thing," I answered. I quickly changed the subject. I had more pressing things to discuss. I confided in her. "I'm finding it difficult at Bella's apartment, all the drugs every night, and getting up early the next day for work.

Star frowned but didn't comment.

"I'm confused about my feelings toward Romeo, and this thing with Justin—it's all just too much!"

She took my hand. "Aw, honey."

"I really need to get out of there."

"My roommate is moving out, so I'll have an empty bedroom. Come live with me, I'd love it."

"I was hoping for something like that to happen."

We hugged goodbye, and I hopped a cable car back to Bella's apartment feeling very relieved. On the ride home, I wondered how I was going to tell Romeo. I couldn't deny I still had deep feelings for him, and if I was being perfectly honest, I was still attracted to him. I knew it wasn't healthy for me, or fair to Bella, that I was living there. Romeo would probably feel deserted. True, he had Bella, but Casey and I were his connection to the commune, and that was a powerful thing we shared. Then again, why did I still care how he felt?

After Casey got out of the hospital he hobbled around on his bum leg for a while. He had a falling out with Romeo on a telephone call from Colombia, and didn't want to be around when they returned from South America. Casey moved to Marin County. I suspected it was over drugs. I remembered something Jenna Maplewood said, "Cocaine makes men out of brothers."

When Romeo and Bella returned from South America, I told them that I was going to move into Star's apartment. Just as I'd expected, Romeo was upset.

He kept repeating, "Why? Didn't I take good care of you? I don't want you to leave."

I hugged him. "I'll always love you, but it's something I have to do for myself."

I'll never forget the look on Romeo's face when I packed my things and left. But as soon as I walked out the front door, I felt as if a heavy weight had been lifted off of me.

There were some great times at Star Green's apartment in North Beach. I loved her creative energy and artistic vibes. I was hoping some of it would rub off on me. I had been creatively numb, except for verse, poems, and pertinent song lyrics I entered in my journal. I felt love for, and had a strong connection to Star. Our communal history kicked in, and for a while it was enough. My head was still in limbo, and I felt like something was about to happen. I was like a plane sitting on a runway in a holding pattern, waiting to take off.

Casey Cutler telephoned me at Star's apartment. "Hey, I've got this great place north of the city in Marin. Why don't I bring you up here for a few days?"

"A weekend in the country sounds like just what I need."

Casey picked me up, and we drove to his place in Marin. We turned onto Saddleback Road and stopped in front of an old wooden house. As soon as we got out of the car, I smelled the country air. I walked around in the yard before I entered the house. I saw blackberries; I picked a few and ate them. The house had a rickety wooden porch, and the stairs creaked as I walked up. Casey was already inside. The screen door slammed as I walked through it. A cat ran up to me, immediately twirling herself around my legs. Casey said, "Oh, that's Moonshine."

A guy was sitting on the couch, playing guitar. He briefly looked up at me, said "Hey," and then continued playing. Casey said, "That's my roommate, Blake Middleton." The guy looked like a real cowboy, sporting jeans, a cowboy shirt, and cowboy boots. He even had a big oval buckle on his belt. He had straight black hair, worn in a long pageboy. His piercing blue eyes added to his attractiveness. I reckoned I was going to enjoy the weekend.

I sat quietly listening to Blake play. When he stopped playing, we chatted for a while. He had a twangy way of talking. Everything he said sounded profound to me. It was like talking to an outlaw from the Old West.

I began spending my weekends in Marin, but my friends warned me that I felt good there because I was still attached to Romeo by hanging out with his best friend Casey, keeping that communal string vibrating. Maybe they were right, but I didn't care. I wasn't walking away from anything that made me feel good.

One weekend on Saddleback Road, Blake took me down to the local watering hole—the saloon. I watched him get ready, putting on his hat and boots. He wore a bolo tie around his neck. Walking into the bar, he said, "Watch this!"

I watched him in action, circulating around the bar, hustling friends, who I sensed had bad opinions of him. He worked humorous magic on older painted ladies, who drew rings of descriptions around him. They told him that he needed a gimmick if he wanted to be successful, and how beautiful his blue eyes were. They filled him with pitchers of beer, and tried to rip off his soul. All the rack-a-rack of the barroom scene was in full swing.

We walked back to his house, arm in arm, and I got the impression he was perpetuating an image of himself in the songs he wrote and sang, like a cowboy living a legend. Blake and I had a strange connection, as if we'd known each other in another life.

At Star's apartment in the city, something was always going on. Jenna Maplewood drifted in one night, with her wild gray hair and nose ring, leaving a trail of patchouli essence behind her. She was smoking a joint and speaking in that animated way she always did. I'd been jealous of her when she came to visit with Romeo on Staten Island a few years back.

She again talked about Romeo as if he were a potted plant—she loved using the plant metaphor when she spoke about him. "You give a plant [the plant being Romeo] to someone [*someone* being Bella] to take care of, and she tries to kill it."

But I saw that situation differently. Romeo was into heroin when I met him years ago, and I figured he was the one who introduced it to Bella, but I wasn't going to argue with Jenna.

She finally stopped complaining and said, "Get dressed; we're going to Winterland to see Stoneground."

I put on my black velvet dress, beads around my neck, and feathers in my hair. We were out the door and on our way to the concert.

Blake Middleton called and said that he had a gig in San Francisco. He gave me directions, and told me to meet him there. I had passed the hat around for him on open-mike nights at various bars in the city. I made my way from Star's apartment to a place called the Holy City Zoo. When I got there Blake was standing at the bar, looking like one of the cast members from *Young Guns*, his guitar case beside him. He watched me saunter up to the bar, where he'd saved me a seat.

Blake said, "The owner got pissed off and put me last on the list to play tonight, because I mouthed off at her about the guy slated to play before me. I mean, who the hell is Oat Willie anyway?"

He was so disappointed I didn't know what to say. We began drinking beer and then shots of tequila. After some weird, drunken conversation about gunfighters, guitar players, and lovers, we walked out.

He put his arm around me as we walked along the street. We stopped in the doorway of another bar. Out of the corner of my eye I caught a glimpse of Star Green sitting at a table by the window. She was with her friend Bailey and an older guy they hung around with, Poncho.

"Blake, there's my friend Star," I said. "Let's go in here."

We walked into the bar and stood next to their table. I introduced everyone to my new friend Blake Middleton. Star heard me talk about Blake, but she was meeting him for the first time. She rolled her eyes at me, and giggled looking at his western garb. There were more pitchers of beer and more shots of tequila—Poncho was buying. Blake took his guitar out of the case and began to play. He blew everyone away. He lit up my soul fierce and feisty, then soft and gentle, depending on the song. What was it with me and musicians? I wished I knew. We all got righteously drunk, and somehow Star got us all back to her apartment. Blake lay down on my bed and closed his eyes. He asked, "Hey, did I play tonight?"

I laughed. "Yes, you played."

He smiled, never opening his eyes. I covered him with a blanket and lay down beside him. The last thing I remembered that night was hearing Star throwing up, and Blake snoring.

I spent the next weekend on Saddleback Road with Blake and Casey. We walked up on the hill behind their house to watch the sunset. That night, a group of musicians came by. Patti was the singer in their group. She was cool, and I liked her. Blake practiced with them on a regular basis, and they sometimes played gigs at taverns. I really enjoyed those jam sessions.

After everyone left, Blake and I hung around talking about love, hate, and the people we'd loved before. I felt close to him, maybe because of our honesty with each other. He knew Romeo and I had been lovers. I'm sure Casey told him my history, but he never mentioned it. Maybe everyone was right. I was hanging on to the communal family thing through Casey, like a lifeline.

Blake picked up his guitar and started strumming and singing. "Easy money, faithless women, and red-eye whiskey, will never kill the pain." We both laughed.

When Blake smiled or laughed his eyes narrowed a bit. He took out capsules from a prescription-sized container, and broke them open on a mirror. He chopped them into thin lines with a razor blade.

"What is that?" I asked.

He lit a cigarette and took a drag. "It's a poor man's coke."

I snorted up a little. It burned my nostrils. I found it edgy and nothing like sweet-sister cocaine. I figured it was speed.

Blake smiled, and even his smile was a smirky cowboy smile. He said, "Hey, Toots!" He took my hand and led me into his bedroom and closed the door. It seemed like a natural progression of things between us. I liked him a lot, and it was good to be made love to by someone I felt so close to. I had no illusions about a big love affair, at least not at that point.

When I woke up in the morning I noticed the blackberries outside his bedroom window.

Blake opened his eyes and said, "Mornin' Toots. Let's see if Casey made breakfast."

Like the lyrics in the John Prine song, "All the snow has turned to water," there was no change in the weather. Instead of snow in the winter, there was rain. I missed the changing seasons which always divided the year. Last winter I was playing in the snow and living at Deer Creek. The memories haunted my brain. Every time I heard a country and western song on the radio, I'd flash on Bud Henderson and the Buckeyes playing at Stormy's Pub. All of us crowding into Finnegan's truck—Wally, me, and Peyton in the back seat, passing a flask around. How we'd dance the night away, talking and laughing; pitchers of foamy beer spilling over the edge and filling thirsty glasses; falling down in the snow filled with the cheer of the Christmas season. In that moment I missed the Catskill Mountains.

It was Christmas Eve, and I had the curse. I lay in bed with bad cramps. When Blake called, I told him I was too sick to come to Marin. As I lay there, I listened to the rain beating on the windows. My mind drifted to the last Christmas Eve at Deer Creek, standing by the fireplace watching the snowflakes drift past the window. Then I was jolted back to reality by the sound of a foghorn in San Francisco Bay. There were no wise men bearing gifts from Morocco or from anywhere else for that matter. I lay in bed miserable for a long time, maybe hours.

I heard a knock at the door. Star opened it, and I heard her say, "Hey, she's in her bedroom."

Blake Middleton walked in and said, "I didn't want you to be alone on Christmas Eve Toots." He bent down and gave me a big kiss on the lips, and I hugged him. He looked around the room for my guitar, grabbed it, and sat on the bed next to me.

I asked, "Where's your guitar?"

"It's in hock."

I frowned at him.

He began to play Christmas carols for me, and it was like a piece of heaven in a lonely hell of a world. It was the most beautiful gift anyone could have given me. His fingers glided along my guitar in a way mine never could. I closed my eyes and felt snow blowing in my face. When he played "White Christmas," I saw my parents toasting each other with glasses of champagne in front of the Christmas tree, with Alfie the cat sitting under it, like a little present. I felt a sudden pang of longing, wanting to be with them again. In reality, I knew it wouldn't ever be that way again.

The moment was like an Old Russian folk song, beautiful but sad. When he stopped playing, I propped myself up on one elbow and said, "Oh, Blake, please don't stop," so he kept playing.

When I was a little girl, I'd sleep under the Christmas tree. I'd watch how the bubbling lights made the ornaments dance. I would make believe I was a figurine living on one of the branches.

Lying there in bed listening to the guitar my mind drifted. I imagined Blake and me in a tent, thousands of years ago. A musician and his concubine passing the time, waiting for the birth of the Naz.

I knew I'd remember the night forever, a moment frozen in time. The candles burned out; it became dark, and everything was still. Blake stopped playing and put my guitar down. He got in bed and made love to me. "God Toots," he said, "You're burning up, but it feels so good."

I knew from the beginning that this relationship was not a big love affair, but I was getting attached, feeling love, and that wasn't a good thing. I began looking for reasons why I should end the relationship, but all reason would get washed away with every drink. I thought perhaps we were just kissing away our memories of those lovers who went before.

Blake would ramble on and say things to me when he was drunk that he never would say sober. I marked it up to the bottle talking. Perhaps we were all just filled with memories, rambles, and dreams.

My weekends on Saddleback Road were filled with music and laughter. Blake had a friend, a nurse, who worked in a hospital. We joined a bunch of people hanging around the nurse's apartment, waiting for him to come home. We sat in a circle on his living room floor.

I asked Blake, "What's going on?"

"Hold on, you'll see," he answered.

The guy finally showed up with a large cylinder that he set in the middle of the floor. It was a tank of nitrous oxide. A mask was passed around, and we all took turns inhaling the gas. It put us in a euphoric state, and none of us wanted to let go of that mask.

I remembered doing research at the university on Staten Island, and reading about laughing-gas parties among the British upper classes in the late 1700s and early 1800s, when it was all the rage. At that time, people regarded it as a vehicle to powerful spiritual and mystical experiences. It was definitely euphoric, and I looked forward to doing it again.

That night Blake and I stayed up into the wee hours of the morning playing music, talking, and writing songs. Then Casey and Blake started drinking heavily, and got into a nasty fight; it was ugly and upset me.

I knew my days on Saddleback Road were waning. I suppose I was waiting for a different life path to unfold before me. In the meantime, for a Christmas gift, I got Blake's guitar out of hock.

Blake took me to his mom's house for Christmas Day dinner. It was a very modern house up on a mountain in Fairfax. His folks were really cool people, although Blake had a tumultuous relationship with his mother. I'd heard all about it during those late-night chats we had. I took photos of Blake in the yard, holding his stepfather's rifle. It reinforced the outlaw image I already had of him. There was an old grandfather clock in the dining room that marked time as we ate dinner. It reminded me that time was flying by.

BLAKE MIDDLETON.

It was January 3, 1975, and I was writing some thoughts in my journal. I was at Suki and Ross's place on the Russian River for the weekend. Oddly enough, I received a phone call from Peyton Parker. We spoke for a long time; we had a lot to say. As he was talking, I closed my eyes and made believe we were back in his bedroom under the covers at Finnegan's house in Forestville. I chuckled at the memory of ice on the inside of the windows. It seemed like it had all been a dream, but Peyton reminded me once again, that our winter together in the Catskill Mountains was forever. Even though I didn't see him anymore, his phone calls were keeping me on a cosmic wave.

After that relaxing weekend on the Russian River, Blake took me to a strange woman's house in Fairfax. He sat at her piano, which he probably had done many times before. He was totally engrossed in his music, as if nothing else was going on around him. It was simply beautiful to watch. Listening to him play, I knew we were all children of God, filled with our own dreams.

But the next day Blake called me at Star's apartment, and he was cold and distant on the phone. I had felt more warmth from my conversation with Peyton Parker, who I hadn't touched in a long time. It was raining heavily outside, and I prayed that the water would wash away my confusion.

Adam Hirschfeld came to stay with Star and me at her apartment in San Francisco. We reminisced about the early days of the commune. We laughed about how Jesse Bob Baker's glasses would get steamed up when he played piano. He had that internal New Orleans fire—it was in his DNA. He'd grown up singing gospel music with a choir in a revival tent. He told us that he had to wear a short wig, with his long hair tucked underneath, when he attended his father's funeral in the Deep South. With his family, he had two strikes against him—he was a hippie with long hair, and he was gay.

I was overjoyed that Adam was with us. He was my only contact left from those early days in that first commune on Charming Way in Berkeley in the late '60s. Adam and I went for a hike in the mountains. We sat on a grassy hillside and talked about what was going on in our lives. We laughed at all the crazy times we'd had over the years. We had a history, Adam and I.

He was quiet for a while; then he said, "You know, our child would have been about five years old by now."

I choked back tears but smiled and reached for him. We hugged each other.

Adam said, "Whatever you're going through in your life right now, it'll soon pass, and everything will turn out okay."

Adam always exuded peace and serenity. He had a way of putting my mind at ease. I was thankful for that—and for him.

TWENTY

VISIONS OF GAUGUIN

Not all those who wander are lost.

—JRR Tolkien, The Fellowship of the Ring

he moon was in Libra, and I sensed uncertainty all around me. I began seeing visions of tropical scenes with endless beaches and palm trees, and I wanted to bake my bones in the sun. I wanted to be Dorothy Lamour in *Aloma of the South Seas*, with a flower behind my ear, standing under a waterfall. I longed for the tropical sun, to be close to volcanic earth, to smell the ocean, and to let my hair fly in the South Pacific Trades. I longed to run my bare toes through the sand. I longed for a lover's hands all over my body, his lips on mine. That's all there is that's worth anything in this crazy life—to live, to love, and be close to the earth. Maybe I was chasing a dream, but damn it, what is life without dreams? I began making plans for a trip to Hawaii.

I hadn't heard from Blake Middleton in a couple of weeks and wondered how he was, and what he was up to. Perhaps he thought we were getting too close. Maybe I wasn't good for him, or maybe he wasn't good for me. I began to think we were better off as just friends. I needed to know if he was dead or alive. I was flipping through the pages of my journal and came across the lyrics of a song that Blake and I had worked on together:

Once It's All Behind
Met a girl the other night, she was so young and fine

Tender as the morning dew, lips like berry wine
Maybe I could love her, but I'd still remember when
I gave my heart to another, only to lose it again
Once again it all went wrong, it all got turned around
Left me here like an old sad song,
But I don't know if it really matters
Once it's all behind

It's weird, the things you miss about someone who's been a friend and a lover. The last time Blake and I were together we walked up on the hill behind his house on Saddleback Road, and I was struggling to make him see his own self-worth, because I didn't think he saw it himself. Later on in town, he begged me to buy him another drink after he was already drunk. I told him I thought booze was killing him. He smiled at me, took my hand, and told me he'd never known anyone like me. He was caught within the legend he'd created for himself.

A few days later, Casey Cutler telephoned me to let me know that Blake was in jail. He had been arrested for driving while under the influence (DUI). At least I knew that if he was in jail he wasn't drinking. I made a decision not to get involved in that mess. I had to cut that string, and this was the perfect time. I couldn't handle watching him die with all the talent he possessed. But I knew our souls had touched and flown.

With Casey, I hated to admit it, but my friends were right. I *was* trying to hang on to that communal thread through him, and it wasn't working for me anymore. It was time to move on.

I had to cut it all loose—lost family, lost friends, and lost lovers. I needed peace in my soul. I wanted it all to stop. I was going through the same things with different people, over and over again. The I Ching says that life is like the seasons, the trees, the mountains, and the waterways. I knew I was just a tiny part of the universe, but nothing was working anymore—or maybe I just wasn't plugged in.

Hawaii was looming on the horizon. I'd heard snippets about Hawaii from friends throughout those early years. I remember Noah Bernstein wanting to check it out when I lived with him on Charming Way in Berkeley in the late sixties. In those days however, a tropical island was the last thing on my mind. Peyton Parker had been to Hawaii and told me it was a slice of heaven. My friend, Loretta Perino in Brooklyn, said that Hawaii was a "Really happening place." She told me that her ex-boyfriend lived on Maui, and she was sure he'd be overjoyed to show me around the island, and that I could stay with him. That sounded like a solid plan to me, and I finally had something new and positive to look forward to.

On my way home from work I saw a flower stand from the window of the cable car. I hopped off one stop before mine to buy fresh flowers. I thought they would cheer up my room. It was the middle of January, and the Christmas ornaments were looking dusty and faded, like yesterday's carnival cotton candy. The Scottish actress Deborah Kerr was on TV, speaking like a stuffed deviled egg, when I walked into Star's apartment.

I said, "Star, guess what—I bought a plane ticket to Hawaii for a month's vacation. I leave February 4."

She looked up at me without much interest, other than to say, "That sounds nice."

I was ready for a break from this place too.

When I told Jackie, the manager at the market research company, about my trip to Hawaii, she said, "No way. February is slated to be our busiest month this year. Let's go for lunch and talk about it."

We left the office and headed to the cafeteria across the street. Jackie was a very together woman. I'd always assumed she had braces on her legs due to a deformity because of the way she walked. We stepped into the street, and a car came from nowhere and ran over her feet. After the car passed my heart was pounding, but she continued walking toward the cafeteria. I thought she must be in shock.

She turned around looking for me, and saw the bewildered expression on my face. She walked back and grabbed my hand, laughing. "I'm sorry. I thought you knew. I have two wooden legs. I didn't even feel that."

Over our soup and salad she told me about her life, which seemed so much more normal than mine. She was married with a husband and two kids. Her husband was a deep-sea construction expert, who helped build the BART (Bay Area Rapid Transit) system under the bay. She said, "My family helps with household chores and bathing, etc."

We chatted over lunch, and I agreed to postpone my trip until spring. On my trolley ride home from work, I was consumed with Jackie's life—how she overcame hardship and difficulty to lead a somewhat normal and happy life.

I remained alone in an attempt to rediscover myself. I did water colors and charcoal drawings of tropical scenes to keep the Hawaii dream alive. I was trying to make sense of the chaotic order that had become my life. I remembered having felt centered in South America. In Colombia, I knew who I was, and I loved the person I had become there. Years later, during a therapy session, I told the therapist about my trip to Colombia—the joy I'd experienced there, and how I felt about myself. I began to choke up as I spoke. She said, "Adriana, the person you were in Colombia was the real you, without societal norms or the expectations of others." With her words, I remember breaking down and sobbing.

Some things remained dark and unformed, and I still had questions, like what did it all mean? Perhaps I chose to ignore reality at times, and live in a world I made up for myself. Maybe I saw fantasy as being better than the reality I observed around me.

"I have made my world, and it is a much better world than I ever saw outside"

~ Louise Nevelson, American sculptor

Somehow, when I stepped off that plane in Miami, Florida from Barranquilla, Colombia, I lost my center. I'd heard that Hawaii was one of the remotest places on earth, and thought I might find myself again on a tiny island in the middle of the Pacific Ocean.

I took a short trip up the coast to the Fort Bragg area in northern California to visit Kelly Cooke and Johnny Doyle, who had just had a baby girl. Kelly told me that the best way to get there from San Francisco was to take a bus. She came to pick me up at the depot. It seemed as if Kelly was always picking me up from a bus depot or a train station. As many times as I had been up the Pacific Coast, the scenery never got old. Kelly and Johnny were in California for a few months to get away from the brutal winter in Upstate New York. They were planning to go back east in the spring. The baby was beautiful. She had Judd Thatcher's blond hair, blue eyes, and facial features. I didn't mention it because Judd was Kelly's former paramour. We took turns holding the baby. She was the tiniest, most precious thing.

I sat on the couch next to the wood-burning stove in the living room. That night I stayed awake listening to the crackle of the fire, just like I did that last winter at Deer Creek. The ocean wasn't far, and I could hear the roar of the waves from inside the house. It was peaceful. I lay down on the couch to sleep.

Johnny came into the living room and put some more wood in the stove. "That should last all night."

I smiled a happy and contented smile, and Johnny smiled back. I fell asleep to the sound of the ocean, and the rain beating on the roof. The wind woke me up a few times during the night, flipping the plastic on the side of the house.

It was almost dark when I'd arrived the night before. In the daylight I noticed a framed photo of Finnegan hanging on the wall in the living room. At first I thought it odd, but then I remembered that Kelly met Johnny through Finnegan, back in the Catskills. I heard somewhere along the line that he and Johnny were tight friends.

Kelly asked, "Would you be interested in renting this place in the spring when me and Johnny go back East?"

"I doubt that I could survive up here by myself."

That weekend, we spent a lot of time gathering and chopping wood for the stove, just to keep warm. The way my life was going, I wasn't making any definite plans.

The next day brought more rain. Johnny and I had just made it back to the house from a walk on the beach, where we'd gathered driftwood for the stove. Kelly had stayed home with the baby. Life up there was certainly rustic and wild. From the kitchen window, over the stove, I could see the ocean.

I was cooking a soup for dinner while watching the waves through the kitchen window. I asked Kelly, "How was the birth?"

"We had a midwife here at the house. All of our friends were here cheering me on."

"Everyone?" I asked.

"Yes, everyone! Johnny held my hand through the whole ordeal. Our friends sat on the bed comforting me, and giving me encouragement when I needed it."

"That doesn't sound like something I would like, with everyone looking at my cucci down there. Who the hell knows what I would be screaming and blurting out during waves of unbearable pain? No, that wouldn't be for me."

Kelly laughed at my depiction of the event.

Johnny said, "We plan to look for some land to buy back East. Land here is too freakin' expensive. You know, Deer Creek is being sold, and they're asking $195,000 for it. I only wish we could afford that place." (Now, a house with a barn, an apple orchard, and a stream, on ninety-five acres of land for that price sounds cheap.)

"God, I loved that place. I'll probably be back East in the summer," I said. But in reality, I had no idea where I would be in the summer.

During the night, I had a disturbing nightmare that I recorded in my journal:

> I dreamt that I was visiting my mother in the Bronx, and I had a baby girl. I couldn't tell her about the baby and avoided showing it to her. I took the baby to a movie, and a friend of hers saw me there, so I ran out of the theater. For some reason, I told my father about the baby. He asked me if I wanted to go on a voyage with him, and I thought he was protecting us in some way. He took me and my baby to the Bronx Sound, and we boarded a sailboat. My father was standing at the bow of the boat, steering it. At some point, we were drifting very slowly down a river, and it was getting progressively darker. I could see dense woods on either side of the boat. The woods, although dark, looked magical with twinkling lights. I felt safe and euphoric. Suddenly everything changed. The water became murky, and the air was cloudy and heavy. My father pulled the boat ashore. Then, he turned to me and said, "Drown the baby."
>
> I was holding the baby tight and screaming, "No, Daddy, I love her. Please, I want her."
>
> My father said, "Adriana, you have to drown the baby, and no one must ever know."
>
> I drowned my baby, and as soon as she disappeared under the surface of the water, I began to scream and cry, and I wanted to die. I was numb as we sailed back to the Sound. On shore there was a crowd of people waiting for us. My mother was there, and she was very angry. I told her what had happened, and she held me and began to cry.
>
> She said, "Why didn't you tell me? You could have kept the baby. Adriana, why did you kill your baby when you wanted it?"

I woke with a start, and the only sound I heard was the crackling of the fire in the wood-burning stove, and the rain beating on the roof. It was obviously a dream about guilt and loss, among other revelations.

Johnny drove me to the bus depot on Sunday afternoon. We must have screwed up the timetable because I missed the bus back to San Francisco. I had to get back—I had to work the next day. It was raining like hell again. Johnny mentioned that he had a friend who was driving into the city, and maybe he could give me a ride back in his truck. Luckily that was a go, and his friend came to get me at the depot. I hugged Johnny goodbye and jumped in the passenger seat of the truck.

On the ride back to San Francisco I took note of the beauty around me. The Pacific Ocean, the cypress trees, and cattle grazing on cliffs. When we passed the Russian River Gulch, I flashed on eight years ago, when I'd stood on one of those cliffs and thought I was observing the dawn of creation. I was twenty-one years old, and Noah Bernstein was twenty-three. He was ready to settle down, but I was still wild and crazy, and thought my life was just beginning.

The sun was setting as we passed the bay in Mendocino. I still had so many questions about life. I didn't know if there would ever be any answers, or just more questions. I thought about past lovers. How different they were from each other, and how different I was with each of them. I think I learned something about myself and about life from each person I came across. I feared that maybe I was meant to be alone

Looking back, I think I pushed away the men who really loved me, and sought men who really didn't care that much about me. I was aware of the concept of polarity. When forces tug at you, it's only natural for you to go in the opposite direction. Although I did observe that behavior, the realization did not help me in the least. I wondered if true love was just an illusion. Was it something that could really last, or was it a fleeting thing? I reached my head out the window of the truck and saw water crashing on the rocks below, and smoke from houses in the distance. As the truck rolled into San Francisco the rain finally stopped.

When I arrived at Star's apartment, there was a letter addressed to me on the kitchen table. It was from Lucas Garzetti back in the Catskill Mountains—the strongest man west of the Hudson River, as Ross liked to refer to him. His letter began: "This is the third time I have ventured forth with pen in hand, looking out over frozen land." I didn't remember answering any of his letters, and I denoted a frustration between the lines. It gave me a warm feeling to know he still thought of me enough to write.

After reading his letter, my thoughts returned to that winter I spent in Upstate New York. I wrote in my journal:

Dreams of beautiful patterns in the snow, but in reality, it's only rain against the window. I remember the time we walked through a frozen wonderland, you and I. But now, that seems like a lifetime ago. The morning it rained after a snowstorm, we were stuck in that old farmhouse on the mountain after a New Year's Eve party. All the trees and bushes were motionless, with droplets of ice freezing the rose hip buds. We stood on the mountain overlooking the valley I lived in. I felt like an Indian squaw, alive again, after hundreds of years of being dead. Maybe I was. But here, it just rains in the winter, and the foghorns in San Francisco Bay make me miss the foghorns in the harbor off Staten Island.

The Godfather, Part II, was playing in downtown San Francisco, and a few of us went to see the movie. Street scenes of New York City, Italian culture, and bowls of spaghetti with sauce, made me miss my family. In some ways my attachment to New York was basic. I was born and grew up there. It was "In my veins" as Jenna Maplewood would say. But sometimes, when I was there I felt like a fly stuck on flypaper. I didn't really know where my home was anymore, or where I belonged. I had different attachments in different places, and I wasn't sure if that was a good or a bad thing.

On the trolley ride to work, I wondered how I could possibly stay focused on work with thoughts of my trip to Hawaii inhabiting my every waking moment. When I walked into the office, my coworkers surprised me with champagne and a bouquet of fresh flowers. They were toasting my upcoming vacation. One of the guys even stayed late at his second job as a baker, just to make brownies for the occasion. They made me feel thought of and appreciated.

I had a warm, fuzzy memory of the time Bobby Becker came to pick me up at the Waverly Street house on Staten Island. The way he handed me a bunch of violets and lilies of the valley he had hidden behind his back. He presented them to me like a magician with a pleasant surprise. The way he looked at me made me feel special. I wondered why I was finding myself in situations where I was almost begging for love and affection. There were people around me whom I loved very much, but I didn't feel a permanent attachment to the place. The truth was, I always felt somewhat adrift in California, flying around looking for a place to land, but never quite finding it.

Kelly Cooke and Johnny Doyle came to visit me at Star's apartment with the new baby. I was happy that Uncle Wally came with them. I hadn't seen him in a while. It was coming on spring, and they were on their way back East in a week or so. For a moment, I wished I was going with them. We laughed, talked, and played music together. It was a high night in the midst of my general malaise. We reminisced about those crazy times we had that winter, bumming around the snowy Catskills. Uncle Wally brought up Peyton Parker as we were talking.

Johnny said, "Let's call Tubs—see what the hell he's up to."

I didn't say anything as Johnny dialed his phone number. I wasn't putting any more juice into that Stormy situation. After all, I was hanging around Marin County, and Peyton was right there yet we never saw each other.

Johnny spoke to someone on the other end, put the receiver down and said, "He's in jail for traffic violations."

Wow, I thought, *there must be something in the air. Two of my ex-lovers are in jail cells. What are the odds of that?*

Kelly and Johnny had brought a bottle of tequila with them, and we proceeded to get wasted. We discussed how we would spend time together back East in the summer. It sounded like fun to me, but at that point, I didn't know if I'd ever get back there.

We went to see Blake's friend Patti. She was singing at a coffeehouse called the Gourd. I handed her a journal as a gift, to record her thoughts in, and she hugged me. She often commented about my writing in my journal when the band practiced at the house on Saddleback Road.

When she stepped on stage, she sang that Merle Haggard song "Today I Started Loving You Again" especially for me. She looked straight at me while she sang the words. Tears welled up in my eyes. It was difficult to hold back my emotions, and I was relieved when the song was over. I was very aware of time slipping by.

I copied this in my journal from a book I was reading:

> *The Dragons of Eden* by [Carl] Sagan on the concept of cosmic calendars: A calendar is more than merely a device for the numbering of the days. All calendars are directly bound to the ever-recurring cycles of nature, most commonly manifested in the rotation of the earth, and its cosmic influence. Their underlying purpose is to help

man to adjust to the cycles and the forces that permeate them, by achieving an organic sense of time. A true sense of partnership in the rhythmic flow of natural events. This brings a sense of harmony with the universe. Everything in the universe is constantly changing and moving. No matter how permanent a thing may appear, it is always subject to change. Times change, and each thing and condition has its period of development, fulfillment and degeneration.

Life's condition remained a mystery to me, and I questioned what I was doing with mine. I avoided making definitive plans and just lived day to day. I figured the universe would sort it out. I continued to get letters from back East, but that didn't feel like home anymore either. I was adrift out there in the cosmos. I thought of Romeo and how we had been so close and so much in love at one time. He was only a trolley ride away, yet we were like strangers. I felt as if everything we shared during that summer of love was a vacuous dream.

I cruised into a bookstore and thumbed through a book of Paul Gauguin's paintings, which I loved. I began reading about his painting methods and composition. Gauguin's style was a big influence on my own painting and drawing.

Later in my life I took a trip to Tahiti and the Marquesas Islands in French Polynesia. I walked up to a remote part in the mountains on a tiny island called Hiva Oa to visit Gauguin's grave. It was very peaceful there under the trees with a view of the bay below. I knew a lot about Paul Gauguin's life, and how much in turmoil he was. In an odd way, I felt my life's condition was similar to his—the way he bounced back and forth between Paris and Tahiti, I was doing something similar between New York and California. I was attracted to the color and composition in Gauguin's paintings—the way he painted nudes and still lifes in tropical landscapes.

I read, "Even though the figures he painted were of large Tahitian women, they retained a delicate quality." I also shared his love for tropical culture. His paintings made me think of the Garden of Eden. I thought that Hawaii might help me conquer the fear I sometimes had of a blank canvas.

Walking through the aisles on my way out of the bookstore, I noticed a book someone had left sitting on a table. I picked it up; it was about psychedelics. I thumbed through the pages, and there was a corner folded on a page about Sapo. It said that the Sapo is a type of frog that exudes a psychedelic substance from the sides of its head. All you have to do is touch your hand to the frog's head, and you will be affected by the substance. Of course, my psychedelic days were long gone, but it was interesting.

The clerk at the desk followed me with his eyes as I walked to the exit. I flashed on the first time I'd seen Erik Eschweiler in that bookstore in Manhattan—how beautiful he looked with his long, straight, blond hair, like a Flemish painting. I smiled at the sweet memory as I walked out the front door.

It was the eve of my trip to Maui, and I sat in my room at Star's apartment, reminiscing about my years of communal living. William Faulkner said, "The past is not dead; it's not even past."

I wrote in my journal:

> Some say, let the past forever remain the past. The bittersweet memories we all shared together during our days of communal living. Vivid scenes of a country road, a swift-moving stream, and a shabby old wooden farmhouse, which at that time seemed divine. In our memories, spring and winter remain intent upon demand of recall, to any newcomer who might ask. Why? Because in spite of ourselves, it still remains with us today and always. Maybe it was our youth or innocence that made it all so grand. Or maybe it was all part of a grand plan. Either way, that time for me remains a magical time, when life unfolded its mysteries. Observing that tree on the hill, I realized that the roots were to the earth, as branches were to the sky.

I was on the plane from San Francisco to Honolulu. I didn't know what awaited me in Hawaii. I had a piece of paper with the name of Loretta Perino's ex-boyfriend written on it, and a PO Box number in Haiku on the island of Maui. I knew I was at a crossroads in my life, and I wanted to explore a more meaningful direction going forward. I wanted a rebirth of art in my life.

Looking back, I realize that I'd led quite a selfish life, and probably used my being an artist as an excuse for some of my actions and decisions. I laughed at the memory of my mother telling neighbors, "Well you know, she's an artist," as an explanation for some of the unconventional things I did. I had developed a wanderlust for new places and new people, perhaps because I was sheltered as a child. It is true that all those who wander are not lost, but I was definitely searching.

When we landed in Honolulu, I walked off the plane, and the balmy air hit me. There was an intoxicating aroma from a flower lei stand I passed that I will never forget. I rushed to my connecting flight to the island of Maui. When I got to the gate I saw a tiny plane, and I immediately flashed on "Aero Crash"—the plane we'd taken from Miami to Barranquilla, Colombia, and I laughed out loud. At that moment I knew I was in for an adventure.

It was a forty-minute flight, and my anticipation grew with each minute. I made friends with the young couple sitting next to me. They were probably my age or younger, who were on their way home. The sun was setting as we descended through the clouds. Out of the window, I could see a tall mountain.

The woman said, "That big mountain you see out the window on the left side of the plane is ten thousand feet high. It's the dormant volcano Haleakala."

As the plane was descending I saw huge fires burning below us, and asked about them.

The guy said, "Don't worry. They're just burning sugar cane down to the root so it can be harvested."

It was an awesome sight.

The plane landed on Maui, and we all walked down the steps onto the runway. The trade winds were so strong they almost knocked me over. The terminal wasn't much of a building, and all I saw around it was fields of sugar cane. I became a little frightened because I wasn't expecting Maui to be that unconstructed. I waited at baggage claim for my bag, and when I got it, I walked outside and didn't know what to do. The couple that I'd met on the plane came over to me, and the woman said, "Hey, you seem a little lost!"

"I wasn't expecting it to be quite this rural," I said.

They looked at each other and laughed. The guy asked, "Where are you going?"

"I have to find a friend of a friend in Haiku."

He said, "It's getting dark. We live in Haiku. You're coming home with us tonight. We'll help you find your friend tomorrow."

I gave a sigh of relief, as if everything was falling into place, and was all going to work out. A friend of theirs picked us up in an open jeep, and my hair blew wildly as we drove away from the airport. I couldn't see much because it was almost dark.

When we arrived at their place, we drove down a bumpy dirt road, and I heard rushing water in the distance. They told me their house was an old cane house, raised up on stilts, so that when torrential rains came the water would run under the house. I walked up the staircase and followed them inside. It was very primitive and sparse, but homey. I was so appreciative.

The woman said, "No worries, Haiku's a small town. Tomorrow we'll take you to the post office and find out exactly where your friend lives."

Everyone was asleep when I woke up early the next morning. I wandered outside to look around. I was in a tropical paradise. The house was set in the middle of a banana grove, and there were mango and papaya trees all around. I followed the sound of rushing water and found myself next to a river in a valley. In the distance was a waterfall, which emptied into a rocky pool. I walked down the path to the waterfall which was lined on either side with guava bushes. I said out loud, "Have I died and gone to heaven?"

Plumeria flowers were floating down on the trade winds from trees overhead, and I saw endless coconut palms swaying in the distance. I walked toward the waterfall and stepped into the rocky pool. I stood under the rushing water and let it wash over me. I dove in and floated around for a while. I swam to the side and pulled myself up onto a rock at the edge and sat down.

Once again, I found myself on the bank of Siddhartha's river. I realized that my life was forever flowing and changing but was still the same river. I began to meditate and tried to clear my mind of everything behind me, all my memories. I tried not to anticipate all that was ahead of me. But like Siddhartha, I struggled to stay in the present. After a while I just concentrated on the sound of the waterfall rushing into the river, and finally, my mind became still.

I don't know how long I was at the edge of the water. Suddenly a myna bird approached and began squawking at me. I opened my eyes and enjoyed the beauty around me. At that moment I realized that I didn't have to say goodbye to any of my memories. All those experiences, all the people I loved, and those who loved me, would be part of me forever. Perhaps being in the present meant that life itself, and the living of it, *is* the journey. I felt happy once again, and smiled at the bird who was watching me.

I walked slowly back to the house, admiring and enjoying everything along the path. I was on life's path once again. Everyone was up having breakfast when I got back to the house. I sat down with them at a very low table. Someone passed me toast with local honey and a cup of strong Kona coffee. I felt at home right away.

One of the guys said, "We want to take you to our favorite beach. After that we'll help you find your friend."

I was overjoyed at the thought. "I'd love that," I said.

After breakfast we drove to the beach which was deserted, except for us. I walked barefoot along the sand and gazed out over the ocean. In the distance I could see another island. I was filled with joy, excitement, and hope for the future.

And so began my adventure on Maui, and my love affair with Hawaii.

PHOTOGRAPH OF KAANAPALI BEACH ON MAUI 1975

Printed in the United States
by Baker & Taylor Publisher Services